The Way of the Archetypes
Volume II

Saturn and Neptune

The Way of the Archetypes
Volume II

Saturn and Neptune

In Psychology, Spirituality, and Culture

KEIRON LE GRICE

ITAS Publications

ITAS
2016

First published in 2024 by ITAS Publications.

Copyright © 2024 Keiron Le Grice.

All rights reserved. No part of this book may be used or reproduced in any medium without permission in writing from ITAS Publications and the copyright owner.

Cover image artwork "Primordial" © 2021 Kathryn Le Grice. www.kathrynlegrice.com.

Astrological charts created using AstroGold software.

The primary sources of astrological chart data used in these volumes are Astro-Databank and Astrotheme.

ISBN: 978-1-7378059-0-8

Jungian Psychology – Astrology – Spirituality – Philosophy – Mythology – Cultural History

CONTENTS

Introduction to Volume II 1

PART FIVE: The Order of Archetypal Realities

16 Structures of the Saturnian World 5

 The Illumination of Suffering 5
 Saturn in Film and Comedy 11
 The Hero and the Wise Old Man 25
 The *Principium Individuationis*: Becoming a "Solitary" 30
 The Soul and Death: The Moon-Saturn Complex 35
 Father and Child 37
 Emotional Distancing and Maturation 40
 Separation from the Mother and the Duty of Care 41
 The Shepherd Tends His Flock 43
 Emotional Rigidity and Domestic Entrapment 44
 Isolation from the Matrix of Being 45
 The Constraints and Certainties of the Logical Mind 47
 The Critical Animus 52
 Love's Lessons and Losses: Venus-Saturn 53
 Aphrodite and Chronos 58
 Social Standing and the Judgment of Beauty 61
 Solider and Senex: The Archetypal Combination of Mars-Saturn 68
 Attack on the Shadow 72
 Efficiency, Stamina, and Resistance 73
 Fear and the Moral Ought 74

17 Jupiter-Saturn Contrasts and Combinations 81

 The Good Life: Jupiter and Venus 81
 The Archetypal Amplifier 85
 Magnification of the Problematic 88
 The Structured Ascent to the Summit 89
 Pragmatism and the Pressure to Grow 91

18	**Case Studies of the Saturn Return: Joseph Campbell and Albert Schweitzer**	94

Themes of the Saturn Return 95
Joseph Campbell's First Saturn Return: 1932–1935 96
Campbell's Second Saturn Return: 1962–1964 102
Albert Schweitzer 106

19	**Idealism and Imagination: The Spiritual Realm of Neptune**	114

Idealistic and Altruistic Heroism 115
The Savior and the Prophet 119
Identity Confusion 127
Portraits of a Psychologist 130
Varieties of the Neptunian Identity 133
The Mythic and the Mystic 135
Dissolution and the Night-Sea Journey: Transits of Neptune to the Sun 138
The Enchanted World of Childhood: Moon-Neptune 140
The Mythic Past and Empathetic Feeling 146
Reverie, Sleep, and Childhood 149
The Idealization of the Maternal, the Feminine, and the Family 150
Sleep and Prophecy, Spirituality and the Unconscious 153
Sanctuary for the Soul 155
Revelation and Confusion: The Receptive and Deceptive Mind 157
Metaphor and the Mythic Imagination 160
Intellectual Synthesis and Universal Theorizing 161
The Idealization of Beauty and the Spell of the Siren: Venus-Neptune 164
The Fairytale Romance and Aesthetic Sensitivity 168
From Eros to Agape: Sublimation and Love for the Divine 171
The Idealized Masculine: Mars-Neptune 172
The Man with No Name 176
The Spiritual Warrior 178
Sensitivity and Spiritual Seeking 181
Aligning with the Tao: The Dissolution and Sublimation of Will 182

20 The Tenor of Faith and Vision: Jupiter-Neptune and   189
    Saturn-Neptune

The Fool's Journey and the Impossible Dream	189
Wish Fulfillment and the Dissolution of Inflation	191
High Ideals, High Expectations	193
The Promised Land	194
Universal Spirituality and the Myths of the World	197
Disillusionment with Hedonism and the Sublimation of Eros	200
The Saturn-Neptune Complex	204
"The Artistic Haunting" and Transcendence through Death	205
Loss of Faith, Alienation from Spirit	209
The Spirit of the Times: Saturn-Neptune World Transits and Culture	210
The Poignant Passing of Time	216
Love's Dreams and Reality	217
The River of Death	220
Spiritual Heroism, Recovery, and Restoration of Lost Ideals	222
Faith in Stone: Saturn-Neptune Personal Transits	234
The Next Destination . . .	239
Bibliography	245
Index	251
About the Author	283

TABLE OF ASTROLOGICAL CHARTS

1	Arthur Schopenhauer	6
2	Woody Allen	12
3	Bill Murray	15
4	Ben Stiller	20
5	Franz Schubert	36
6	Helen Keller	51
7	Billy Joel	55
8	Gertrude Stein	62
9	Leo Tolstoy	65
10	Demi Moore	71
11	Agnetha Fältskog	83
12	Winston Churchill	86
13	Bruce Lee	91
14	Joseph Campbell Personal Transits 1934	97
15	Joseph Campbell Personal Transits 1963	103
16	Albert Schweitzer Personal Transits 1904	108
17	Linda McCartney	117
18	Diego Maradona	125
19	David Bowie	129
20	Carl Gustav Jung	131
21	Owen Wilson	134
22	William Wordsworth	142
23	Friedrich Hölderlin	147
24	Marcel Proust	152

25	Sigmund Freud	154
26	Carl Gustav Jung Personal Transits 1923	156
27	Georg Friedrich Hegel	163
28	James Stewart	167
29	Kate Bush	174
30	Clint Eastwood	177
31	Morihei Ueshiba	179
32	Jim Carrey	193
33	Bruce Springsteen	196
34	Mircea Eliade	198
35	Federico Fellini	201
36	Ingmar Bergman	205
37	Release of Keane's *Under the Iron Sea*	212
38	Premiere of *Life on Mars* (UK Television Series)	215
39	Joni Mitchell	218
40	Release of Don McLean's "American Pie"	221
41	Robert F. Kennedy, Jr	224
42	Carl Gustav Jung Personal Transits 1927	236

INTRODUCTION TO VOLUME II

In this second volume of *The Way of the Archetypes*, we begin our survey of the themes and experiences associated with planetary alignments featuring the five outermost planets usually included in astrological analysis: Jupiter, Saturn, Uranus, Neptune, and Pluto. We will focus here mostly on alignments involving Jupiter, Saturn, and Neptune (with the Pluto and Uranus the primary topic of concern in Volume III). These alignments, periodically formed as the planets complete their cyclical rounds through the zodiac, indicate the activation of archetypal powers in the depths of the unconscious psyche, which, in combination, form dynamic archetypal complexes. Each of these complexes gives rise to discernable themes, impulses, yearnings, and modes of experiencing reality, yet each is distinct and varying in the way it actually comes to expression in the personal details of our lives, shaped by socio-cultural historical context and a range of other factors. The aim in conducting this survey is to better understand how the different archetypal complexes tend to manifest, and how they drive, animate, and determine the course of the psychological process of transformation that C. G. Jung called individuation. To do this, we will consider themes presented in the lives and works of individual artists, philosophers, psychologists, and other well-known figures, as the basis for reflection on the nature and experience of particular archetypal complexes and their significance for individuation. We will also consider the presence of archetypal themes in the events of cultural history, which, impacting us all, influence the course of our evolution, individually and collectively.

PART FIVE

The Order of Archetypal Realities

Chapter 16

Structures of the Saturnian World

The fundamental reality of our experience—structures and material conditions, labors and struggles, responsibilities and pressures, time and mortality, sufferings and limitations—all pertain to the archetype of Saturn. In this respect, it offers us a natural starting point for exploring the archetypal dimension of human experience through astrology.

The Illumination of Suffering
"Unless *suffering* is the direct and immediate object of life, our existence must entirely fail of its aim."[1] Arthur Schopenhauer's opening proclamation in "On the Sufferings of the World" sets the tone for his essay and his philosophy of life in general. Schopenhauer was born in February 1788 under a conjunction of the Sun and Saturn (see Chart 1), and his focus on suffering, in this essay and elsewhere, provides an excellent point of entrance for understanding the range of archetypal themes associated with this alignment. Through Schopenhauer, the light of conscious awareness, associated with the Sun, starkly illuminates a range of phenomena and themes at the heart of the experience of the Saturn archetype.[2]

As we saw in Volume I, Saturn is connected to the psychodynamic principles and archetypes of the shadow, the *senex*, and the super-ego. More broadly, it is associated with death, old age, illness, toil, depression, and the entire gamut of human experiences that bring limitation or cause suffering, of one form or another. In Schopenhauer's case, reflecting the archetypal meaning of the natal Sun in a conjunction with Saturn, throughout his life he was able to direct his consciousness towards this dimension of experience, in focusing, more than any philosopher before him, on the inescapable sufferings and hardships of life. It is for this reason that he became known as the philosopher of pessimism.

Chart 1

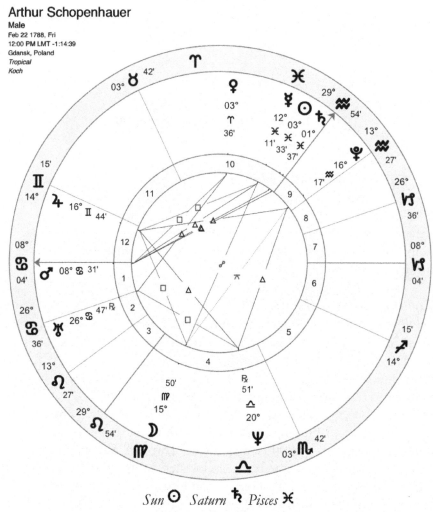

Sun ☉ *Saturn* ♄ *Pisces* ♓

The chart above shows the positions of the Sun and Saturn in the zodiac sign Pisces, at 3 degrees and 1 degree, respectively, at the moment of Schopenhauer's birth. The two planets therefore form a close conjunction—they were only two degrees apart when Schopenhauer was born. The presence of this conjunction indicates that the two corresponding planetary archetypes exist in a mutually stimulating, dynamic relationship, shaping Schopenhauer's character and biographical experiences.

In this essay, he proceeds to detail a litany of traits and themes associated with Saturn, which in his experience constitute the fundamental reality of life. Suffering, he insists, should be our primary focus if we are to face up to the truth of what life is, as unpalatable as this may be.

> It is absurd to look upon the enormous amount of pain that abounds everywhere in the world, and originates in needs and necessities inseparable from life itself, as serving no purpose at all and the result of mere chance. Each separate misfortune, as it comes, seems, no doubt, to be something exceptional; but misfortune in general is the rule.[3]

Pain, misfortunes, needs, necessities—Schopenhauer draws attention here to core Saturnian themes. He illuminates a basic truth of existence, which for Schopenhauer is his primary revelation and experience of what life truly is. There is indeed a truth here, we cannot deny: suffering is inherent to life—the notion of *dukkha* in Buddhism, influential on Schopenhauer, connotes the suffering in its multiple forms that arises from the temporal, transient, and unsatisfactory nature of all things. But suffering is not the whole truth, of course, only the truth as seen from within a particular archetypal vision, one especially connected with the Sun-Saturn combination and other prominent Saturn alignments. Each particular archetypal combination will construe the world in its own manner in a range of ways all consistent with the themes of that particular complex. Schopenhauer continues:

> We are like lambs in a field, disporting themselves under the eye of the butcher, who chooses out first one and then another for his prey. So it is that in our good days we are all unconscious of the evil Fate may have presently in store for us—sickness, poverty, mutilation, loss of sight or reason.[4]

In this dire situation, unconsciousness would be preferable. Greater consciousness, associated with the Sun, serves only to further illuminate the various horrors and dismal plights that may befall us in life. The archetypal Sun, that is to say, shines a light into the Saturnian dimension of reality, into the painful content of the shadow and the reality of *samsara*. In astrology, Saturn has long been associated with the afflictions of fate and is known as the "great malefic," the cosmic principle inflicting suffering and "evil" upon us. Yet its meaning, as we have already seen in Volume I, is not essentially a negative one.

Next Schopenhauer's focuses on another Saturnian theme: time.

> No little part of the torment of existence lies in this, that Time is continually pressing upon us, never letting us take breath, but always coming after us, like a taskmaster with a whip. If at any moment Time stays his hand, it is only when we are delivered over to the misery of boredom.[5]

From suffering, evil, and labor, he then turns to the ultimate Saturnian inevitable: death.

> But all this contributes to increase the measures of suffering in human life out of all proportion to its pleasures; and the pains of life are made much worse for man by the fact that death is something very real to him.[6]

Like the Freudian super-ego, the image of "Time" as a "taskmaster with a whip" is a striking portrait of key aspects of Saturn—the unrelenting pressure of material existence, in which we are continually reminded by circumstance and the force of necessity of what we must do, ever aware of the inexorable ticking of the clock as we move towards old age and ultimately death. Schopenhauer remains fixated on the negatives in these passages, but others, such as Martin Heidegger, have viewed the encounter with mortality more favorably, indeed as essential to the living of an authentic life.[7] A focus on death can help us determine what is truly important in life. Similarly, the awareness of the passing of time and aging can push us, like the stern hand of fate, to do what we must in life, to heed our innermost conscience and make necessary changes, facing whatever challenges and problems these changes entail. Death can focus the mind immediately on the practical necessities and tasks at hand, foster a pragmatic and realistic attitude, and enable us to commit our efforts to making the best of our life. For Schopenhauer, however, it is more a question of running down the clock, gradually discharging the onerous and futile burden life places upon us: "Life is a task to be done. It is a fine thing to say *defunctus est*; it means that the man has done his task."[8]

This position leads—understandably given such a view—to Schopenhauer's well-known conclusion that life is something that should never have been. It would have been better, he reasons, had we not been born.

> If you try to imagine, as nearly as you can, what an amount of misery, pain and suffering of every kind the sun shines upon in its course, you will admit that it would be much better if, on the earth as little as on the moon, the sun were able to call forth the phenomena of life; and if, here as there, the surface were still in a crystalline state.[9]

Birth brings us into the field of suffering and sin, where the oppressive weight of Saturn is with us from the first.

> . . . like the children of a libertine, we come into the world with the burden of sin upon us; and that it is only through having continually to atone for this sin that our existence is so miserable, and that its end is death.[10]

The unfolding of life does not permit any respite or improvement, leading Schopenhauer to conclude: "every man desires to reach old age; in other words, a state of life of which it may be said: 'It is bad to-day, and it will be worse to-morrow; and so on till the worst of all.'"[11]

No one could accuse Schopenhauer of downplaying the problematic side of life, which touches us all in many, if not all, of these ways. Yet he is able to find, even amidst this gloomy vision of the desperate misery of life, as it reveals itself to him, that suffering has a valuable purpose:

> But misfortune has its uses; for, as our bodily frame would burst asunder if the pressure of the atmosphere was removed, so, if the lives of men were relieved of all need, hardship and adversity; if everything they took in hand were successful, they would be so swollen with arrogance that, though they might not burst, they would present the spectacle of unbridled folly—nay, they would go mad. And I may say, further, that a certain amount of care or pain or trouble is necessary for every man at all times. A ship without ballast is unstable and will not go straight.[12]

This is Saturn as grounding, as the reality principle, and as the positive limitation and containment that create the structure of our experience, countering the Jupiterian tendency towards inflation ("swollen with arrogance") and ignoble ease. Despite the misery it brings, Saturnian hard labor, in Schopenhauer's judgment, spares us from even greater sufferings.

> Certain it is that *work, worry, labor* and *trouble*, form the lot of almost all men their whole life long. But if all wishes were fulfilled as soon as they arose, how would men occupy their lives? what would they do with their time? If the world were a paradise of luxury and ease, a land flowing with milk and honey, where every Jack obtained his Jill at once and without any difficulty, men would either die of boredom or hang themselves; or there would be wars, massacres, and murders; so that in the end mankind would inflict more suffering on itself than it has now to accept at the hands of Nature.[13]

I have quoted Schopenhauer at length here because I know of no finer example, unflinchingly detailed, of many themes central to the Saturn archetype, illuminated by Schopenhauer's own experience of life. The Sun archetype shows what is most immediately real for us and those aspects of the world to which we are most consciously attuned. Through Schopenhauer, the solar archetype brings Saturnian themes squarely into the light of day, revealed in one stark passage after another.

It is important to keep in mind, however, in the context of our discussion of archetypal multivalence in Volume I, that Schopenhauer's experience is but one of many, perhaps innumerable, ways that the Sun-Saturn complex can find expression in life. No one else's experience of Sun-Saturn will be quite the same as Schopenhauer's, although it will share many thematic similarities. We will consider examples demonstrating both this similarity and difference below. We should keep in mind, too, that we have focused here on Sun-Saturn in isolation as a single archetypal complex even though it functions alongside all the other archetypal complexes depicted in the configurations in Schopenhauer's chart. Schopenhauer's Sun-Saturn conjunction was also in significant geometric relationship to Mercury, the Moon, and Jupiter. These other archetypal principles inflect the way in which the Sun-Saturn combination is expressed and would be included in a fuller analysis. Thus, for example, the centrality of Saturn in Schopenhauer's experience is reinforced by the Mercury-Saturn alignment in his chart. The Saturn archetype impressed itself on his thoughts and his perceptions; his mind naturally dwelled on the problematic side of life, its suffering and hardship, and this is reflected in the language he used. That his insight into the misery and suffering of life should constitute his entire worldview and should be stated, or perhaps overstated, in such sweeping terms reflects the influence of Jupiter, which tends to expand and amplify. Jupiter is in a close-to-exact square with Mercury. And the focus on being condemned by sin even from childhood reflects a theme associated with the Moon (in relation to Saturn) and its connection with the child archetype. In Schopenhauer's chart, the Moon is brought into relationship with Saturn through its placement in the complex T-square involving all of the planets mentioned above. We will unpack these other correlations with Saturn aspects more fully in later examples.

Saturn in Film and Comedy

Given the fixation on the problematic side of life in Schopenhauer's exegesis of the central themes associated with Saturn, one could be forgiven for concluding that the experience of Saturn must give us nothing to smile about, leaving us utterly devoid of humor. There is little in the quoted passages above, save for the dramatic overstatement, to bring us any amusement. Yet often, of course, it is the grave and tragic elements of life, and our shared experience of misfortune and failings, that provide the context for humor, if only as a mechanism of survival. For this reason, Saturn is often prominent in the lives of those who bring laughter into our lives.[14]

Of all the figures in comedy, one who we might immediately call to mind as an exemplar of archetypal themes associated with Saturn is Woody Allen. While his personal life has been embroiled in controversy and allegations, his films offer us a vivid illustration of the creative expression of the Saturn archetype.[15] We might not be surprised to discover that Allen has major natal hard-aspect alignments of Sun-Saturn, Moon-Saturn, and Jupiter-Saturn in his birth chart, indicating that the experience of Saturn is prominent in his life. Thus Allen's characteristic portrayals, in one film after another, of neurosis, doubt, worries, inferiority (with humorous attempts to compensate), and a morbid preoccupation with aging, illness, and death.

A famous scene in *Annie Hall* has Allen, as Alvey Singer, in a Manhattan bookstore with Annie (played by Diane Keaton), introducing her to Ernest Becker's *The Denial of Death* and sharing the benefit of his own decidedly Saturnian view of the world—a view with which Schopenhauer would surely have concurred:

I feel that life is divided into the horrible and the miserable. That's the two categories. The horrible are like, I don't know, terminal cases, you know, and blind people, crippled. I don't know how they get through life. It's amazing to me. And the miserable is everyone else. So you should be thankful that you're miserable, because that's very lucky, to be miserable.[16]

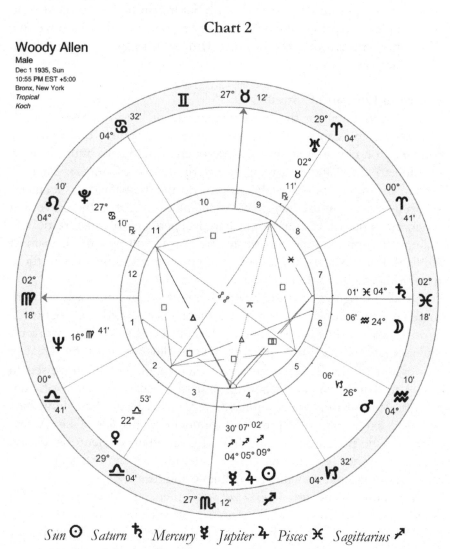

Chart 2

In Woody Allen's birth chart, the Sun is positioned at 9 degrees Sagittarius in a square alignment with Saturn, positioned at 4 degrees Pisces. Note also the close squares between Jupiter and Saturn and Mercury and Saturn.

Again, as was the case for Schopenhauer, Woody Allen's fundamental experience of the world is shaped by a direct and immediate apprehension of core themes associated with Saturn. Allen's view has remained unswervingly consistent over time. A 2010 Cannes Film Festival conference interview on the release of the film *You Will Meet a Tall Dark Stranger* gave him the opportunity to make his position unequivocal.

> Questioner: "It seems that the only happy people in this movie by the end are slightly crazy, and they are the future Mr. and Mrs. Wunch—a lovely name—and they're the ones who don't believe you may even need happiness in the present life. So everyone else seems to be left miserable and I'm curious if you are being playful with this or if this is a serious comic commentary on what life looks like to you at this point."

> Woody Allen: "This is my perspective, and has always been my perspective, on life. I have a very grim, pessimistic view of it. I always have since I was a little boy and it hasn't gotten worse with age or anything. I do feel that it's a grim, painful, nightmarish, meaningless experience and that the only way that you can be happy is that you tell yourself some lies and deceive yourself . . . and I'm not the first person to say this or the most articulate person on it; it was said by Nietzsche, it was said by Freud, it was said by Eugene O'Neil. One must have one's delusions to live. If you look at life too honestly and clearly life does become unbearable because it's a pretty grim enterprise, you will admit."[17]

In Allen's case, the Saturnian problematic dimension of life is magnified to humorous proportions, reflecting the archetypal influence of Jupiter, as indicated by Allen's Sun-Jupiter-Saturn configuration. Like Schopenhauer, who also had Jupiter in major alignment with Saturn, Saturnian themes impressing themselves on the basic experience of reality and sense of identity are dramatically amplified, even overstated, constituting an entire worldview and philosophy for both men. Yet Schopenhauer draws on his own experience and disposition to write philosophical treatises while Allen uses his as a source of comedic commentary on life, with similar themes expressed in quite differing ways.

Other eminent figures in comedy with major natal Sun-Saturn alignments include Bill Murray, Jim Carrey, and Ben Stiller who each draw out different inflections and forms of expression of the Sun-Saturn archetypal complex through their various film roles, with the characters they portray affording an opportunity to give expression to the archetypal potentialities symbolized in their birth charts. It often seems to be the case, moreover, that actors are drawn to, and serendipitously cast in, roles for which they are well suited. This is especially true for those parts and characters for which they become best known.

Bill Murray's role as Frank Cross in the 1988 film *Scrooged*, a modern variation of Dickens's *A Christmas Carol*, portrays almost to caricature the negative *senex* aspect of the Sun-Saturn complex. As shown in Chart 3, Murray was born with a Sun-Saturn conjunction (as part of a larger, four-planet configuration involving Mercury and Venus), and is able to draw on the archetypal qualities and experiences associated with that configuration in his portrayal of this and other distinctly Saturnian roles. As Frank Cross, he is the miserly Scrooge-like television executive, trapped inside the walls of his own ego, closed-off, judgmental, bored, and seemingly in danger of losing his humanity, until, as in the Dickens original, the haunting visitations on the eve of Christmas force him, facing the prospect of his own death, to confront his past wrongs and the stark reality of what he has become. Saturn here manifests as the archetypal judge.[18] Central to Frank Cross's experience in this film is the loss of his former love, pertaining to the Venus principle, a motif reflected in the alignment between Saturn and Venus in Murray's chart. The confrontation with mortality explored in this film generates the necessary inner pressure for Cross to overcome his egoic defensiveness and remoteness from life, and thus to reclaim the love that had escaped him.

Similar traits are evident in the cynical television weatherman Phil Connors, played with aplomb by Murray in the film *Groundhog Day*.[19] Here again, Murray portrays a distinctly brash and arrogant character, trapped in his own egocentric world.[20] The topic of the film is the annual custom of celebrating the appearance of the groundhog from its hibernation, a ritual especially popular in Punxsutawney, Pennsylvania, where the film is set. As the folk wisdom has it, if the sky is overcast that day (February 2nd) spring will come early; if there are sunny skies, the groundhog ("Punxsutawney Phil") will see its shadow and retreat into its burrow, indicating an extended winter period and the late arrival of spring. The premise of the story is Phil Connors's encounter with his own shadow, anticipated not only in the groundhog custom, but also in the opening scene of the film in which we see Connors giving a weather report, with the studio lighting casting his shadow onto the wall behind. Note here again Saturn's specific association with the Jungian shadow archetype. As the film unfolds, Connors is to become more fully aware of and acquainted with his shadow, as circumstances contrive to trap him in a situation that forces upon him a period of repeated life lessons, moral improvement, and character maturation.

Chart 3

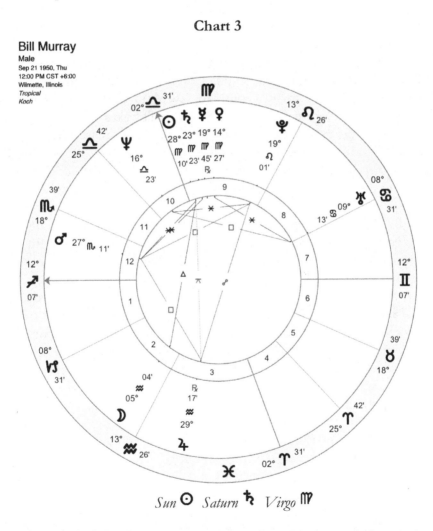

From the outset, Connors is cynical, judgmental, and disparaging, resenting what he sees as the tedious assignment of giving a report on the Groundhog Day weather, direct from the scene in Punxsutawney. His judgment and cynicism are often conveyed through dry, put-down, and deadpan humor, characteristic of Saturn, with much of the humor directed at his colleague Rita Hanson (played by Andie MacDowell), for whom he has a romantic attraction. After the perfunctory and disinterested delivery of the television report, Connors is eager to leave town as quickly as possible but circumstance, showing its Saturnian face, contrives to thwart him and block his path. Forced to remain in Punxsutawney for another night due to a snow blizzard, he wakes the next morning to find himself reliving the same day over again, in virtually the exact same detail—a consequence, we are left to assume, of the magical influence of Groundhog Day.

Connors finds himself caught in a cycle of seemingly endless repetition, the eternal return of a single day. For him, time is stuck—there appears to be no way out, not even through his attempts to commit suicide. Whatever Connors does he still wakes on February 2nd and experiences exactly the same sequence of events, played out on that single day. His own responses to the events, however, are not fixed, and he has some latitude (within the parameters of his own slowly evolving character and understanding of the situation) as to how he will interact with the all-too-familiar events as they unfold. Sure enough, little by little we witness something like a progressive wearing down of the walls of his ego, as circumstances present Connors with the opportunity to consider again and to amend how he conducts himself and treats the people he encounters, not least his love-interest, Rita. Time and again he is tripped up by his own ego, with the repeated cycle of events exposing the flaws in his character, even in spite of his increasing efforts. Gradually, however, he comes to terms with the situation and accomplishes what is required of him, drawing on his by now innumerable experiences of past missteps until he perfects the performance of the day and earns the love of Rita.

The film conveys a sense of lessons being learned, with Saturn evident as the wise old man, teacher, and taskmaster forcing upon Murray's character Connors the concentrated repetition of experiences he needs in order to outgrow the pattern of cynical defensiveness and thus to begin to come to terms with this dimension of his own shadow. We see here too the characteristic BPM II experience of no-exit, associated with the Saturn principle, of being stuck in a painful situation from which there is no escape, with accompanying feelings of moral judgment, even damnation. The film is illustrative of the way Saturn is often experienced—as concentrated pressure and enforced limitation in which time passes excruciatingly slowly, with the pressure remaining until one has been able to do what one really must if one is to move forward in life. In *Groundhog Day*, time and limitation combine to force the maturation of Connor's ego personality, associated with the Sun. By the end, Connors has become a master at living that day, having assimilated into his personality the instructive wisdom and lessons of the Saturnian situation in which he found himself.

Whereas one might immediately identify Woody Allen and Bill Murray as distinctively Saturnian personalities, although in different ways, the presence of the Sun-Saturn conjunction in the birth chart of Jim Carrey (see Chart 32) is perhaps more surprising, although, like Murray in *Scrooged*, Carrey reprised the role of a character who detests the open-hearted spirit of Christmas in his portrayal of Dr. Seuss's the Grinch. Carrey's best-known roles—in *Ace Ventura*, *Dumb and Dumber*, *The Mask*, *Bruce Almighty*, and so forth—are of over-the-top characters, typically naïve and idiotic or extravagant and flamboyant, traits which are the very antithesis of Sun-Saturn, and which bear more obvious connections with the Jupiter-Mercury-Neptune alignment in his chart, to be discussed in Chapter 20.

Yet in many of his films the Sun-Saturn complex is evident either in the restrictive circumstances forming the setting for the story or in the form of an alter-ego, such as the downtrodden bank clerk in *The Mask*, who is oppressed by the littleness of life.[21] In *Bruce Almighty*, similarly, Carrey plays Bruce Nolan, a television news reporter overlooked for promotion and frustrated by the tedious, even belittling, assignments he is given, causing him much consternation, leading him to judge himself and his life a failure.[22] In *The Truman Show*, Carrey plays Truman Burbank, trapped within an artificial television-studio world, in which the fake sky at the edge of the ocean is essentially a prison wall of his false reality.[23] In *Liar, Liar*, as an attorney whose success depends on his capacity to lie, Carrey's character Fletcher Reede finds himself bound by his young son's magical birthday wish that his father not tell any more lies.[24] The resulting restriction, and Carrey's attempts to handle it, then provides the source of the film's humor. In each case, Carrey's characters are in some way restricted or even oppressed by the circumstances in which they find themselves, with the Saturnian circumstantial or internal pressure producing the impetus for the facing and overcoming of character flaws or for psychological maturation. In many roles, Carrey, expressing not only the Sun-Saturn archetypal pairing, but also Mars-Saturn, battles vigorously against the restriction, depicting the struggles through an overtly physical kind of humor. Mars, you will recall, is associated with anger, aggression, action, and physical energy. Mars-Saturn is the signature of frustrated will, when one's energies hit against an obstacle, and it feels like bashing one's head against a brick wall. The restriction, in Carrey's case, gives rise to the thwarted energies that he embodies in the most vivid physical manner, often in contorted postures or protests.

Another comic actor with a major Sun-Saturn alignment in his birth chart is Ben Stiller, and in his case again we see prominent Sun-Saturn themes in many, if not all, of the roles he has taken on. As in the other examples, however, Stiller's expression of Sun-Saturn draws out different sides of this archetypal complex. In the series of the hugely popular films *Meet the Parents*, *Meet the Fockers*, and *Meet the Little Fockers*, directed by Jay Roach, Stiller plays Greg Focker who finds himself repeatedly trying to win favor with Jack Byrnes (played by Robert De Niro), the father of Focker's fiancée, Pam Byrnes (played by Teri Polo). Viewers witness the painfully humorous encounters between Greg and Jack, with De Niro perfectly cast as the former CIA agent father-in-law, who is something like an over-zealous super-ego, subjecting the unfortunate Focker to constant monitoring by hidden surveillance cameras and, at one point, even forcing him to take a lie-detector test. With Jack Byrnes hovering in the background, judging his every move, Focker finds himself always trying to live up the standard, to meet the requirements for admission into Byrnes's "circle of trust."

The comical, and often excruciatingly awkward and embarrassing, situations in which Focker finds himself, vividly exemplify the experience, often associated with Sun-Saturn, of living in the shadow of a dominant father figure or controlling internalized super-ego that determines how one should be and act, simultaneously inhibiting and molding the development of the conscious personality. When this side of the Sun-Saturn archetypal complex is accentuated, it can be difficult to step into one's own authority and therefore to be oneself. The judgment, doubt, and desire to meet the standard and prove oneself can lead people with this archetypal complex to seek approval and confirmation from others, often those with more experience, such as elders or mentors, who seem to embody the very authority they believe they lack. The conscious personality then develops by assimilating the wisdom of such elders. Slowly maturing, under the influence of the Sun-Saturn complex, people might ultimately embody for themselves the wisdom of hard-earned experience.

A glance at Robert De Niro's chart, in the context of these films, is also illuminating as he has a natal Moon-Saturn alignment, correlating with an archetypal complex that he draws on to great effect to play Jack Byrnes as the authoritarian ruler of the home, upholder of Byrnes' values, and systematic planner and controller of all family activities—recall the Moon's association with the home and family. Byrnes's rigid Saturnian exterior cloaks his soft lunar underbelly, as we see the contrast between the hard disciplinarian ex-CIA agent and Vietnam War prisoner, on the one hand, and Byrnes's emotionality, on the other, evident especially in his sentimentality around the passing of his mother and his doting relationship with his daughter and his cat. To put this in Jungian terms, behind the hard-edged, rigidly disciplined persona lies an overly sentimental and needy anima and mother complex, perhaps even a needy child. Similar themes, incidentally, are explored in *Analyze This* (1999, directed by Harold Ramis) in which De Niro plays a mafia boss seeking the help of a psychotherapist (played by Billy Crystal) to work through emotional issues—the act of working on one's emotions is another leitmotif of Moon-Saturn.

Ben Stiller also has a major Moon-Saturn alignment, in addition to the Sun-Saturn combination, and in this series of films we witness him in one embarrassing family scene after another, as the Saturnian judgment and sense of inferiority is experienced in a domestic family situation, pertaining to the Moon. Everything Focker tries to do to meet with the approval of Jack Byrnes and his fiancée's family goes wrong. This type of situation is not uncommon when one is dealing with those areas of life in which the Saturn principle is most acutely experienced. Recall that Saturn as the shadow pertains to the areas of life in which we experience a sense of weakness, inferiority, embarrassment, guilt, and judgment. To try to live up to societal standards at the expense of behaving authentically and naturally invariably does not work out. One's own ignored energies trip one up, for, in areas of life under the influence of Saturn, naturalness and authenticity are simply not available to us, until we have worked through the resistances, emotional complexes, and internalized standards that determine how we live. In *Meet the Parents*, Focker is placed in a situation in which his every impulse falls foul of the standards and conventions that hold sway in Pam's family. He is ridiculed, for instance, for being a male nurse—the Saturnian conventional judgment of a caring and traditionally female role associated with the Moon. We also feel his sense of inadequacy, when, in the company of the wealthy Byrnes family and Pam's even wealthier ex-boyfriend (played by Owen Wilson), he admits, with a sense of inadequacy, to not being a home owner—another expression of a Saturn-Moon theme.

Chart 4

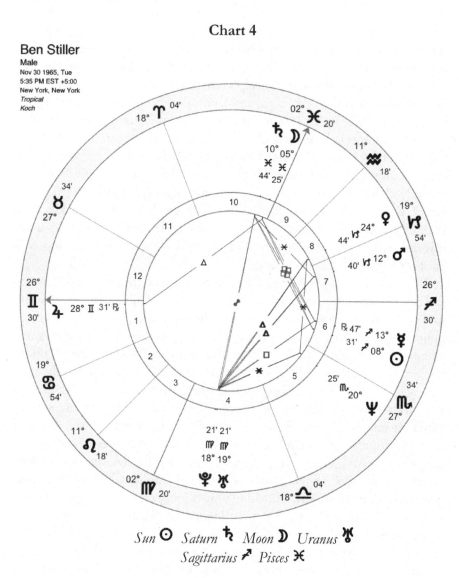

Sun ☉ Saturn ♄ Moon ☽ Uranus ♅
Sagittarius ♐ Pisces ♓

Born in the mid-1960s, Stiller's Saturn is in an opposition alignment with Uranus, and in this sequence of films we can recognize the presence of the Uranus archetype as the trickster, undermining his attempts to meet the standard, tripping him up, and thereby activating feelings of embarrassment and inferiority, bringing them into conscious awareness. Uranus awakens and liberates the Saturnian experiences of judgment, guilt, shame, self-consciousness, and so forth. The opposition of Saturn and Uranus here yields acute and excruciating moments of awkwardness and disruptive mishaps that expose the Saturnian shadow and sense of inferiority. With the opposition these tensions are not readily resolved, but rather have to be endured. It is a struggle to reconcile oneself to both poles—here social respectability and convention, on one side, and authenticity and the freedom of following one's own inclinations, on the other side. This struggle of opposites is acutely apparent in the role of Focker. If Focker attempts to play by the rules, and to do what Jack Byrnes expects of him, the Uranus principle comes to the fore and leads to mishap, accident, or a faux pas. If he blithely ignores or breaks the rules, which often seem to him ridiculous, Saturn is constellated, as Byrnes's judgment and Focker's own feelings of failure and inadequacy come to bear on him. That the situations are often extreme reflects the presence of the Pluto archetype in that configuration, with Pluto in a conjunction to Uranus and in opposition to Saturn—aspects we will consider in detail later.

Trying even harder to make things work only worsens Greg Focker's plight. Saturn inspires us to effort, but sometimes effort towards inappropriate goals, or goals that do not come out of our authentic being. We try to fit in or win approval or to accommodate ourselves to social expectation. Unconsciously responding to the fear and judgment associated with Saturn pushes us to meet some external standard that we deem to be important, and prompts us, through feelings of judgment and inadequacy, to try to meet these standards and prove or justify ourselves. Saturn also exposes us to failure, until, in time, we have developed enough confidence in ourselves and proven our abilities that we can live and act with competence and confidence, trusting our own judgment.

Teri Polo has a Venus-Saturn conjunction, corresponding to an archetypal complex that she gives expression to in the role of Focker's fiancée Pam. As a "daddy's girl," Pam's capacity to give and receive romantic love, the anima-eros function associated with Venus, is bound-up with her father, inhibited by her father's presence, expectations, and values—the Saturnian element. Equally, her relationship with Greg is, one can assume, the cause of much embarrassment to her, once the family dynamics and dramas start to unfold. The entire context of her romantic relationship with Focker is dominated by her father and the rules of conduct in her household.

In the second film, *Meet the Fockers*, Greg, now in the role of family organizer himself, has to take on the responsibility of managing the coming together of his own parents with Pam's, again with embarrassing consequences, as disastrous as they are entertaining. Bearing the weight of responsibility for one's family is a typical form of expression of the Moon-Saturn combination, with the Moon as the impulse to care and associated with the home and family, and Saturn as the pressure of responsibility and duty. In this film, Greg's own parents (played by Barbra Streisand and Dustin Hoffman) are a source of embarrassment to him, with their eccentric hippie values, style, and ways of being completely at odds with the staid East-coast conservatism of the Byrnes family, and divergent too with Greg's somewhat reserved manner and his attempts at control, to make the course of events run smoothly.

Whereas the Sun-Saturn hard-aspect combinations can often manifest as a father complex, the Moon-Saturn combination can be expressed as a mother complex or as a difficult, emotionally distant, or burdensome relationship with the mother.[25] Ben Stiller's characters are often subject to one of both of these complexes. In *Starsky & Hutch* (2004, directed by Todd Phillips), spoofing the 1970s television series, Stiller portrays David Starsky as a detective dwarfed by the glittering police career of his mother and also as a fastidious follower of the rules, always playing by the book. Living in the shadow of his mother and her celebrated career in the force, at one point, early in the film, Starsky protests in exasperation "I am not my mother!" as he attempts to assert his own identity, associated with the Sun.

Another variation of the rule-follower motif, connected to Sun-Saturn, is evident in *Along Came Polly* (2004, directed by John Hamburg) in which Stiller plays Reuben Feffer, a life-insurance risk assessor, jilted by his new bride while on honeymoon, and then romantically involved with the carefree Polly, played by Jennifer Anniston. Much of the film's humor centers on Feffer's aversion to risk and his conditioned tendency to see dangers wherever he goes, and thus to play it safe, assessing and avoiding all potential hazards. Again, Saturn gives the eye for the problem, the fault, and the impetus to protect and to make safe—tendencies valuable and admirable within reason, unless they become the guiding principles of life itself.

In Wes Anderson's *The Royal Tenenbaums* (2001) Stiller plays Chas Tenenbaum, a single parent wounded by the death of his wife, and, as a result, excessively regimented and overprotective in his fathering style, with Saturnian laws, structure, and discipline impinging on parenting and his attitude towards his children, associated with the Moon. With a Moon-Saturn astrological aspect in one's birth chart, the role of caregiver can sometimes be felt as particularly burdensome or limiting, as a heavy emotional weight to bear. Yet, as much as we might resent the restriction it brings, the Saturn principle, in the form of responsibilities, duties, and necessities, also provides our lives with binding structure, serving to anchor us in the real world, thus bringing counterbalance to our more escapist, obsessive, indulgent, or fickle tendencies. The imposition of structure is one response to the emotional pressure of parenting associated with the Moon-Saturn complex, for the structure permits a sense of order, security, and control in an area of life that tends not to come naturally to the person with major natal Moon-Saturn alignments and in which he or she may suffer from doubts and insecurities. On the other hand, however, the pressure and pain can prompt the total avoidance of those areas of life pertaining to Moon-Saturn, fostering a kind of emotional detachment from the family and the past or relational barriers that are difficult to break through.

In Stiller's portrayal of Walter Mitty in the 2013 remake of *The Secret Life of Walter Mitty* (directed by Sean Penn), we learn that the death of Mitty's father prematurely brought to an end his youthful aspirations for a life of adventure. Instead, he was saddled with responsibilities to the family that imposed upon him an early psychological maturation or, as not infrequently happens, repression. Again, Stiller's character here reflects themes associated with Moon-Saturn. Burdened by responsibilities, the Moon, as the inner child, cannot be freely expressed, and the dimension of experience associated with the Moon can remain undeveloped, as if frozen in time. The Sun-Saturn complex is plainly evident in this film too. In Stiller's Mitty, unconscious fantasy compensates for the littleness of his existence in a dingy basement room of *Life* magazine, where he is subject to the embarrassing ridicule of his employers. Despite this, he shines through the exemplary fulfillment of his work responsibilities—a characteristic trait of the Sun-Saturn complex, that of a sensible, hardworking, and responsible person, inhabiting an orderly if sometimes uninspiring world. With Sun-Saturn, one can become a shining embodiment of the rules and laws of life, as in the struggle to become an honest and decent upright citizen, or in the assumption of the role of judge and arbiter, deliberating on transgressions or shortcomings, and enforcer of the rules and standards. Saturn is associated with conventional morality and the laws of the land, at least until such a time one can become one's own moral authority, attuned to the inner law of the Self.

Contrary to what one might initially assume, having major alignments of Saturn in one's birth chart, such as hard aspects to the Sun, does not preclude the attainment of success and happiness in life. Indeed, Saturn gives us, or draws out of us, what it takes to face the reality of the world, adapt to its demands, and prosper through our own efforts. For some people, Sun-Saturn manifests as a kind of worldly realism, a matter-of-fact acceptance of material reality as it is, shining the light of consciousness on what needs to be done, fulfilling one's task, shouldering responsibility, and so forth. Sun-Saturn can impart, or extract from us, the capacity to be grounded and to keep things real, with a keen awareness of our limitations, thereby countering any tendencies towards inflation. Naturally, such attitudes can often foster success, as one shines through one's endeavors or climbs to the top through persistent effort and hard work. In some instances, though, with major Sun-Saturn alignments a person's identity can be utterly shaped by a focus on work or the fulfillment of responsibilities of an assumed life role. Saturn as the negative *senex* can be singular and oppressive, like a controlling tyrant-ogre that does not permit us to stray from the straight and narrow path of order and duty.

Often the Sun-Saturn complex, especially when associated with hard-aspect alignments, can manifest as the constant struggle for self-expression and creativity, the struggle to give concrete form to one's experience of life, to define oneself, and to shine forth through one's creative endeavors. Self-expression does not tend to come easily, however, for with these alignments the Saturn archetype tends to hold creative and expressive urges in check, or inhibits and impedes, as one is forced to struggle each step of the way under the pressure to give tangible form to what one is, or what one seeks to express, and to develop confidence in one's abilities. As noted, with Sun-Saturn one can be constrained and conditioned by tradition, by an overly deferential attitude towards the achievements of those who have gone before, or defined by a sense of lack and inadequacy when measuring oneself against others, society's standards, or one's own expectations. Accordingly, the opportunity to shine and to find success might well come later in life, when one has been able to assimilate and go beyond tradition, incorporate Saturnian qualities into one's being, and build one's confidence through demonstrated achievement.

The Hero and the Wise Old Man

Turning now from film and comedy to sports provides further examples of prominent themes associated with Sun-Saturn. Most notably, here the presence of Sun-Saturn alignments is an indicator, in a number of cases, of the dominant influence of parental figures as coaches. In tennis, for instance, in the last few decades many of the most successful players who were trained and mentored by parents or other relatives have major Sun-Saturn alignments in their birth charts, including Andre Agassi (Sun conjunct Saturn), Rafael Nadal (Sun opposite Saturn), Martina Hingis (Sun-Saturn-Jupiter conjunction), Venus Williams (Sun square Saturn and Mars), and Serena Williams (Sun-Saturn-Jupiter-Pluto-Mercury stellium). Sun-Saturn hard aspects are often indicators that in some sense the person's entire life and personality have been influenced to a high degree by these parental coaches.

Martina Hingis was coached and managed by her mother, by all accounts an ambitious figure, who named her daughter after the other famous Martina in tennis—Navratilova—and reportedly began to prepare her for a tennis career, while carrying her during pregnancy.[26] The Williams sisters, Venus and Serena, were coached by their father, Richard Williams, who intentionally set out to make them tennis champions, taking on responsibility for their tennis development from an early age, and enabling them to rise to the pinnacle of the sport and to dominate for many years.

In the case of Agassi and Nadal, their popular autobiographies of 2009 and 2011 detail how their childhood experiences were defined by the stern discipline of their father and uncle, respectively, who were dominant figures forging the character of the two tennis stars, for better and worse. Agassi's father was a former boxer who seems to have transferred his own unfulfilled aspirations for sporting success onto his son, imposing training on the young Agassi with an iron fist. To assist in training, Agassi senior created what Andre referred to as "the dragon," a fearsome machine, relentlessly spewing tennis balls at speed in the direction of the then seven-year-old Agassi. As he describes it:

> My father says that if I hit 2,500 balls a day, I'll hit 17,500 balls each week, and at the end of one year I'll have hit nearly one million balls. . . . A child who hits one million balls each year will be unbeatable.

> Hit *earlier*, my father yells. Damn it, Andre, hit *earlier*. Crowd the ball, crowd the ball.
>
> Now he's crowding me. He's yelling directly into my ear. It's not enough to hit everything the dragon fires at me; my father wants me to hit it *harder* and *faster* than the dragon. He wants me to beat the dragon. The thought makes me panicky. I tell myself: You can't beat the dragon. How can you beat something that never stops? Come to think of it, the dragon is a lot like my father. Except that my father is worse. At least the dragon stands before me, where I can see it. My father stays behind me. I rarely see him, only hear him, day and night, yelling in my ear.[27]

Another incident described by Agassi in his autobiography saw the young Andre receive a trophy for good sportsmanship during a tournament, but not the winner's trophy. Agassi recollects his own feelings and his father's reaction.

> It *is* an awfully cool trophy. And I *have* been a good sport. I walk out to the car, clutching the trophy to my chest, my father a step behind me. He says nothing, I say nothing. . . . Finally, I break the silence. I say, I don't want this stupid thing. I say it because I think it's what my father wants to hear. My father comes alongside side me. He rips the trophy from my hands. He lifts it over his head and throws it on the cement. The trophy shatters.[28]

On another occasion, when Agassi skipped a tennis practice to play soccer with his friends, Andre's father unceremoniously marched him from the soccer field, telling Andre: "You're never playing soccer again."[29] When Andre pleads with him, the response is even more unequivocal: "You're a tennis player! You're going to be number one in the world! You're going to make lots of money. *That's the plan, and that's the end of it.*"[30]

Unsurprisingly, later in life Agassi grew to deeply resent this imposed heavy-handed authority, ambition, and discipline, to the point that, despite all his success, he began to hate tennis. His father effectively became a militant super-ego, hovering in the background, bellowing instructions, and imposing on Andre the endless repetition necessary to achieve sporting excellence. While the training was clearly effective, Agassi felt he was not able to be or to express himself, exemplifying one problematic side of the Sun-Saturn complex.

Although a Sun-Saturn hard-aspect alignment can indicate the presence of a dominant, overbearing parent or other authority figure, as in this example, the presence of such an authority can be the foundation for future achievement, as the identity is crucially molded by the severe discipline or exacting judgment or even the threat of punishment. Without this structure and early conditioning, in all probability Agassi would not have been able to realize his innate talent and emerge as a tennis champion—the discipline and suffering we resent can often prove to be our greatest strength and provide the foundation for our life. The experience of Saturn can often come to us seemingly from outside—from other people or from circumstance—such that we tend to think that it is something alien to us, something external imposed on us that prevents us being ourselves. We do not identify with the Saturnian influence, but see it as something "other." Viewed astrologically, however, we can recognize that even external influences are in some sense our own. Astrology, that is, encourages us to see all the events of our lives, all the things that arise within our life-field, as a manifestation of the psyche as it focuses on us individually. The external circumstance is but the mirror image of our own unconscious or the medium through which the unconscious finds expression. "In the final analysis," as Nietzsche observed, "one experiences only oneself."[31]

Agassi has the Sun and Saturn in a tight conjunction (within three degrees), as part of a larger configuration involving Mercury, Venus, and Mars in a broad stellium—that is, all the planets are forming a single conjunction, extending from the sign Taurus into Gemini. This stellium configuration indicates a greater archetypal complexity than a two-planet conjunction, of course, with each of the corresponding planetary archetypes in a mutually stimulating dynamic relationship.[32] The additional alignment of Venus and Mars, in a trine to Uranus, is associated with another prominent theme in Agassi's character. He is well known not only for his tennis accomplishments, but also, in his younger years, for his rebellious fashion sense, with bleached blond highlights, pony tail, and acid-washed cut-off denim shorts breaking the mold for tennis attire and the look of tennis players in the late 1980s and early 1990s. Here Venus is associated with style and image, Mars with sport, and Uranus with the archetypal rebel. In this act of rebellion, the solar identity asserted itself against Saturnian authority that had so shaped the young Andre's life experience.

The Saturnian influence on Rafael Nadal came from his uncle, Toni Nadal, himself a former professional tennis player with unrealized aspirations of becoming an international champion. From the first, the young Nadal was treated more sternly than the other young players under Toni's supervision. Toni, we learn in Rafael's autobiography, treated his young nephew with "undisguised injustice in the company of his peers, while requiring him never to complain."[33] Rafael was obedient ("he would bow his head and do as he was told"), even if he sometimes resented his uncle's heavy-handed authority.[34]

As he began to compete and play in tournaments, Rafael was repeatedly told that his opponent was better than him. Rather than foster an inferiority complex, however, Nadal was instilled with a healthy awareness of shortcomings such that throughout his career he would never underestimate an opponent nor rest content with his achievements, as he dedicated himself to hard work to constantly improve and overcome flaws. An awareness of deficiencies compared to other players, such as the supremely gifted Roger Federer, fostered in Nadal the humility for which he is widely known, and his dedication to the sport enabled him to prosper in many encounters against players with more natural ability, Federer included.[35]

John Carlin, the co-author of Nadal's autobiography, observes that Nadal's "feet-on-the-ground civility" is a direct consequence of the way he was raised by his parents and guided by Toni, who instilled positive Saturnian virtues.

> Were he to end up a superstar, Toni and his parents would make damn sure he would end up a humble one. Were he to be applauded for his humility, as he often has been, that too would be disdained as excessive praise. "Humble is the way you have to be, period," Toni says. "There's no special merit in it. What's more, I wouldn't use the word 'humble' to describe Rafael. He just knows his place in the world. Everybody should know their place in the world."[36]

Carlin describes Toni Nadal as "cold-eyed and resolute," as someone who, although sometimes kindly and generous, is "a moralizer, opinionated, always up for the argument," "unbendingly doctrinaire," and as "severe in his certitudes as a black-clad Catholic in the Spanish Court during the age of [Hernán] Cortés."[37] In these respects, his character was perfect for the Saturnian role of mentor in Rafael Nadal's life. "Toni is my tennis coach and my life coach too,"

Rafael stated. "His medium is words: he urges me on, berates me, gives me advice, teaches me."[38]

A later development of the Sun-Saturn complex in some cases sees the transition from the aspiring hero, tutored by the father figure or wise guide, into the master and then the teacher, as the hero of youth becomes the wise old man in maturity and later life. In the case of Agassi and Nadal, both men established centers for the training of young players, feeling a responsibility to nurture young talent. In 2017 Agassi also moved into the role of coach of Nadal's rival Novak Djokovic, hired especially to pass on the wisdom and understanding from having himself achieved success later in life, when youthful motivations and aspirations had long since disappeared. We recognize, in this life pattern, the combination of the Jungian archetypes of the hero and the wise old man, symbolized by the Sun-Saturn pairing in major aspect.

Returning to film, we meet a classic cinematic portrayal of the hero-to-mentor transition in the character of Luke Skywalker, played by Mark Hamill in George Lucas's *Star Wars*. Hamill, too, has Sun-Saturn in major alignment in his birth chart, and in his portrayal of Skywalker we witness his personal maturation guided by the two Jedi masters Ben Kenobi and Yoda, who temper his youthful over-eager heroism and mold his character. Saturn invariably provides us with ample opportunity to cultivate moral virtues—patience, steadfastness, self-discipline, responsibility, and good judgment—even if the labor of developing such qualities can be the cause of much frustration. Key to Skywalker's own transformation is the willingness to curb his enthusiastic individualism in order to assimilate the necessary lessons from his mentors, and, at a crucial threshold of his training, to muster the courage to meet his greatest fear: coming face-to-face with his foe and dark father, Darth Vader. We see here a cinematic portrayal of the archetypal encounter between ego-consciousness and the shadow, and the mythic motif of the solar hero standing up to the tyrant-dictator—both reflections of Sun-Saturn themes. In the seventh installment of the *Star Wars* series, *The Force Awakens*, we witness Skywalker emerge from his hermetic solitude as the wise old man, primed to serve as a mentor to others.

In a variant form of expression of the Sun-Saturn complex, the individual's experience can be defined by the absence of a father (which is the case with Skywalker, of course), just as with Moon-Saturn aspects the relationship with the mother can be absent, obstructed, or problematic—perhaps a source of tension, anxiety, or embarrassment.

Without adequate guidance from parents, or with a heavy-handed influence, one's sense of one's own inner authority can be difficult to develop, but in addressing the inferiority and building up one's confidence and personal authority one step at a time, one can come to deep and profoundly satisfying realization of having actualized one's potential, of having met the challenge of one's destiny, as it were. As the alchemists realized, the lowly starting point—the base metal of the *prima materia*, which is repugnant and vile, despised and rejected, deemed of no worth—can become the foundation stone for the realization of the *lapis*, the alchemical gold.

The *Principium Individuationis*: Becoming a "Solitary"

As we can see, the Sun-Saturn archetypal complex obviously has a significant bearing on the course of individuation. One key challenge is the struggle to express oneself in spite of the fear of judgment or embarrassment, and in spite of any sense of guilt or shame that risks of creative self-expression entail. Saturn inclines us to abide by the rules of the game and to look for approval, imbuing a strong sense of right and wrong. One is challenged to assimilate what is best in tradition, to learn from elders, guides, and authorities in one's field. Of course, one can be crippled as much as guided by the weight of authority or by the psychological pressure one feels from one's own expectation and inner critic. Hence, there has to be a progressive re-education of the super-ego or the critical animus, as one's inner conscience becomes attuned to the dictates of the Self rather than parental or societal expectation. This allows a transition to a state in which one becomes one's own authority—a key element of the spiritual journey and individuation. As one logion in the Gospel of Thomas declares, we must become as "solitaries," learning to stand apart.[39] The Sun-Saturn combination is especially associated with the *principium individuationis* by which one is differentiated into a definite, separate individual, carved out in space and time. The willingness and ability to stand apart, in one's integrity and solitude, and perhaps in isolation, are imperatives of a realized individuation process.

Such themes are often pronounced in the lives of people with major Sun-Saturn aspects in their birth charts. For instance, we see precisely these capacities and tendencies articulated by Friedrich Nietzsche, in an expression of his own natal Sun-Saturn alignment—a square, in his case. His was a life of solitude and isolation from the world, which had a crucial influence on the nature of his philosophy. His solitary path took him away from the crowd, away even from the historical moment, to stand in judgment on present-day humanity from the perspective of his revelation of the coming *Übermensch*, his ideal of distant human possibility. The solitude and sufferings of his life forged his character in such a way as was necessary to formulate his philosophical revelation. A major element of Nietzsche's life path was also the assimilation and subsequent rejection of all forms of authority—virtually every settled religious and philosophical teaching and every intellectual mentor and authority in his own life, notably Arthur Schopenhauer and Richard Wagner, who had initially served as substitute father figures in Nietzsche's life. Nietzsche felt compelled to become his own authority, to live by his own self-forged laws and values within an otherwise meaningless world. As Jung remarked, even as Nietzsche rejected all forms of meaning in his embrace of creative nihilism, he became, in the figure of Zarathustra, a living embodiment of the wise old man, espousing his judgments and teachings to every audience—a veritable mouthpiece for meaning. In short, Nietzsche unconsciously identified with the wise old man archetype, expressing in one form a tendency associated with the Sun-Saturn complex. Such a tendency was especially pronounced and extreme given the presence of Pluto, which is in hard aspect to the Sun and Saturn in Nietzsche's chart, as we will consider in Volume III.

In another example, William Wordsworth (see Chart 22), in the most famous line of his poetry, gave voice to sentiments associated with his own natal relationship between these principles (he had Sun square Saturn): "I wandered lonely as a cloud." Similarly, in music, singer-songwriter Neil Diamond, who has the Sun in square aspect to Saturn, explores Sun-Saturn themes in a number of his songs. In "I Am . . . I Said," one of his most popular tracks, Diamond brings together the solar experience of being, the "I am," with the Saturnian experience of solitude and loneliness:

> "I am," I said
> To no one there
> And no one heard at all
> Not even the chair
> "I am," I cried
> "I am," said I
> And I am lost, and I can't even say why
> Leavin' me lonely still.[40]

In another song, he is the "Solitary Man," coming to terms with the possibility of remaining alone:

Don't know that I will
But until I can find me
The girl who'll stay
And won't play games behind me
I'll be what I am
A solitary man. [41]

The archetypal Saturn can build walls around us, as it were, as we assume the isolation of some particular life role that can mold our character and our capacity to function as responsible, autonomous agents, able to do what must be done. Indeed, the transits of Saturn—periods of life in which the current position of Saturn in its orbit through the heavens is in major geometric relationship to the position of the planets in a birth chart—can often indicate periods when one must learn to stand alone, accepting isolation as a necessary element of individual maturation. Such experiences serve to strengthen and differentiate the individual nature of our being, pushing us to more fully move into and affirm our separateness, even as we dispassionately fulfill the roles and responsibilities our community places on us.

We have noted already in relation to the shadow that the experience of Saturn, as one matures into adulthood, often entails the building up a life structure around one's weakness. The impulse towards self-preservation and self-protection pushes us to unconsciously eschew that which is most painful and uncomfortable, removing ourselves from these dimensions of our character and experience. The result can be a defensiveness or acute sensitivity towards those aspects of our life. During individuation, however, when the structure of the ego and its persona are disrupted, broken, or dissolved, we are presented with the opportunity to face the shadow and integrate that which has been discarded. Individuation thus demands the willingness to rebuild one's life on firmer foundations by facing and accepting one's own inferiority and sensitivity to judgment. To individuate one must affirm the pressure that Saturn brings, accept the pain and suffering as necessary elements of psychological transformation and growth. One's suffering, if affirmed, can become the source of deep life meaning. As difficult as this path is, the pain of avoiding Saturnian responsibility is invariably worse than the pain of facing it and accepting it. And avoidance or denial may close doors, shut one off from life in alienation and isolation, defensiveness and cynicism.

Tests and Thresholds: Transits of Saturn to the Sun

In addition to correlations involving Sun-Saturn alignments in natal charts, any of these themes might manifest in one's life for periods of limited duration during personal transits of Saturn to the Sun—lasting for anything up to a year or so, depending on speed of movement and retrograde motion.[42] Personal transit analysis, you will recall, maps the moving positions of the planets over time onto the planetary positions in birth charts, focusing on periods when the orbiting planets form significant aspects with these natal planetary positions.

Saturn hard-aspect transits to the Sun occur roughly every seven years (keeping in mind that Saturn's orbital period is 29 years so that every seven years it forms a conjunction, square, or opposition with the Sun in the birth chart). In addition, Saturn also forms other significant aspects with the Sun during this time—the trine and the inconjunct (quincunx) are especially noteworthy. The qualitative feel and dominant mode of one's experience come to reflect Sun-Saturn themes during such times.

For instance, Saturn transits to the Sun often accompany the shouldering of worldly responsibilities and encounters with limitations that come from the assumption of a particular life role, one that is typically associated with one's profession or work in the world. Periods of these transits can subject one to constant pressure of responsibility as if one's consciousness is being forged, pressed into a cast that shapes the personality. One's life can feel restricted, time seems to pass more slowly, and one's horizons narrow to focus on the tasks at hand and labors to be performed.

Sometimes during these transits one has to bow to the authority of superiors and supervisors, or the judgments of others and of society at large, which might feel oppressive or uncomfortable, particularly if one is used to following one's own direction and natural impulses. There can also be a tendency towards self-judgment and a loss of confidence in oneself. Yet equally, Saturn forges the identity associated with the Sun, bringing experiences in which we must assimilate past traditions or fall in line with the way things have been done before. Saturn, in its association with the wise old man archetype, introduces us to the rules and requirements of life at that moment. On other occasions, one might assume the position of authority oneself, and thus be forced to bear the burden of decision and command that this authority entails, carrying the weight of responsibility to oneself and others.

At a deeper level, looking beyond the specific challenges these transits bring, they can be experienced often as periods of trial, tests, and occasionally of torment. Given Saturn's association with endings, dividing lines, and time, they can also manifest as thresholds marking the end of one life phase and the entrance into another. Invariably, such threshold experiences mold us by imposing on us pressure, isolation, sufferings, and sometimes a greater awareness of mortality. The transit can be especially testing if the outer planets are also involved—in aspect to transiting Saturn or to the Sun or Saturn in one's natal chart.

Experiences arise that can push us into the reality of our separateness. We might, for instance, experience the isolation of our position in the world, as if we are cut-off from those around us, and therefore can become more acutely aware of our separate existence, as consciousness is called to stand alone and support itself—the isolation of the "I Am" experience. An encounter with death and suffering might also serve to separate us from others and from the world, as if we were becoming further incarnated as separate beings, unable to rely on anything apart from ourselves for support. In addition to a perceived slowing down of time, there can be a felt compression of experience, and an entrapment in a situation from which there seems to be no escape. The transits tend to call forth a focus on necessities, doing only what must be done, fulfilling one's duties. As well as bringing to an end a life phase, these transits can even challenge the validity or continued existence of the person one was. In mythic and religious terms, Saturn is at once the threshold to be crossed and the experience of karma or the hard knocks of fate. In one way or another, the challenge of self-sustaining autonomous existence (associated with the Sun) can be difficult to manage during major Saturn transits to the Sun; it can be a struggle just to be, to exist. An acceptance of the difficulties the Saturn transit brings, however, can enable one to affirm the experiences as necessary, no matter how undesirable or painful they might be, and thus to attune to the deeper meaning of the transit and its value for individuation.

*　　*　　*　　*　　*

The Soul and Death: The Moon-Saturn Complex

As we have seen, with Moon-Saturn natal alignments the experience of Saturn is often experienced most immediately in the sphere of one's emotions, family relationships, and domestic life. The Moon, let us recall, is also connected to the soul and the inner child, whose emotional sensitivity and vulnerability form a stark contrast to the often hard and harsh conditions of material reality, pertaining to Saturn. Under the influence of this archetypal combination, it can seem that the world is cold and unforgiving, utterly indifferent to our emotional needs and all-too-human feelings.

The mood of this side of the archetypal combination is conveyed well by the music of Franz Schubert, especially the Schubert *Lieder*, performed by a solo singer with piano accompaniment. Schubert was born with the Moon and Saturn in a square alignment, part of a larger T-square with Jupiter and Uranus, a configuration reflected in his ability to convey, often in a dramatic and magnified manner, sentiments and experiences close to the essence of the Moon-Saturn complex.

We can feel these sentiments and moods acutely in Schubert's song cycle *Winterreise*, set to the story of the suffering of a lonely man, moving through the harshly cold and desolate landscape of wintertime Germany in a world that cares naught for his plight. Although the Moon-Saturn complex is the prevailing mood throughout—the sensitive soul and fragility of the human condition in cold, uncaring, remorseless world—other archetypal complexes are also in play. For example, the song's protagonist is moved by the desire for and the pursuit of love—a theme resonating with Schubert's Mars-Venus complex (and a theme we will encounter again in Bruce Springsteen's lyrics discussed in Volume III):

> I dreamed of love reciprocated,
> Of a beautiful maiden,
> Of embracing and kissing,
> Of joy and delight.[43]

This desire for romance and the embrace of the beautiful maiden gives rise in turn to the lonely man's restless seeking and journeying, which are resonant with themes associated with the Jupiter-Uranus alignment in Schubert's chart, perhaps accounting for his attraction to this story. These other archetypal dynamics serve as supporting context for the core experience of sorrowful suffering, however. For, throughout, the journey is met with disappointment, sadness, pain, loneliness, and the approach of death. Through Schubert's music, put to the words of Wilhelm Müller's poems, one feels the pain of the soul unable to come to a place of home or rest in life, finding comfort only in the prospect of old age and death.

Chart 5

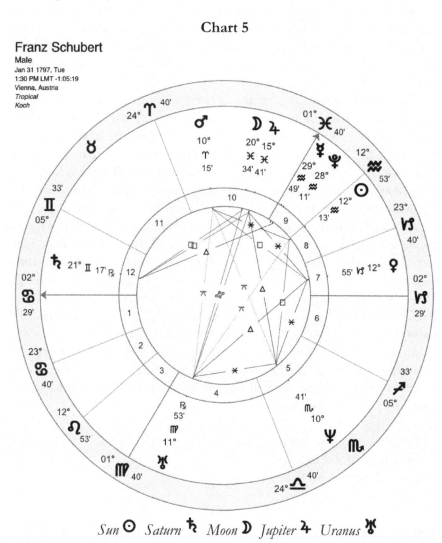

In Schubert's chart, the Moon and Saturn form a square aspect, less than 1 degree from exact. Note also the opposition between the Moon-Jupiter conjunction and Uranus, which form a broad T-square with Saturn. and the square between Venus and Mars. Schubert also has the Sun square to Neptune, an archetypal combination to be discussed later in this volume.

We encounter here a similar Saturnian reality to that described in the Sun-Saturn examples but the emotional quality of the experience, associated with the Moon, is more prominent—the lonely suffering soul, an inhospitable world in which one finds no comfort or place of home, the soul's emotional draw to death, and so forth. We are made aware of the vulnerability and fragility of the human condition, of the plight of the isolated individual estranged from the supporting warmth of the human community, of the person whose heart is frozen, like the landscape of the poem.

One finds the same themes manifesting during specific periods of time in coincidence with Saturn transits to the Moon. For instance, during these transits we can feel emotionally weighed down and serious, perhaps somber and sorrowful. We might also become more distant from our feelings, with the Saturnian tendency towards repression and negation coming to bear on our emotional life. Hurtful episodes in life can obviously trigger such responses, causing a hardening of the heart as we shut down emotionally. In the mood of *Winterreise*, at these times we might feel more acutely the isolation and suffering of the soul within the hard and unforgiving reality of the world. The suffering, however, as difficult as it can be to bear, enables us to become more aware of the soul, to feel into that dimension of experience. Our emotional reactions to the suffering that might arise during this transit can pull us away from the worldly ego or make us aware of the absence of soul in our lives. We can feel more acutely the needs of the soul or the inner child, its longings for home, for belonging, and perhaps for solitude or even for death.

Father and Child

The Moon-Saturn combination also brings together the father principle and the child archetype, with the father representing the authoritative voice of experience, which can often be painfully distant from the felt reality of the child's emotional world. Goethe's poem, providing the lyrics for the Schubert *Lied* "The Erlking," ("Der Erlkönig") exemplifies this dimension of the Moon-Saturn experience. Goethe too had a major Moon-Saturn alignment—in his case a trine—as did Dietrich Fischer-Dieskau, the eminent baritone best known for his dramatic and moving rendition of *Winterreise* and other Schubert *Lieder*, who had natal Moon in a square to Saturn. In "Der Erlkönig," a father holds his son close as they travel through night and wind. Soon the child becomes alarmed by the presence of the Erlking, with crown and tail, visible only to him. The father tries to reassure and comfort the boy, until events take a tragic turn.

> "My father, my father, and don't you see there
> The Erlking's daughters in the gloomy place?"
> "My son, my son, I see it clearly:
> There shimmer the old willows so grey."
>
> "I love you, your beautiful form entices me;
> And if you're not willing, then I will use force."
> "My father, my father, he's touching me now!
> The Erlking has done me harm!"
>
> It horrifies the father; he swiftly rides on,
> He holds the moaning child in his arms,
> Reaches the farm with great difficulty;
> In his arms, the child was dead.[44]

Here, the father's care for his child takes the form of the correction of the boy's emotional responses, an appeal to the facts of the matter, the commonsense explanation associated with Saturn. There is a refusal to take seriously the claims of the emotions, and thus to deny them, a tendency consistent with one form of expression of the Moon-Saturn combination. Themes of the frightened child, a distance from the child's experience, and the child's death are all also expressive of the Moon-Saturn complex. Saturn manifests here as death, the Grim Reaper, claiming the life of the child (associated with the Moon) in the stark ending—and in this case death comes suddenly and unexpectedly, reflecting one theme associated with the Saturn-Uranus hard aspect, present in Schubert's chart. As Richard Capell notes in his study *Schubert's Songs*, "Der Erlkönig" addresses the "terrors of a child," which to the adult have no reality. "But fears are born in the sensitive child, who must painfully learn to banish the visions of the dark and to cease in defiance of nature to quake."[45]

For comparison, a parallel might be drawn in popular music with Robert Smith of The Cure, who has a Moon-Mars-Saturn T-square (in a grand cross with Mercury). One of the band's most popular early hits, from 1980, was "Boys Don't Cry," co-written by Smith, a title conveying well the Saturnian cultural prohibition on boys and men (Mars) expressing emotion (the Moon). The lyrics of "In Between

Days," from 1985, penned solely by Smith, touch specifically on the theme of the frightened child, as in Schubert's *Lieder*, and the emotional problem or block, typical of this complex. "Yesterday I got so scared, I shivered like a child. Yesterday, away from you, it froze me deep inside."[46] And 1989's "Lullaby" relates the experience of a child being frightened by the visitation of a terrifying "Spiderman":

> On candy stripe legs the Spiderman comes
> Softly through the shadow of the evening sun
> Stealing past the windows of the blissfully dead
> Looking for the victim shivering in bed
> Searching out fear in the gathering gloom and
> Suddenly
> A movement in the corner of the room
> And there is nothing I can do
> When I realize with fright
> That the Spiderman is having me for dinner tonight
>
> Quietly he laughs and shaking his head
> Creeps closer now
> Closer to the foot of the bed
> And softer than shadow and quicker than flies
> His arms are all around me and his tongue in my eyes
> Be still be calm be quiet now my precious boy
> Don't struggle like that or I will only love you more
> For it's much too late to get away or turn on the light
> The Spiderman is having you for dinner tonight.[47]

The inspiration for the song was Smith's own experience. He recalls:

> When I was really young I had a very strange uncle (also called Robert!) who delighted in finding as many ways to scare me witless as he could. One of his favorites was to whisper grim bedside stories into my ear, stories that often related the twisted deeds of a horrible boy-eating creature called simply "the spiderman." One night he actually went so far as to climb in through my bedroom window after the lights had been put out . . . . I screamed for what seemed like days. The "spiderman" stories ended that night, but my fear of the dark and spiders persisted for quite some time.[48]

Aspects involving the Moon—in both natal charts and transits—have much to do with childhood experience, from the perspective of both parent and child. In a reality shaped by the Moon-Saturn archetypes, care can be expressed as the firm hand of discipline, imparting worldly wisdom and the benefit of years of experience to the children in one's charge.

Another form of manifestation of this complex follows from the tendency of Saturn as *senex* to literalize, and to limit, and oppress us, which in relationship to the Moon can give rise to a style of being in which one becomes nothing but a parent or caregiver—one's entire existence can become trapped within a narrow life role, for one feels the heavy weight and seriousness of Saturn to the exclusion of all else. The seriousness associated with Saturn is often a response to feelings of inferiority and sensitivity to others' judgments—in this case, concerning one's capacity to be a good parent, for instance, or it might take shape as a feeling of awkwardness around personal relationships, perhaps especially with women or family.

For the child with a significant Moon-Saturn complex, parental discipline and correction, if applied too emphatically, might manifest in adulthood as emotional caution, perhaps even a profound mistrust, with the Moon-Saturn complex prompting a judgment of the emotional reactions, questioning whether feelings and natural reactions are correct and permissible, and believing they stand in need of validation or improvement. Yet there is a positive dimension to this impulse, for Saturn's influence on the Moon can press us to squarely face up to our emotions and to work over the years to come to terms with them. Through meeting the Saturnian challenge, in whatever area of life it manifests, we develop patience, perseverance, discipline, and a deep understanding of life. Saturn provides an opportunity to turn a former weakness into a strength, slowly attained.

Emotional Distancing and Maturation

When our experience is significantly shaped by the Moon-Saturn complex, the innocent, pure, gentle, sensitive child within us can suffer not only amidst the pressures and expectations of the world, but also from the judgments of others or of our own inner critic. This situation can on occasion lead to a kind of emotional distancing, repression, and aloof detachment from the past, with the erection of emotional boundaries between oneself and others. Equally, we can become stuck emotionally in the past, wrapped up in our own emotional world, with the archetypes of child and anima, associated with the Moon, remaining relatively underdeveloped, concealed behind a protective screen of the ego structure. The deep life feeling of the anima can become imprisoned in attachments to old forms—perhaps in memories of the happy times of childhood or in lost relationships or woundings that triggered some kind of emotional shutting down. During individuation, the challenge might then arise of breaking through the protective walls of the ego, undoing Saturnian repression and defensiveness, so that we can recover a sense of soul, allowing the emotional core of the child within us to resurface. Jung had the Moon in a square aspect to Saturn, and his own loss of soul and his attempts to recover it were recounted in the mythic, almost biblical, narrative of his *Red Book*.

Simultaneously, however, with Moon-Saturn natal aspects and under transits of Saturn to the Moon, Saturn, manifesting as the senex and wise old man, can force upon us a maturation so that we grow beyond the emotional neediness of the child in us. Life circumstances impel us to leave behind the world of childlike dependence, to put away childish things, and to bring control and discipline to bear on our feelings. Saturn brings to an end the innocent and supported world of childhood, associated with the Moon, for entrapment in the emotional world of youth can signal stagnation and spiritual death as it does not permit the psychological development necessary for continuing growth. As painful as it is to leave behind the comfortable feelings and habits of the past, we must if we are to realize our calling and potential in the world. Saturn pushes us towards actualization.

Separation from the Mother and the Duty of Care

As the child's emotional world is so intimately connected with the relationship to the primary caregiver, most often the mother, themes associated with the Moon-Saturn complex also include a literal separation of mother and child. In this respect the Moon-Saturn combination is related to what Jung has called the orphan archetype. This particular archetypal pattern is exemplified by Marilyn Monroe, who was orphaned as a child, and was born with the Moon and Saturn in a ninety-degree square alignment.

At other times, the Moon-Saturn complex can manifest as some kind of block or obstacle to the expression of maternal care and the role of mother, including the experience of post-partum depression, which was vividly documented by Brooke Shields in her 2006 memoir, *Down Came the Rain: My Journey through Post-partum Depression*. Shields was born during a Moon-Saturn square. In this book she describes her experience of multiple life events associated with the Moon-Saturn complex: her relationship with her mother, living alone with her mother as an "only child" even as she had step siblings at her father's home, physical problems with her cervix following surgery, struggling to get pregnant, feelings of inadequacy as a mother, a deep struggle with depression following the birth of her daughter, and the supportive role of antidepressant medication in helping her work through the condition (a theme associated with the Saturn-trine-Neptune aspect in her chart). Thus again Saturnian themes—problems, delays, difficulties, isolation, a sense of inferiority, and melancholic episodes—impinge on the lunar experiences of the past, childhood, motherhood, and pregnancy. Distancing from the maternal experience can, in more extreme circumstances, produce cynicism and a deadening of the emotions until such a time that we can deconstruct the walls of resistance and fully feel the fear, loss, and vulnerability locked up in this form of the Moon-Saturn complex.

The same Moon-Saturn complex, however, in a variant form of expression can enable one to assume a burden of care for others in one's life, often children or elderly family members. Needless to say, such responsibilities can force upon us an emotional maturation, as we put our own needs to one side in attending to the needs of others. One is challenged to fulfill roles and responsibilities to others even in spite of one's feelings. In this way, we can learn to break the hold our feelings have over us.

The Moon-Saturn archetypal complex, positively experienced, imparts the gift of emotional consistency and solidity, with the capacity to stand with grounded emotional integrity in relation to the world. A developed relationship to themes and patterns of the Moon-Saturn combination can also promote a deep feeling for life's maturations and transitions, its endings and separations that we all experience: the parent no longer relied upon by the growing child, waving goodbye to the teenager leaving for college and moving out of the family home, or the passing of an elderly relative. The Moon archetype is associated with the capacity to feel into the loss and the sadness, as the heart tries to adapt to the painful but necessary separations life brings our way. Especially under the supportive trine or sextile aspects between these planets, one can develop a deeper appreciation of the importance of family and home, and a feeling for the value of the past and tradition to support and nourish us, providing continuity and stability from generation to generation.

The Shepherd Tends His Flock

A number of Moon-Saturn themes are marvelously conveyed in the selection of biblical quotations describing the life of Jesus in Händel's great oratorio *Messiah*.[49] Expressing the archetypal complex associated with the Moon-opposite-Saturn aspect in his birth chart, Händel was able to attune to those elements of the Christian narrative that reflect themes of this complex and enable us all to feel into them more fully through his music.

Moon-Saturn themes are present from the beginning. The infant Jesus, though born into difficult, humble circumstances, is destined to rule, and is laden with responsibility for the wellbeing of the human race, with the Moon pertaining to the childhood experience and care for humanity, and Saturn to the weight of responsibility:

> For unto us a child is born, unto us a son is given, and the government shall be upon His shoulder.

Jesus is to become the comforter of the people in their suffering. He is the good shepherd, in a Saturnian role, gently tending to the sheep in his flock. Astrologically, we might say that the archetypal Moon provides the tender comfort to relieve the Saturnian sufferings and hardships of life, just as Saturn, as the wise guide, leads the people, like lost sheep and children, from the condition of darkness into the light.

> He shall feed His flock like a shepherd; and He shall gather the lambs with His arm, and carry them in His bosom, and gently lead those that are with young.

> Come unto Him, all ye that labour, come unto Him that are heavy laden, and He will give you rest.

> Take his yoke upon you, and learn of Him, for He is meek and lowly of heart, and ye shall find rest unto your souls.

Not least, as Jesus meets his fate, we encounter again the theme of the suffering soul, in a harsh world, rejected and judged by men, weighed down with grief and sorrow, finding no comfort for himself even as he gave comfort to the people:

He was despised and rejected of men, a man of sorrows and acquainted with grief.

Surely He hath borne our griefs, and carried our sorrows!

Thy rebuke hath broken His heart: He is full of heaviness. He looked for some to have pity on Him, but there was no man, neither found He any to comfort him.

Behold, and see if there be any sorrow like unto His sorrow.[50]

Throughout *Messiah*, these Moon-Saturn themes are intermixed with the triumphant glory and epic quality associated with the Jupiter-Pluto complex—Händel also had natal Jupiter square to Pluto. We will return to consider this complex in Volume III.

A different Moon-Saturn theme lies at the heart of another celebrated Händel oratorio, *Solomon* (based on stories in the Old Testament books I Kings and II Chronicles), with the wise Egyptian king called upon to act as the judge in a bitter dispute between two women who both claim to be the biological mother of a newborn baby and desperately press their claims for custody. Astrologically, the Saturnian act of judgment is brought to bear on the fate of the baby, reflecting the Moon's association with motherhood, pregnancy, and infancy.

Emotional Rigidity and Domestic Entrapment

In another theme associated with the Moon-Saturn complex, either as a natal aspect or during a Saturn transit to the Moon, one can find that one is unable to feel at home. There might be a tendency to feel uncomfortable or inadequate in domestic situations or to feel judged by one's family—recall the example of Ben Stiller as Greg Focker in *Meet the Parents*. During transits of Saturn to the Moon, there can also arise a sense of separation from home—whether a literal separation (if one is forced to live away from home, for instance) or the feeling that one cannot find home and a sense of belonging. One might be forced by a change in circumstance to move away from a comfortable domestic situation or away from one's family, leaving behind the familiar world of the past. Or the complex might give rise to an impulse for domestic order and structure, even taking the form of an austere and spartan domestic environment, minimally decorated and devoid of home comforts. Even if circumstances change little, one's home environment might start to feel more claustrophobic, with the psychological shift impressing upon one the need for change.

At a psychological level, this complex can also give rise to the experience of being stuck in one's emotional patterns, or being stuck in one's home or hometown, imprisoned in the habits and familiar scenes of the past. Equally, under the Moon-Saturn pattern, one might find oneself trapped in rigid domestic routines, which can serve to shield one from being present in the moment. Saturn generally shows where we are trapped or experience binding limitation.

Actor Jack Nicholson's portrayal of Melvin Udal in 1997's *As Good as It Gets* (directed by James L. Brooks), to present one example from film, gives expression to a number of these themes and characteristics, reflecting the Moon-Saturn conjunction in Nicholson's birth chart. Nicholson is able to draw on the complex of experiences associated with that aspect in taking on the role of Melvin. While his neighbor, Simon Bishop (played by Greg Kinnear), convalesces after suffering a violent attack at home, Melvin becomes saddled with unwanted domestic responsibilities, first caring for Simon's dog and then looking out for Simon himself. Ordinarily, Melvin's life is dominated by rigid daily routines and patterns. He is emotionally withdrawn, grumpy, and cynical. In his dealings with waitress Carol Connelly (played by Helen Hunt), he is at once harshly judgmental and yet also, in his own way, caring, in that he goes to great lengths to help Carol's son, footing hefty medical bills to provide treatment for the boy—Saturnian judgment is coupled here again with the lunar impulse to care. Inspired by his feelings for Carol, the film shows Melvin being forced by circumstance to develop qualities of responsible care, to temper his harsh judgments, and to move beyond his rigid habit patterns and emotional barriers.

Isolation from the Matrix of Being

Behind a number of these forms of expression of the Moon-Saturn complex, and behind the personal separation of child and mother or the distancing between them, stands the transpersonal dimension of a felt separation from the matrix of being, with the Moon-Saturn archetypal dynamics taking the form of an existential alienation from the experience of life as nurturing, caring, and supportive. Unsurprisingly, then, we see major elements of the Moon-Saturn complex in one of the most influential existential thinkers of the last century—Jean-Paul Sartre, who had a Moon-Saturn conjunction. Although Sartre in many ways had a happy childhood experience, and was doted upon by his mother, even spoilt and pampered (reflecting the archetypal association with the Venus-Jupiter conjunction in a square to the Moon in his birth chart), his childhood also left him isolated and alone, a pattern arising out of the Moon-Saturn complex. As Sartre expresses it in his autobiographical memoir of childhood, *The Words*, "I was nine years old. As an only child and without a friend, I did not imagine that my isolation could end."[51] Periods of loneliness later in life, he noted, would take him back to his childhood experience.

We have seen that Saturn is associated with BPM II in Grofian perinatal psychology, the phase of the birth process in which contractions begin. People reliving the birth process in non-ordinary states of consciousness report the experience of this matrix as one of exile and alienation, with the loss of the condition of preconscious unity with the mother, as one is thrust into a world of entrapment, limitation, toil, suffering, and separation. The experience of Saturn in our lives partakes in the themes of this matrix for Saturn brings endings, often tinged with sorrow and sadness, and it pushes us, in spite of our emotional attachment to past comforts and familiarities, into the separation and often alienation of egoic selfhood, in service of the *principium individuationis*. One has to experience the "fall," be cast into exile, awaken to *samsara*, and face one's finitude to become a separate carrier of self-reflective consciousness, and to actualize the pattern and potential of the Self.

Underlying these variant forms of expression of Moon-Saturn themes is the principle of individuation, pressing us to leave behind our emotional containment in the world of childhood, which persists within us all, long into our adult years, especially in the absence of meaningful rites of passage in the modern West. During the hard-aspect transits of Saturn to the Moon, we will tend to pass through experiences that force us to sever the emotional bonds to an earlier, more habitual, more unconscious way of being in the world. Saturn brings a further "fall" and exile from the preconscious world of childhood, for this is also a movement towards the actualization of separate individual consciousness. The archetypal dynamics arising during these transits create circumstances in which we are forced to resist the demands of our own emotional nature—for nourishment, comfort, security, care, and past attachments and familiarities.

In Jungian terms, we might say that Saturn, in its association with the father archetype, as the principle of the spirit that furthers our individuation into separate autonomous beings, opposes the pull of the mother archetype, back to comfortable unconsciousness and the familiar instinctive emotional patterns of the past, which were less burdened by the demands of self-conscious awareness and responsibilities. The father negates the neediness of the child-anima within us, while simultaneously bringing to maturity the playfulness of the child such that it is expressed in more valuable ways, in service of one's higher calling.

* * * * *

The Constraints and Certainties of the Mind: Mercury-Saturn

We were introduced to the Mercury-Saturn complex in our earlier discussion of Schopenhauer, noting his tendency to be intellectually preoccupied with the problematic dimension of experience, and pressed to articulate his understanding of the centrality of suffering in human life. More generally, as Richard Tarnas has noted, the Mercury-Saturn combination is often associated with negative thoughts or an eye for the fault or error, which fill the scope of one's perception. It can manifest, too, he observed, as thought patterns that become stuck, perhaps in morbid contemplation, or as in those moments when you cannot get a particular idea or problem out of your mind. One notable example of this phenomenon, Tarnas proposed, is Albert Einstein, born during a Mercury-Saturn conjunction, who, from 1917, became fixated on the idea of a "cosmological constant" to support the view of a static universe, despite evidence to the contrary which suggested that the universe was expanding.[52] Einstein took issue with quantum physics, famously claiming that "God does not play dice," and attempted, until the end of his life, to debunk the theory.

In the case of René Descartes, who had a natal trine between Mercury and Saturn, an aspect that is considered to be supportive of the expression of the corresponding archetypes, he was able to draw on the intellectual doubt associated with this complex as the sole foundation of his certainty about his existence in formulating his *cogito ergo sum*: I think therefore I am. Isaac Newton, another major intellectual father of the modern era, who had Mercury square to Saturn, formulated the laws of motion, and the mathematics and measurement of the mechanistic functioning of reality—foundational principles that defined an entire worldview and provided the basis for classical physics.

A Mercury-Saturn alignment can indicate a mind structured and perhaps constrained by the rules of logic or the adherence to certain fixed principles or ruling ideas. In philosophy, Immanuel Kant's focus on the innate categories of the human mind—principles that structure and condition all cognition and perception, and that define the boundaries of human knowledge—is a fine example of this type. The knowledge and cognition pertain to Mercury; the boundaries and structuring principles pertain to Saturn. He had the two planets in a square aspect. Themes of the Mercury-Saturn complex are also strikingly evident in Kant's concern with the rational basis of morality, which he articulates as the "categorical imperative"—the idea that human actions and decisions are moral to the extent that they conform to duty and may be upheld as a universal ethical principle applicable in all situations. Kant's Saturn was also in a square alignment with Mars, associated with the archetypal principle of action, with Mercury square to Mars, forming a T-square.

In popular culture, one ready example of these elements of the Mercury-Saturn complex is Leonard Nimoy, with a natal Mercury-Saturn conjunction, whose *Star Trek* character, Mr. Spock, became known to television and cinema audiences as the very embodiment of reason and logic, often in defiance of the intuitive and emotional responses of those around him, and occasionally his own. His refusal, in the face of speculation or the lack of hard evidence, to formulate opinions not grounded in known facts gave rise to his oft-repeated retorts—"illogical" and "insufficient data"—both conveying well a Mercury-Saturn position. His logical mind and his firm commitment to scientific evidence became part of *Star Trek* folk lore, just as much as his Vulcan ears.

Born less than one week apart from Nimoy, and starring alongside him as Captain James T. Kirk, William Shatner has the same Mercury-Saturn conjunction yet portrays it in *Star Trek* in a quite different way—often encountering it through Spock or in the situations in which they both find themselves. Both characters were adherents to the United Federation's "prime directive" (prohibiting any action that would interfere with the autonomous life and development of an alien civilization—a kind of categorical imperative) and subject to the statutes of Federation law, which shaped their thinking and provided a consistent reference point in moments of doubt and uncertainty about whether or how to act. Kirk was bound by Spock's logic and often suffered from the frustrating lack of data or knowledge of the alien life they encountered. And both Shatner and Nimoy also have Uranus in aspect to the Mercury-Saturn conjunction in their birth charts, an archetypal combination that in *Star Trek* is most apparent in Kirk's struggle to overcome the limitations of the logical course of action propounded by his First Officer. In this configuration, the archetypal Uranus—the rebel and awakener—can give rise to the intuitive hunch or brilliant idea that breaks through rationality and logic, often in a crisis moment when life is on the line and all rational options are exhausted. In episode after episode, Spock likewise encounters the same dialectic between sure-footed logic and the unpredictable and unexpected emergence of intuition. They are also occasionally shown aboard the Enterprise playing a form of three-dimensional chess, and this too is associated with Mercury-Saturn in the intellectual straining and strategizing that one might also get from playing word games, doing quizzes, and the like, as the mind grapples with problems, questions, and quandaries. In their chess duels, as in the adventures in space, Kirk's intuitive approach tends to triumph against the pure Vulcan logic of Spock. Perhaps, in the final analysis, intuition holds the upper hand in life too.

The Mercury-Saturn complex pertains not only to the mind and thought, but also to communication. This can manifest in a number of ways: as a concise and efficient, or even curt and cutting, manner in speech; as a slow, impaired or unnatural spoken voice; and as a tendency towards critique in content of speech and writing. While communication and perceptual challenges can arise in association with a number of different Mercury aspects (especially to Uranus, Neptune, and Pluto), in each the defining quality of the associated experience reflects the nature of the planetary archetype interacting with the Mercury principle. With Mercury-Saturn complexes, people can, in some instances, face obvious barriers or impediments to communication, such that dialogue with others requires considerable effort but also brings with it the potential for deep satisfaction if the obstacles can be overcome.

Helen Keller is a striking example of this type. Blind and deaf before her second birthday after an illness, Keller faced enormous obstacles, and yet, aided by the dedication of her guide and teacher, Anne Sullivan, she was able to develop the remarkable capacity to communicate using her other senses. As one documentary reports, showing footage of Keller: "She is deaf and blind, but if you enter a room she will know it. Your lightest footfall will tell her," for her capacity for physical feeling was developed to such an incredible degree that she could feel the vibration of every step. "In reaching out beyond her dark and soundless life," the narrator continues, "Helen depends most on touch." She learned to rely on touch, aided by taste and smell, to recognize people and objects. Her hands became her primary bridge to experience, for she used her hands to read other's lips. She gave answers in her own voice, but, with no access to sound, the voice was "unnatural." For Keller, this was the source of "great sorrow." "For all her years of effort, Helen has never learnt to speak clearly. . . . Since she was a baby she has not heard a word spoken or seen lips form one." As Keller said herself: "It is not blindness or deafness that bring me my darkest hours" but her " . . . acute disappointment at not being able to speak normally." "Longingly," she adds, and in keeping with a negative Saturnian assessment of lack or disappointment, "I feel how much more good I could have done if I had acquired normal speech. . . . But after this sorrowful experience, I understand more fully all human striving, thwarted ambitions, and infinite capacity for hope."[53] Thus, communication, associated with Mercury, became the greatest obstacle in Keller's life and drew forth the talent, fortitude, and accomplishment for which she became known. Her achievements were nothing short of astonishing: she became the first deaf and blind person to earn a Bachelor's degree; she published twelve books; and she established the Helen Keller foundation, which has helped millions of people. Although Saturn aspects can indicate areas of weighty burden, limitation, and difficulty, they can also indicate the moral capacity to face and overcome these conditions through steadfast and patient effort. Saturn often establishes the basic conditions of life, the structure in which experience will unfold, but, as we all in time come to realize, those areas of life that bring the greatest difficulty can also provide deep life meaning and satisfaction arising from hard work and perseverance over many years.

In considering Mercury-Saturn's significance for the individuation process, we might recognize again Saturn's association with the shadow in the form of inferiority, judgment, embarrassment, and guilt. In this case, feelings of inadequacy or uncertainty in the area of knowledge can give rise to the pressure to learn, to make sure one knows enough, so that one cannot be exposed for one's ignorance in communication with others—Mercury-Saturn can manifest as acute embarrassment from saying the wrong thing or having insufficient knowledge. Dimly aware of the discomfort and suffering this might bring, the defensive structure of the ego can be built up around one's intellectual capacities and knowledge, which seemingly provide certainty in the face of doubts and insecurities, offering a kind of intellectual fortress against life. Locked away in an ivory tower of one's rational intellect or fixed ideas, one is partly shielded from the pain of life and the vagaries of chance perhaps, for one can rest secure in the apparent certainties of one's knowledge, but one might also effectively lose one's life—that is, the capacity to live, think, and feel authentically and openly—in the process.

Chart 6

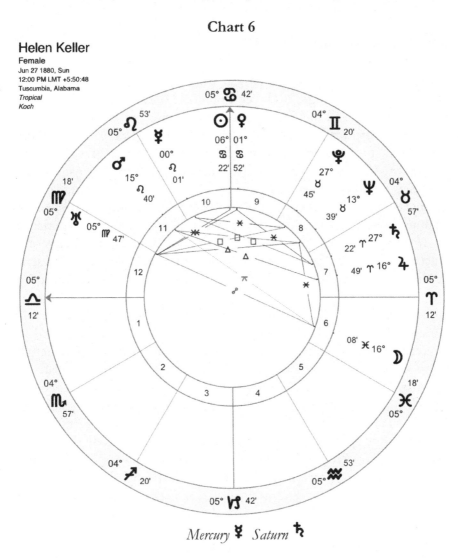

Mercury ☿ *Saturn* ♄

To meet the challenge posed by Saturn during individuation, it is necessary to recognize, accept, and enter into the inferiority and embarrassment. Passing through such emotions and judgments feels acutely painful, sometimes excruciatingly so—this is Saturn as the "narrow passageway" of the shadow, leading out of the prison walls of a defensive ego into the fuller reality of the unconscious and the depths of our humanity. One must pass through the fear associated with Saturn, otherwise one can remain a prisoner of it, always unconsciously avoiding painful experiences, and thus unable to pass beyond the Saturnian threshold guardian to meet one's life adventure.

The Critical Animus
The Mercury-Saturn combination is particularly relevant to the challenge of overcoming the critical animus, with its stern judgments, lack of self-knowledge, and yet dogmatic unconscious convictions. When the animus functions unconsciously, one can be subject to the Mercury-Saturn propensity to be rigidly attached to certain fixed ideas, even to the point of defensiveness, for often these ideas provide a form of security in the face of life's unpredictable twists and turns. Yet this complex is also associated with the critical scrutiny and careful formulation of ideas necessary to overcome the unconsciousness of the animus, by testing ideas against the empirical reality of one's experience.

It could be said that attempts to counter life's insecurity and uncertainty, for better and worse, underlie modern Western civilization's dominant worldview and scientific paradigms. The quest for rational understanding and positivistic scientific knowledge is motivated, to a large extent, by the desire to render life knowable, orderly, and controllable, and thus to attain more security and to preserve us from illness, sufferings, and loss, and perhaps ultimately to stave off death. The archetypal background helps us to appreciate the defensiveness and resistance towards those aspects of experience that challenge the hegemony of the reigning scientific paradigms and that appear as cracks in the walls of the academe's cathedral of knowledge. The scientific spirit, in its truest sense, however, is precisely the attitude one needs to cultivate in dealing with the animus during individuation: the challenging of accepted assumptions in the light of one's actual experience, the questioning of inherited beliefs weighed against facts, and the commitment to a continual openness in the face of new experiences rather than falling back on old truths. All these exemplify positive dimensions of the Mercury-Saturn complex, which we might experience if we have these planets in a major aspect in our birth chart and during periods in life when Saturn transits the position of Mercury in one's own individual birth chart.

* * * * *

Love's Lessons and Losses: Venus-Saturn

The combination of Venus and Saturn gives another inflection to the experience of Saturnian themes. When Venus is paired with Saturn in an astrological birth chart, indicated by a major geometric alignment between the two planets, we see the dynamic combination of the corresponding planetary archetypes such that the Saturnian themes discussed above are manifest in the areas of life to do with love, romance, beauty, art, happiness, pleasure, and friendship—the domain of the archetypal Venus.

Typically, with a pairing of these archetypes the experience of romantic love is felt as weighty and important, sometimes too important, in that efforts in this direction can be motivated by fear, tinged with self-protection and self-concern or defensiveness. In some cases, this might lead people to avoid romantic entanglements entirely; in others the style of romantic relating might be dutiful and conservative, while slowly ripening into a long-lasting devoted relationship; and in others still the Saturnian sense of inferiority regarding relationships might be masked by a confident persona, as if one must prove oneself in defiance of a perceived weakness. One way or another, the sense of separateness, perhaps even alienation, associated with Saturn, comes to the fore in the midst of relationships.

The struggles and disappointments of romantic love have provided plentiful material for popular and classical music (perhaps even more so than the joys of love), and the Venus-Saturn complex can give a developed understanding of this dimension of experience. Rather than indicating only difficulty in romantic relationships, however, Venus-Saturn is associated with a complex and varied range of expressions of themes consistent with the archetypal meanings of this combination. Contrary to what one might assume from a simplistic interpretation of its meaning, the Venus-Saturn combination does not preclude happiness in love and in friendship; indeed, it can indicate deep satisfaction in these areas of life.

To enter into the experiences associated with the Venus-Saturn complex, we can again turn to examples from the arts. One popular singer-songwriter with a Venus-Saturn natal alignment (a square) is Billy Joel, and many of his best-known songs provide illustrative examples of some of the many forms of expression of the Venus-Saturn complex.

"An Innocent Man," from the album of the same name, explores themes of self-protection in relationships, the erection of barriers to protect from possible hurt, and the denial of love.

Some people stay far away from the door
If there's a chance of it opening up.
They hear a voice in the hall outside
And hope that it just passes by.[54]

As a result, Joel adds, these people begin to "see through the eyes of the old" and run out of the Saturnian quality of patience; they are unable to "wait any more" so the Venusian romantic dimension of experience is rejected and denied.[55] The *senex* experience of old age here impinges on the romantic experience of Venus, and the delays and obstacles to finding enduring romantic happiness cause a shutting down in the sphere of love relationships. Saturn negates Venus, as it were. Past hurts, failures, and suffering reinforce the negative judgment of one's romantic prospects ("the love you've been denying you could ever feel").[56] The result, as Billy Joel describes, is the familiar sense of Saturnian aloneness, in this case fueling a cool distance, cruelty, bitterness, and resentment:

Some people sleep all alone every night
Instead of taking a lover to bed
Some people find that it's easier to hate
Than to wait anymore.[57]

Saturn as *senex* can foster cynicism and negativity that result in closing oneself off from life in attempts at self-protection: "I know you're only protecting yourself"—Joel names the Saturnian motivation.[58] In mythic terms, one could say that the old king (Saturn) has taken possession of the princess, symbol of the anima (Venus), keeping her locked away in a castle or dungeon, waiting to the liberated by the heroic ego or animus figure, symbolized by the Sun.

This dynamic plays itself out in Joel's lyrics. Reflecting the presence of the Sun in this three-planet configuration in Joel's chart, in this particular song we see the intervention of intentional ego consciousness, the solar archetype, shining a light into the painful shadow that Saturn can cast on romantic relationships, and choosing, through an act of will, to face the root of the experience—the moral challenge of facing the shadow, in Jungian terms—in the belief that life might then take a different path. The protagonist in this song is the solar hero, who knows this experience of romantic hurt and disappointment only too well, has learnt from hard knocks of rejection and pain in love, but has come through the other side, and is now in a position to draw on his life wisdom to help his beloved escape the clutches of her emotional entrapment:

> I know you don't want to hear what I say,
> I know you're gonna keep turning away.
> But I've been there and if I can survive
> I can keep you alive
> I'm not above going through it again.[59]

We saw earlier that Saturn pertains to those aspects of life we find acutely painful, perhaps the source of shame, embarrassment, and guilt, and that we might thus seek to avoid, often unknowingly. The ego structure and the circumstances of our life are unconsciously erected to protect us from the painful experience. As a result, however, the structure of one's life can be built on a false foundation, and one can thus fall into inauthenticity because the prime motivation for how one lives comes out of fear and the desire to avoid pain. Invariably, the path of psychological development forces us to address, and brings us face to face with, the uncomfortable or painful aspects of life we have long sought to deny.

In the song's chorus, we meet Saturn as the judge, the super-ego, delivering a verdict as if in a courtroom, in the area of romantic relationship, presided over by Venus. Here, Joel's character, having assimilated the hard lesson of Saturn, has moved through it, walked through the valley of the shadow, and can proclaim his innocence:

> And although this is a fight I can lose
> The accused is an innocent man.[60]

Other alignments in Joel's chart might also be included in understanding the motivations and themes of this song, not least the Moon-Neptune conjunction. Passing beyond the Saturnian judgment, the protagonist returns to the state of innocence (the "innocent man")—an archetypal theme associated with the Moon-Neptune complex in its expression of the purity of the child archetype, and of an emotional condition devoid of the stain of the sin and corruption of the world. Remember that Neptune pertains to the state of paradise before the Fall. Recall too that the Moon is also associated with the mother archetype, and these principles together pertain specifically to the universal mother, extending empathy and care to all. Joel draws on this impulse in his compassionate identification with the emotional experience of his beloved as he tries to lure her out of the womb-like world of emotional sanctuary to which she has retreated—another theme associated with the Moon-Neptune complex. The song's lyrics, then, explore the combination of the fragile emotional sensitivity associated with the Moon-Neptune pairing and the Venus-Saturn experience of a protective, defensive attitude in romantic relationships, believing things can never work out, because of past hurt and failure.

Chart 7

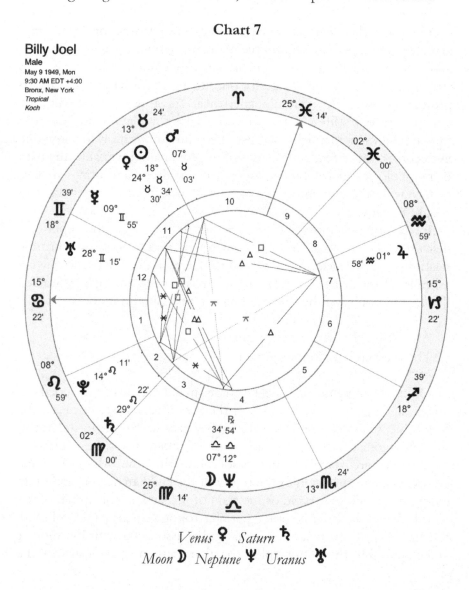

Another aspect in Joel's chart is deserving of mention here: Uranus in a sextile alignment with Saturn. This archetypal combination, in a potentially helpful and supportive sextile relationship, suggests the opportunity of breaking through the Saturnian protective boundaries, and thus to live again, and to live authentically, in spite of the pain romantic relationships might bring. Additionally, Uranus is in a wide square to the Moon—thus the archetypal theme of awakening from the womb-like withdrawal and passive stance that will merely "accept the world as it is," play the martyr, or long in childlike fashion for a "miracle cure."[61] Moon-Neptune archetypally tends towards passivity and refuge in the safe world of childhood dreams. Uranus, as we will explore more fully in Volume III, comes as the liberator, the awakener, and the rebel—suggested here by the awakening disturbance (the opening door, the voice in the hall, the repeated petitions to open the heart to love once more) bringing the possibility of liberation from old emotional patterns, even if this awakening call is initially felt to be disruptive and unwelcome, as an intrusion rather than a release.

In "Uptown Girl," on the same album, the barriers to love are primarily circumstantial—prohibitive class and wealth divisions rather than emotional walls. Again, in this song other archetypal complexes play a role in the story. Here we see Joel drawing on his Mars-Pluto complex (he has a Mars-square-Pluto natal alignment), as he casts himself in the role of the hot-blooded "downtown man," memorably depicted in the song's video as the oil-stained car mechanic, standing in stark contrast to the "white-bread world" of the "uptown girl"—a motif associated with the spotless purity of the Moon-Neptune complex. In this song too, he explores particular elements of the Venus-Saturn experience:

Uptown girl
You know I can't afford to buy her pearls
But maybe someday when my ship comes in
She'll understand what kind of guy I've been
And then I'll win.[62]

The downtown man is unable, through the limitation of material circumstance, to express love through conventional means—suggested by the giving of pearls. Saturn is susceptible to literalize, to make concrete, but also to deny—here the song's protagonist is unable to be romantic in the usual ways because of his lack of money. He is therefore forced to move beyond material displays of affection, and win love in other, deeper ways. Saturn, as always, forces upon us maturation and a deepening of character.

The song's hero, we are led to assume, is to reap the rewards of Saturnian virtues. Unable to meet the socially expected standards of providing fine gifts for the uptown girl, and separated by a class barrier, he is forced to bide his time, waiting for his ship to come in, cultivating the Saturnian moral qualities of patience and persistence. In a pattern characteristic of a Saturnian maturation, starting from a position of disadvantage, weakness, blockage, or failure, the downtown man, through exercising patience and consistency, finds himself in a position of strength, in which he can "win."

Aphrodite and Chronos
In "Piano Man," one of Joel's earlier recordings (released in 1973), the varied characters of the bar's clientele are "sharing a drink they call loneliness" for this is "better than drinking alone," again juxtaposing Saturnian isolation with Venusian pleasure and friendship, with their social life with friends and the piano man's music alleviating and providing solace from feelings of loneliness.[63] Venus can serve to sweeten life's sorrows and sufferings. Indeed, as we hear in Joel's words, the piano man provides a sad, sweet melody, from long ago, bringing a remembrance of the passing of years and of lost happiness. The music is to compensate for or to "forget about" life's struggles and disappointments and limitations.

"Piano Man" also juxtaposes the Saturnian themes of time and old age with Venusian love making:

> It's nine o'clock on a Saturday
> The regular crowd shuffles in
> There's an old man sitting next to me
> Making love to his tonic and gin.[64]

Similarly, in the "Longest Time," on *The Innocent Man*, Aphrodite meets Chronos, as it were, as the song explores the experience of romantic love, which "hasn't happened for the longest time."

> Who knows how much further we'll go on
> Maybe I'll be sorry when you're gone
> I'll take my chances

> I forgot how nice romance is
> I haven't been there for the longest time.[65]

The song reflects on the rewards of patience and the willingness to take a chance on love and life again, in spite of the risk it entails. Risk taking can be the perfect antidote to Saturnian protectionism, conservatism, and caution. Yet, on the other hand, brazen risk taking can be a screen for Saturnian insecurity, and one would be better to appease and honor Saturn by proceeding with caution. There is no universally applicable strategy here, alas. One has to make the determinations as to the right course of action for oneself.

But in "Tell Her About It," also on *An Innocent Man*, having suffered his own hard knocks, Joel seeks to pass on the wisdom or "good information" gleaned from his experience of romantic relationships:

> Listen boy, don't want to see you let a good thing slip away
> You know I don't like watching anybody make the same mistakes I made.[66]

Joel embodies Sun-Saturn as the wise old man, who has become learned in handling the pitfalls of romance, associated with Venus. He has made all the mistakes; he knows the rules of the game and understands the challenges.

A primary strategy is to combat feelings of insecurity that arise during relationships—another Venus-Saturn theme—for, as he tells us, "When you love someone you're always insecure."[67] Out of the Saturnian insecurity and inferiority in affairs of the heart comes a self-protective strategy to prevent the relationship turning bad or ending:

> Listen boy, it's not automatically a certain guarantee
> To insure yourself you've got to provide communication constantly.[68]

He advances a kind of unwritten rule of relationships, emerging from the desire to prevent things from going wrong. The basic motivation here is fearful and self-protective, the very opposite of trust and confidence, for when Saturn is involved confidence does not come naturally; it has to be earned. The rules, the advice, the strategies provide some structure and security in response to the doubt and inferiority arising when involved in the romantic experiences pertaining to Venus.

And, as in the other songs we have considered, here too Joel brings together themes of time and romance, in his role as the judge and wise guide:

> The girl don't want to wait too long
> You got to tell her about it
> Tell her now and you won't go wrong.[69]

In another inflection of the combination of time and love, in some instances Venus-Saturn can manifest in significant age differences between partners, as Richard Tarnas has observed, where the older partner (usually) is cast into a parental role. To give one classic example of this kind of notable age difference, in the film *The Graduate*, Dustin Hoffman, born with a Venus-Saturn square, plays college graduate Benjamin Braddock, the young man seduced by the significantly older Mrs. Robinson (played by Anne Bancroft) who, in a famous scene set in a hotel room, initiates him into love-making. The older partner effectively functions as a kind of mentor (albeit in this example a somewhat predatory one), drawing out the expression of Venus in love, romance, and sexual attraction. In Bancroft's birth chart we find a Sun-Venus conjunction in a trine to Saturn, aptly symbolizing her role as the older romantic guide in this film, with Venus also in a sextile alignment with Pluto, which correlates with, among other things, the archetypal motif of the predatory lusting seductress, which she portrays so convincingly.

Saturn prompts us to seek out and cultivate the security and sensible maturity of age. People with Venus-Saturn complexes might thus be inclined to look for these traits and qualities in an older partner, although this might not mean literal age, but those who are older in character or Saturnian in their realism, reliability, and seriousness. Sometimes, where this archetypal complex is present, the partner embodies conservative qualities or is an authoritative power in one's life, bringing into one's life order, limitation, and perhaps discipline and exacting judgments. As is often the case with all archetypes, the assessment of whether these experiences are positive or negative is ambiguous and relative to one's perspective. Living with the Venus-Saturn complex can bring the realization that marriage or the primary romantic relationship is at once limiting and perhaps even oppressive, and yet provides essential structure for one's life, a binding tie to reality, and grants the opportunity to cultivate the virtue of responsible love. The limitation often is just what is needed even if it feels restrictive or one blames it for one's unhappiness. With Venus-Saturn alignments, one can find oneself bound to another in relationship through some kind of practical necessity or by adversity—such as the older couple caring for each other through decaying powers and health in later life, even if feelings of romantic love have long since departed or they manifest conservatively and are expressed with reserve or through practical acts as much as romantic gestures.

We are often motivated to try to free ourselves of the burden or restrictive circumstance that comes through the experience of Saturn. However, if one can accept the limiting pressures of one's life and resist the desire to break free of uncomfortable situations, this can provide a container for psychological transformation. If our circumstances do not change, we ourselves are forced to change and adapt psychologically through an inner transformation that is essential to individuation. Thus, what is at one time perceived as a frustrating restriction can at another time—and from another place of consciousness—be appreciated as a grounding, steadying, and stabilizing factor, perhaps even as a source of deep satisfaction and fulfillment. With Venus-Saturn alignments, the responsibility of romantic relationships, the work that comes from committing to love, and perhaps even the critical judgment of one's partner, can, for instance, be precisely what one needs to counterbalance any tendencies towards inflation and escapism or to oppose the turbulence of psychospiritual transformation when the instincts and fantasies are often powerfully stirred.

Social Standing and the Judgment of Beauty

We have been concerned with the dimension of the Venus archetype pertaining to romantic love, with a selection of Billy Joel's song lyrics as our guide. But Venus also "rules" (to use astrological parlance) beauty and aesthetic experience. One theme associated with Venus-Saturn, then, is the judgment of beauty, in all its forms, whether discerning or otherwise. One example is the 45th and 47th US president, Donald Trump, with a Venus-Saturn conjunction, who was roundly chastised during the Republican Party primaries of 2016 for his critical judgments of women's appearances, directed, for instance, at fellow candidate Carly Fiorina (who also has a major Venus-Saturn alignment). Trump is well known for his television celebrity past, of course, and for running the Miss Universe competition over many years—a conspicuous form of the judgment of female beauty in the culture, and another expression of the complex of archetypal meanings associated with the Venus-Saturn complex.

Chart 8

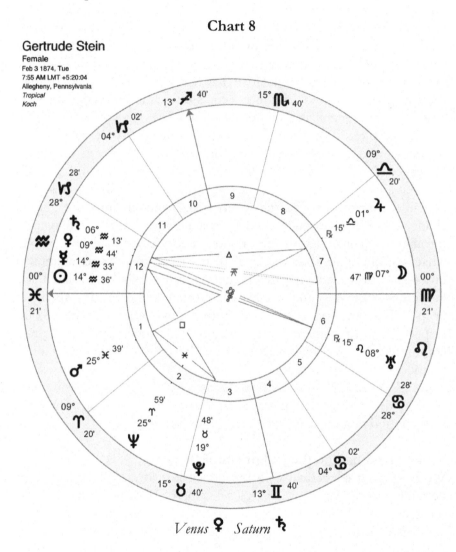

Venus ♀ Saturn ♄

Gertrude Stein (born February 3, 1874) represents an altogether different expression of the Venus-Saturn combination. The American modernist writer was born with a Sun-Mercury-Venus-Saturn conjunction (all opposite Uranus) and she embodied defining themes associated with the corresponding archetypal complex in becoming not only a remarkably shrewd and discerning judge of paintings and literature, but also a mentor and sounding board for a number of prominent modern artists and writers in her Paris salon, including Pablo Picasso, Henri Matisse, Ernest Hemingway, and F. Scott Fitzgerald. We see again the role of Saturnian judgment on aesthetic matters, with Stein's personality shining through her involvement in the arts, particularly new developments in modern art (reflecting the presence of Uranus in the configuration), as she became one of the most influential figures in the art scene in the first half of the twentieth century.[70]

We noted earlier that Saturn is often experienced as a felt pressure to meet and maintain a certain standard; the Saturnian impulse is experienced as a "should" or an "ought," something we feel we absolutely must do. When that planet is in major geometric relationship with Venus, particularly the hard aspects, this pressure can be felt as the impulse to meet some standard in one's appearance or manner of social engagement, by wearing certain labels or brands perhaps, or by a felt need to invest in items of enduring high quality or to adhere to a formal conservative style. Venus and Saturn underlie the linking of beauty or style and social status. This archetypal combination can often promote a leaning towards a classical, traditional, or formal style in taste and in artistic sensibility. Yet, in a quite different expression, demonstrating the multivalence of archetypal complexes, some people with natal Venus-Saturn aspects remain totally indifferent to fashion, with the Saturnian concern for utility and practical economy outweighing style and aesthetics.

Ray Davies of the celebrated British rock band the Kinks—with a Sun-Venus-Saturn triple conjunction, all opposite Neptune—could be describing a particular form of expression of this three-planet conjunction in two of the band's best-known songs from the 1960s. A "well-respected man," who is always "doing the best things so conservatively" while living a perfunctory existence of routine and respectability, is a playful parody of a Sun-Venus-Saturn figure, as is the "dedicated follower of fashion" who believes he is a "flower to be looked at."[71] Davies was poking fun at, and thus critiquing, the 1960s Carnaby Street set in London (aptly expressive of his Venus-Saturn opposite Neptune).[72]

With Venus-Saturn in major aspect, there can be an investment in upholding what is considered good taste in the right social circles and a concern with the rules of social discourse, doing what should be done to meet with approval and not cause embarrassment. This topic is approached by Emily Brontë in *Wuthering Heights*, reflecting themes associated with her own Venus-opposite-Saturn alignment, with the class division and a concern with social respectability and good manners persuading protagonist Catherine Earnshaw, mindful of social status, to marry the refined and genteel Edgar, rather than the uncouth and uneducated Heathcliff for whom she had stronger romantic feelings.

Yet in determining and assessing how these archetypes manifest, so much depends on the individual's value system and the context. Trump's values, for instance, seem to be driven to a large extent by financial and business interests, with an ethic based on getting the best business deal—the "art of the deal" (the title of Trump's memoir) is another expression of the Venus-Saturn pairing. Equally, however, in other instances this archetypal complex can take the form of the person who is steeped in the classics, such that he or she becomes a connoisseur of enduring cultural values and refined aesthetic tastes.

As we have seen, Saturn relates to that part of us that needs to know how to live, that looks for rules and scripts, and that needs permission or social sanction to guide and support our actions. Its position in the birth chart indicates dimensions of life where we are particularly sensitive to social convention and to the perceived judgment of others. An unconscious subservience to external rules and standards can obviously alienate us from our own inner truth, as we live according to assimilated values and ways of behaving, prompted by Saturn to consistently meet these standards, almost as a moral imperative. Needless to say, then, if one's consciousness and conduct are bound to acceptable standards of social discourse and appearance, it can prohibit the furthering of individuation. The one-sidedness of a narrow identification with accepted patterns and values can alienate one from the Self, although living in this way can also, however, precipitate a crisis through which one might move into a more authentic way of being and thus further one's individuation.

Leo Tolstoy's novella "The Death of Ivan Ilyich" provides a fine example of a situation of this kind. In Tolstoy's birth chart Venus and Saturn are conjunct, both opposite to Uranus, and he draws on the archetypal complex associated with this planetary configuration as he narrates the tragic liberation of Ilyich from a life of inauthentic social discourse and a loveless marriage—the latter theme mirrored by Tolstoy's own marriage.[73]

After securing a new position of employment and moving to St. Petersburg, Ilyich had a seemingly innocuous accident while decorating his new apartment. Until that mishap, his difficult relationship with his wife became much improved when they were involved in the joint project of getting the apartment into order—the work and arrangements providing a screen from the painful reality of their otherwise loveless and joyless relationship. Beyond this, the grip of the Venus-Saturn complex permitted small enjoyments mostly through rather superficial social gatherings and card-playing evenings: "Ivan Ilyich's pleasures were little dinners, to which he invited ladies and gentleman of good social position."[74]

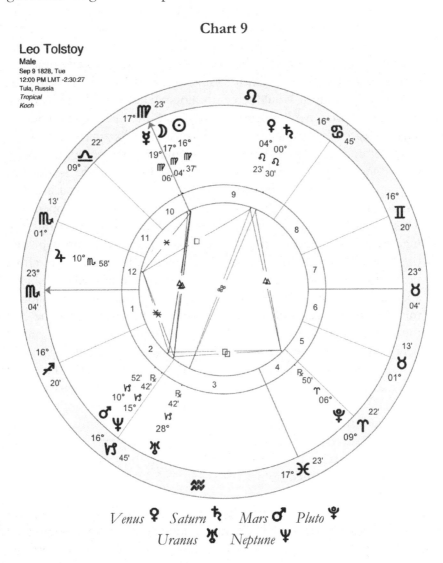

Chart 9

Further evidence of the interplay between Venus and Saturn comes through in Tolstoy's description of Ilyich's daily routine:

> He got up at nine, drank his coffee, read the newspaper, then put on his official uniform, and went to the court. There the routine of the daily work was ready mapped out for him, and he stepped into it at once. People with petitions, inquiries at the office, the office itself, the sittings—public and preliminary. In all this the great thing necessary was to exclude everything with the sap of life in it, which always disturbs the regular course of official business, not to admit any sort of relations with people except the official relations; the motive of all intercourse had to be simply the official motive, and the intercourse itself had to be only official. A man would come, for instance, anxious for certain information. Ivan Ilyich, not being the functionary on duty, would have nothing whatever to do with such a man. But if this man's relation to him as a member of the court is such as can be formulated on official stamped paper—within the limits of such a relation Ivan Ilyich would do everything, positively everything he could, and in doing so would observe the semblance of human friendly relations, that is, the courtesies of social life. But where the official relation ended, there everything else stopped too. This art of keeping the official aspect of things apart from this real life, Ivan Ilyich possessed in the highest degree; and through long practice and natural aptitude, he had brought it to such a pitch of perfection that he even permitted himself at times, like a skilled specialist, as it were in jest, to let the human and official relations mingle. He allowed himself this liberty just because he felt he had the power at any moment if he wished it to take up the purely official line again and to drop the human relation. This thing was not simply easy, agreeable, and decorous; in Ivan Ilyich's hands it attained a positively artistic character. In the intervals of business he smoked, drank tea, chatted a little about politics, a little about public affairs, a little about cards, but most of all about appointments in the service. And tired but feeling like some artist who had skillfully played his part in the performance, one of the first violins in the orchestra, he returned home.[75]

This passage illustrates the particular form of influence of Saturn on Venus discussed above, as the Venus archetype is narrowly expressed within the rules and expectations of public office. We might note the "official relations" and the "courtesies of social life," and the Venusian description of "the easy, agreeable, and decorous" manner in which Ilyich moves in and out of his official persona. The fulfillment of his duties of his impersonal bureaucratic role, and negotiating the boundary between human and official relationships, are compared to an artistic performance, with his Venus-Saturn character flourishing in the Saturnian formal rule-bound interactions required of his position.

Ilyich's relationships are utterly dominated by his official role, and his working life is punctuated by superficial social interactions offering mild pleasures within a humdrum and largely inauthentic existence. Saturn can manifest as the daily grind of working life, which gives little regard to the claims of the spirit and the soul; Venus serves only to sweeten the experience and thus to make it bearable, for a time. For although Ilyich's way of living conforms to themes associated with the Venus-Saturn complex, it is, of course, one of but many ways this complex can find expression. The unconscious will not permit us to remain in such a life-negating and inauthentic pattern indefinitely, merely going through the motions of social discourse, and sees to it, in real life as in this story, to impose change through crisis and suffering.

Ilyich's fall while hanging a curtain at home, although at first seeming to amount to little, develops, as the days and weeks pass, into a serious physical problem, incurable by all medical means. The incident can be recognized as the disruptive awakening call (associated with Uranus, as we will consider shortly) that breaks the Saturnian mechanized monotony and turns Ivan's world on its head, forcing upon him authenticity in the face of his impending death.

As always, there are multiple archetypal players in the plot. The Venus-Pluto combination (Tolstoy had these planets in a trine alignment) is evident in Ilyich's loathing of his wife and the disgust at her shows of affection, and apparent too in his wife's hatred of him, with the Venusian love relationship serving as the medium through which the seething underworld energies of Pluto find expression. Praskovya Fyodorovna, we read, "began to wish he were dead; yet could not wish it, because then there would be no income. And this exasperated her against him even more. She considered herself dreadfully unfortunate, precisely because even his death could not save her . . ."[76] Through Tolstoy's access to his Venus-Saturn complex came forth from his imagination a situation in which the husband and wife were bound to each other by circumstantial necessity, even as their feelings revolted. Saturn—manifest in the inescapable circumstantial limitation—provided the containing vessel for the unfolding episode of transformation through suffering, ultimately bringing about, with

Ilyich's demise and approach to death, a slow and painful reversal of what he considered pleasurable and a deepening into an authentic response to life.

We see themes associated with the Mars-Neptune complex (corresponding to Tolstoy's natal conjunction between these two planets) in Ilyich's idealization of his young male assistant, Gerasim, and the youth's selflessness and compassion in service to the dying man. And not least, we see experiences corresponding to the themes of Tolstoy's Saturn-trine-Pluto, in the agonizing pain of a slow death. Paired with the Saturn-Uranus alignment, the details of the agony of death jump out in one jarring account after another of the acute suffering Ilyich experienced, with death finally coming as liberation. Uranus pointedly accentuates the Saturnian episodes of pain and constriction, and ultimately, through the chain of events following his accident, frees the poor man from his hell of suffering. Uranus is the archetypal liberator and tends to manifest in sudden moments of jolting, acute experience, like a lightning bolt of electrical charge. We will meet this principle again later, in Volume III.

*   *   *   *   *

Soldier and Senex: The Mars-Saturn Archetypal Combination

We turn now to an exploration of the Mars-Saturn archetypal combination, which provides an opportunity to remind ourselves of the archetypal multivalence that is so critical for a correct understanding of astrological symbolism. This multivalence, you will recall, implies that the universal meanings ascribed to the planetary archetypes take on a wide variety of forms at the level of manifestation, often markedly different and sometimes even seemingly opposite, yet still remaining consistent with the nature of the planetary archetypes—Tarnas has described this as "archetypal coherence and concrete diversity."[77] Thus, the archetypal complex associated with a Mars-Saturn planetary aspect can manifest as a pattern of defensive aggression and retaliation or as an inability to express anger and to assert oneself; it could be present in the chart of the athlete or fighter engaged in a punishing regime of physical training or in the chart of someone for whom physical activity is impossible because of restrictive circumstance; it refers equally to people who have disciplined themselves to fight and be aggressive and to people who have been conditioned *not* to fight and to refrain from aggressive behavior. Although, on the surface, the difference between these forms of expression could not be more marked, on closer inspection we can see that they all partake in a common archetypal meaning arising from the combination of the Mars principle, pertaining to self-assertion, aggression, striving and struggle, fighting, physical energy, anger, and the warrior archetype, and the Saturn principle, relating to restriction, limitation, concentrated pressure, discipline, structure, repression, fear, and a sense of inferiority. The person who trains to fight—who accentuates and improves their ability to fight—is imposing discipline and structure (Saturn) on their physical and aggressive energies (Mars). The person who refuses to fight or show aggression and anger, although ostensibly pursuing a totally opposite course, is similarly applying Saturnian discipline to aggressive, assertive, energetic impulses. We can see, therefore, that both possibilities are archetypally consistent—that is, they both conform to the underlying meaning of the Mars-Saturn planetary combination, and often many of these seemingly opposing patterns of behavior are interchangeably or simultaneously present, such is the dynamic complexity of an archetypal pairing.

To recognize archetypal meaning in widely varying modes of expression one often has to examine more deeply the underlying motivations behind patterns of behavior. In the case of Mars-Saturn, one might find that defensive retaliation is a sign of fighting to protect one's unacknowledged weakness; physical training and muscular armoring may serve to bolster or conceal a fragile ego; and the hard-edged disciplinarian, similarly, might be motivated primarily by fear. On the other hand, weak passivity may indicate the unconscious repression of anger; and pacifism—ruling out anger or violence because it is perceived as morally wrong or socially unacceptable—might cloak a deeper fear of facing and expressing anger. To uncover the underlying archetypal meanings of our actions we have to discern just what our motivations are behind these actions. Astrology, in this way, encourages a greater depth of insight and understanding of one's nature, which, in time, can give rise to a penetrating self-knowledge—the prerequisite for individuation.

In psychodynamic terms, the Saturn archetype, when activated by Mars, can manifest as a militant super-ego, which can order one around like an inner dictator. If the ego identifies with this tendency, it can cause one to take on the role of enforcer, judge, and prosecutor all at once, policing and censoring one's world, ensuring that others do not fall out of line, flout the rules, or avoid their duty. The Mars-Saturn complex, in one mode of expression, inclines us towards defensive reactions and to making efforts to control one's environment with an iron fist, laying down the law, aggressively enforcing the rules to keep everything in order. Of course, such behavior can be the result of acting out one's own frustration, with the Mars anger, although originating from elsewhere, finding an outlet through the medium of Saturnian laws, rules, and punitive judgments.

In this archetypal pairing, the conservative and traditional Saturnian *senex* meets the Mars warrior principle in other ways too. One can feel, from within this complex, that one has to live up to a perceived standard of traditional masculinity—to be tough and strong, or protecting, practical, and reliable—with Mars, the archetypal masculine, conditioned by Saturnian judgment as to how one should be and act, with the judgment informed by established patterns of masculinity in the wider culture or embodied by men in one's own upbringing. Expressing this dimension of the complex might come rather naturally if Mars is in a conjunction, trine, or sextile with Saturn, but bring conflict and tension with the squares and opposition.

In acting, it is little surprise that a number of traditional Hollywood "tough guys" and combat stars have Mars-Saturn natal aspects, including Charles Bronson, Chuck Norris, and Jean-Claude van Damme, although it should be borne in mind that an understanding of the particular character of Hollywood action heroes and stars of combat sports can reflect a range of aspects to Mars—we will consider later, for example, Clint Eastwood's film personas in light of his Mars-Neptune trine. This correspondence with natal Mars-Saturn aspects is apparent even in comedy, exemplified by figures such as Paul Hogan in the *Crocodile Dundee* films, playing the practical, no-nonsense, and uncouth Australian, hardened by the wilds of the Outback, for whom the urban jungle of New York holds no fears.

Similar themes are evident in the lives of women with major Mars-Saturn aspects, who can find themselves called to develop toughness, resilience, and fortitude in environments often dominated by men and masculine energy, such as the military and—until recent decades, at least—politics. Film stars Goldie Hawn and Demi Moore, with Mars-Saturn natal alignments, both took on the role of a woman in the military—in *Private Benjamin* (1980) and *G. I. Jane* (1997), respectively—in which their characters undergo tough basic training or intensive selection testing and, in the case of Moore's character Jordan O'Neil, are subject to brutal, bullying treatment.

Chart 10

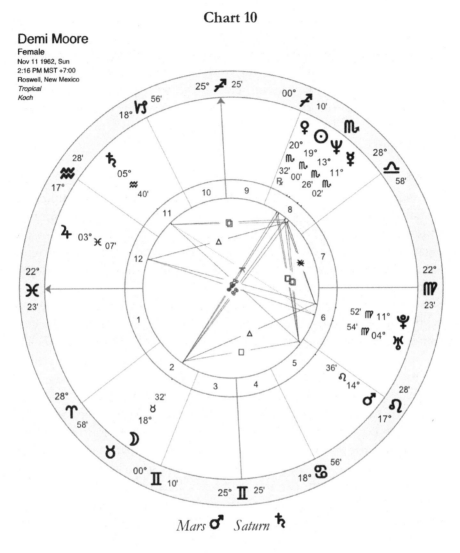

In Demi Moore's chart, note also that the Mars-Saturn opposition is part of a larger T-square involving the Sun and Mercury (as well as Venus and Neptune).

In politics and international affairs, too, many of the most influential female politicians of recent years who have been able to prevail in this most unforgiving of arenas have major Mars-Saturn alignments in their birth charts, including Hilary Clinton, Condoleezza Rice, Christine Lagarde (President of the International Monetary Fund), and Sarah Palin, with the Pluto archetype, associated with power, also prominent in many such cases. Even if one does not consciously identify with a particular archetypal complex symbolized in one's birth chart, or if it is not central to one's personality, that complex still invariably shows up in one's life, as a particular theme of one's experience or in projected form, coming to one from the outside or through other people. Individuation, as we have seen, entails the withdrawal of projections and the integration of aspects of one's experience and of one's personality that have fallen into the shadow and are yet to be consciously realized.

Attack on the Shadow
The impulses coming out of the Mars-Saturn complex can manifest as hostility towards that which is perceived as weak, inferior, morally reprehensible, or threatening, in an attempt to beat down or destroy the negative—Mars attacking the Saturnian shadow, as it were. In extreme cases, if fueled by warped ideologies, the tyrannical dimension of Saturn coupled with the aggression and violence of Mars has assumed pathological form in the lives of a number of dictators or military and political leaders known for their cold brutality, sometimes directed against those people perceived as inferior, with all human feeling banished from the heart and mind—the list includes Ivan the Terrible, Benito Mussolini, Adolf Hitler, and other infamous Nazi figures Josef Mengele, Walter Schellenberg, and Herman Goerring.

As we can recognize in several of the examples above, Saturn is associated both with the sense of inferiority that is intrinsic to the shadow and the protective screen of the ego boundaries that shield us from the shadow through repression and censorship. In the case of Mars-Saturn combinations, there can often be an armored or aggressive outer shell.[78] Mars, the warrior principle, leaps to the defense of the Saturnian weakness, beating down any perceived attack that threatens to encroach on areas of life in which one feels judged or sensitive. Individuation might therefore entail overcoming this "strong man" in order to come back into contact with the inner feelings and to reconnect to the vulnerability and innocence of the child archetype as it becomes more centrally established in the psyche.

In literature, central elements of the Mars-Saturn complex, including the strong man or bully motif, are vividly portrayed in the work of Charles Dickens in its focus in story after story on hard labor, punitive actions, and brutal taskmasters and bullies, but also the experience of standing up to bullies, facing down fears, and prevailing in "hard times" and through adversity. Dickens had Mars square to Saturn in his birth chart, but also the Moon conjunct Neptune, associated with an archetypal complex expressed in his sensitive feeling for the human condition and his capacity to imaginatively enter into the experience of childhood, giving rise to his compassion and empathy, for children, the weak, the vulnerable, the poor, and the infirm.

Efficiency, Stamina, and Resistance
Another trait associated with the Mars-Saturn complex is the capacity to execute tasks with clinical efficiency. We see this in sport, for instance, with major Mars-Saturn aspects in the charts of a number of famous sports stars renowned for their capacity to "finish" with cool control, including record goal-scorers of the German football team Gerd Müller and Miroslav Klose, and, in tennis, Björn Borg and Roger Federer. In all cases, these figures are recognized for their efficiency and ability to execute under pressure. Mars-Saturn can also furnish one with tremendous defensive capacities to withstand attack after attack and with a solid and consistent level of performance, notably exemplified by Borg's almost flawless and tireless style of play in the seventies and early eighties, and manifest in a different way by Federer's remarkable consistency and longevity, with his record of having reached the quarter-finals or better in 36 consecutive tennis grand-slam tournaments between 2004 and 2013—indeed, he was still competing at the highest level after his 40th birthday.

The Mars-Saturn dimension of the personality also takes the form of the figure of the practical problem-solver, as Tarnas has noted, in which the Saturnian problem draws forth the decisive action (associated with Mars) to address it, pushing us to get the job done, and to drive things to completion. Simultaneously, Saturn conditions the Mars energy such that we are able to assume responsibility and act according to the needs and necessities of the moment—this capacity usually comes more naturally with trines and sextiles than with hard aspects between these planets. Under the influence of the Mars-Saturn complex, whether present in the birth chart or as a personal transit, we are often pressed to do what needs to be done in spite of circumstance, and in spite of emotional protestations, tiredness, illness, anger, frustrations, and attacks to one's position. This archetypal complex calls us to squarely face reality in the dispassionate fulfillment of duties and commitments, and elicits the disciplined use of our energies in slow, consistent activity, pushing against and through resistances and smashing down obstacles that stand in our way.

Problematically, however, Mars-Saturn in combination can succumb to a singular hero-*senex* type of consciousness in which one's entire life becomes fixated on problems and their solutions, the execution of duties, keeping on top of things, keeping everything in order, sticking to a routine, and being reliable and disciplined. This leaves little room for the wealth of other emotions and ways of being that are simply not permitted to arise into consciousness. James Hillman (see Chart 82 in Volume III) had a natal Mars-Saturn square aspect, as part of a T-square involving Jupiter and Neptune, and was especially aware of this tendency, which informs his critique of both *senex* consciousness and the singular style of heroic consciousness.

Fear and the Moral Ought
Again demonstrating the multivalence of these archetypal complexes, the same combination is associated with fears and inhibitions crippling one's capacity to act. Displays of strength or aggression can be impaired by moral censorship, often established early in life, or a prohibitive awareness of rules and the consequences of one's actions, or the fear of punishment or injury, and so forth. From a position of weakness, however, in the working through of the Mars-Saturn complex there can be an emphasis on the building up of courage and strength through experience. To put this in mythic terms, Saturn stands in our way as threshold guardian, a personification of ingrained fears and psychological resistances. Mars can supply us with the courage and strength to meet the fear head on and to keep on pushing through our resistances, in spite of our limitations and deficiencies.

As we have seen, conditioned by the Saturn archetype, we can unconsciously build a life structure and personality structure that prevent authentic, natural expression. In the case of natal Mars-Saturn alignments, one might, for instance, learn from one's upbringing or parental authority that one has to be strong and courageous, able to stand up for oneself, to fight, and be nerveless in the face of fear. Inevitably, one would thus try to develop these capacities, and come to feel that one *should*, one *must*, possess and display strong martial qualities in the way one lives one's life and conducts oneself. The unconsciously motivated effort to be a certain way because one feels one *should*, has the effect, however, of impeding natural expression. One cannot truly develop confidence and courage if one is *trying* to be a certain way, for then one's motivation arises from the Saturnian impulses to conform, to meet societal standards, rather than from one's own nature. We see here the difference between the cultivation of a persona, or "self-image" actualization, and genuine psychological development or individuation in which one's own natural character unfolds as it will regardless of societal norms or past conditioning. One becomes what one is rather than *trying* to be a certain way because one has come to believe it is important.

The erection of a personality structure built upon trying, effort, moral imperatives, and societal conditioning invariably leads at some point to a crisis of transformation, when the old structures are torn down and one has to face the buried fear that had been cloaked by the veneer of the persona. In terms of the Mars-Saturn experience, during individuation one might have to face and accept one's feelings of fear and weakness before one can realize one's authentic capacity for confidence, courage, and strength, just as with Venus-Saturn one might have to unlearn the rules of the game in love and romance in order to express oneself more naturally and spontaneously in this area of life. As we have seen, this process can take many years (recalling Saturn's association with Chronos, the god of time), as the walls of one's ego and conditioned defensiveness are gradually eroded through hard knocks such that one's true inner nature can emerge into consciousness.

Saturn's association with the wise old man or teacher is also evident in Mars-Saturn configurations. This theme is portrayed by Tom Hanks in a moving performance as John H. Miller in Steven Spielberg's *Saving Private Ryan* (1998). Drawing on themes associated with the Sun-Mars-Saturn grand trine in his birth chart, Hanks plays a schoolteacher obliged to assume the role of captain in the US army, commanding his battalion of men in the face of mortal danger and the horrors of battle during the 1944 Normandy Invasion in World War Two, leading by example and with quiet but firm authority, and serving as a life mentor to the men in his charge. Throughout the film we witness Miller drawing on reserves of stamina and fortitude in the struggle not only against attrition and the enemy, but through his own worsening physical tremors, as he fights to hold himself together on behalf of those who are depending on him—a noble expression of the Mars-Saturn complex.

Notes

[1] Schopenhauer, "On the Sufferings of the World."
[2] My analysis here was prompted by Richard Tarnas's discussion of Schopenhauer in a graduate lecture in 2005.
[3] Schopenhauer, "On the Sufferings of the World."

4 Schopenhauer, "On the Sufferings of the World."
5 Schopenhauer, "On the Sufferings of the World."
6 Schopenhauer, "On the Sufferings of the World."
7 In Heidegger's chart, there is a very close trine between Jupiter and Saturn (approximately a one degree orb). He also had Mercury sextile Jupiter and Sun square Jupiter.
8 Schopenhauer, "On the Sufferings of the World."
9 Schopenhauer, "On the Sufferings of the World."
10 Schopenhauer, "On the Sufferings of the World."
11 Schopenhauer, "On the Sufferings of the World."
12 Schopenhauer, "On the Sufferings of the World."
13 Schopenhauer, "On the Sufferings of the World." Emphasis in original.
14 Early in my academic career, I had the good fortune of working as a teaching assistant for a course at the California Institute of Integral Studies taught by Richard Tarnas and John Cleese, entitled "Comic Genius: A Multidisciplinary Perspective," which looked at figures from comedy in terms of the astrological configurations in their birth charts. Among the comedians considered was Woody Allen, whose work and birth chart I discuss in this volume.
15 An archetypal astrological perspective invites us to consider people and their life experiences in terms of their thematic archetypal content rather than their ethical value. It enables us to better understand root motivations behind human behavior, whether these be elevated or debased. As Jung noted, archetypes are, like nature itself, not inherently moral. It should be emphasized, too, that invariably creative people live in close proximity to the unconscious—the source of their creative inspiration but also, on occasion, the impetus behind ethically dubious actions.
16 Allen, *Annie Hall*. Diane Keaton also has a major Sun-Saturn alignment—an opposition, with Mars in a conjunction with Saturn.
17 "Woody Allen on Life" (recording of Cannes Film Festival press conference, 2012), accessed July 31, 2021, https://www.youtube.com/watch?v=5yVPS8XBoBE.
18 Charles Dickens had the Sun in a semi-square (45-degree aspect) with Saturn. See also my discussion of the Mars-Saturn square in Dickens's chart later in this chapter.
19 *Groundhog Day*, directed by Harold Ramis (Columbia Pictures, 1993). The film was released during a square between Saturn and Pluto—a world transit. Among the archetypal themes of that combination is repetition compulsion—of becoming stuck in a pattern and repeating it over and over again. Nietzsche formulated his idea of the eternal return during a Saturn-Pluto conjunction in 1882. For a discussion of the Saturn-Pluto complex, see Volume III.

20 The arrogance and sense of superiority in Phil Connors reflect traits associated with Bill Murray's Jupiter-Mars-Pluto T-square, in a one form of expression. See my discussion of the Jupiter-Pluto complex in Volume III.
21 *The Mask*, directed by Chuck Russell (New Line Cinema, 1994).
22 *Bruce Almighty*, directed by Harold Ramis (Universal Pictures, 2003).
23 *The Truman Show*, directed by Peter Weir (Paramount Pictures, 1998).
24 *Liar Liar*, directed by Tom Shadyac (Universal Pictures, 1997).
25 A point made by Alexander Ruperti in *Cycles of Becoming*, 134–135.
26 Writing on Martina Hingis and her mother, Melanie Molitor, Dana Kennedy notes that "their quest . . . began back when Melanie was pregnant with Martina in their native Czechoslovakia. Their mission, and it didn't really matter if little Martina chose to accept it, was officially launched when Molitor placed a sawed-off wooden racket in the tiny hands of her two-year-old daughter and hit balls to her every day for 10 minutes. "Since I was in her stomach, she was thinking I was going to be a great tennis player," says Hingis of her mom, who played professional tennis in Czechoslovakia for nine years and was ranked as high as 10th in her country. "She never thought I maybe wouldn't have the talent. In the beginning she wanted it more than I did." See Dana Kennedy, "Blue Skies," accessed October 26, 2021, https://web.archive.org/web/20010124000100/http://sportsillustrated.cnn.com/features/1997/womenmag/blueskies.html.
27 Agassi, *Open*, 28.
28 Agassi, *Open*, 56.
29 Agassi, *Open*, 57.
30 Agassi, *Open*, 57.
31 Nietzsche, "The Wanderer," in *Thus Spoke Zarathustra, Part III*, 173.
32 In combination with Saturn, we see the signature of Mercury-Mars especially in the particularly militant and aggressive character of his father's training—the yelling of instructions like a sergeant-major conducting a drill. Agassi also had a wide orb midpoint configuration of Mercury=Sun/Mars, reinforcing this theme.
33 Nadal, *Rafa*, 51.
34 Nadal, *Rafa*, 51.
35 The following article, by Christopher Clarey in *New York Times* (June 12, 2017, https://www.nytimes.com/2017/06/12/sports/tennis/something-old-something-new-at-french-open.html), also draws attention to Nadal's humility and struggle with doubts—traits associated with his Sun-Saturn archetypal complex:

> Rafa is a normal person doing abnormal things," said Guillermo Vilas, the former French Open champion and part-time poet from Argentina. Nadal's life has, of course, been anything but normal since he became a star in Spain by leading his country to the Davis Cup title in Seville in 2004

by defeating Andy Roddick of the United States in the opening match at age 18. He is treated like a celebrity in Spain and abroad and is certainly accustomed to his luxuries, but his upbringing and connection to family and his home island of Majorca have—against the odds—kept him grounded. "For sure, I have doubts," he said when asked about the three-year gap between his last Grand Slam singles title, in 2014, and the title he won Sunday. "During that three years, I had doubts. Right now, I'm going to have doubts even in a few days, because in tennis, every week is a new story, and that's part of the beautiful thing of our sport. Life is not that clear. So if you have no doubts, probably it's because you are too arrogant. I don't consider myself arrogant at all." In Nadal's mind, humility has pushed him to keep pushing. "For that reason, I am having the success that I had," he said.

[36] Carlin, *Rafa*, 51.
[37] Carlin, *Rafa*, 50, 52–53.
[38] Carlin, *Rafa*, 70.
[39] See, Ross, *Gospel of Thomas*, logion 29.
[40] Neil Diamond, "I Am . . . I Said," on *Stones* (New York: Uni Records, 1971).
[41] Neil Diamond, "Solitary Man," on *The Feel of Neil Diamond* (New York: Bang Records, 1966).
[42] Retrograde motion is the apparent backwards (that is, east to west) movement of a planet, against the frame of the zodiac, caused by the relative speeds of movements of planets in orbit around the Sun relative to the Earth's orbit. Retrograde motion is a real astronomical phenomenon, although the planets do not actually move backwards, of course. In astrology, symbolic significance is placed on the phenomenon. Transits, particularly of the slower-moving outer planets, will often include periods of direct and retrograde motion, such that exact transits are formed three or even (on rare occasions) five times. In this case, I have observed that the different exact passes of the transit manifest rather like different acts in a play, with the middle exact retrograde transit often indicating a turning point in themes and events unfolding within the duration of the transit. See also, note 20 to Chapter 18.
[43] Goethe, "Erlkönig," accessed July 31, 2021, https://www.oxfordlieder.co.uk/song/1420. Translation © Richard Wigmore, author of *Schubert: The Complete Song Texts*, published by Schirmer Books, provided courtesy of Oxford Lieder (www.oxfordlieder.co.uk).
[44] Goethe, "Erlkönig," accessed July 31, 2021, https://www.oxfordlieder.co.uk/song/1420.
[45] Capell, *Schubert's Songs*, 109 (London: Pan Books, 1973).

46 The Cure, "In Between Days," on *The Head on the Door* (Fiction/Elektra, 1985).
47 The Cure, "Lullaby" on *Disintegration* (Fiction, 1989).
48 Robert Smith, notes on The Cure, *Galore: The Singles* (Fiction/Elektra, 1997).
49 Händel's precise time of birth is unknown, although it is believed to be between 4 am and 6 am. At any time on his day of birth (March 5, 1685, Gregorian calendar), however, the Moon is in an opposition with Saturn. The Moon is also conjunct the Sun. See https://www.astro.com/astro-databank/H%C3%A4ndel,_George_Friedrich.
50 Georg Friedrich Händel, "Messiah: *A Sacred Oratorio*," accessed December 6, 2023, http://opera.stanford.edu/iu/libretti/messiah.htm.
51 Jean-Paul Sartre, *The Words*, 181.
52 Tarnas, "Archetypes, Art, and Culture," lecture at the California Institute of Integral Studies, spring term 2005.
53 "Helen Keller Speaks Out," accessed December 6, 2019, https://www.youtube.com/watch?v=8ch_H8pt9M8.
54 Billy Joel, "An Innocent Man," on *An Innocent Man* (Family Productions/Columbia, 1983).
55 Billy Joel, "An Innocent Man," on *An Innocent Man*.
56 Billy Joel, "An Innocent Man," on *An Innocent Man*.
57 Billy Joel, "An Innocent Man," on *An Innocent Man*.
58 Billy Joel, "An Innocent Man," on *An Innocent Man*.
59 Billy Joel, "An Innocent Man," on *An Innocent Man*.
60 Billy Joel, "An Innocent Man," on *An Innocent Man*.
61 Billy Joel, "An Innocent Man," on *An Innocent Man*. The miraculous intervention is a Uranus-Neptune theme. This complex is discussed in Volume III.
62 Billy Joel, "Uptown Girl," on *An Innocent Man*.
63 Billy Joel, "Piano Man," on *Piano Man* (Family Productions/Columbia, 1973).
64 Billy Joel, "Piano Man," on *Piano Man*.
65 Billy Joel, "Longest Time," on *An Innocent Man*.
66 Billy Joel, "Tell Her about It," on *An Innocent Man*.
67 Billy Joel, "Tell Her about It," on *An Innocent Man*.
68 Billy Joel, "Tell Her about It," on *An Innocent Man*.
69 Billy Joel, "Tell Her about It," on *An Innocent Man*.
70 The Sun-Uranus combination, as we will consider in Volume III, takes form in the figure of the creative genius—as in the list of artists with whom Gertrude Stein was involved.
71 The Kinks, "A Well-respected Man," on *Kinda Kinks*, and "Dedicated Follower of Fashion," on *The Kink Kontroversy* (Pye/Reprise, 1965).
72 John-Paul Gautier, for instance, has Saturn conjunct Neptune opposite Venus.

[73] Historian A. N. Wilson remarked that Tolstoy's own marriage was "one of the most miserable in history." See *Tolstoy—A Biography* (New York: W. W. Norton, 2001), 196.
[74] Tolstoy, *Death of Ivan Ilyich and Other Stories*, 99.
[75] Tolstoy, *Death of Ivan Ilyich and Other Stories*, 98.
[76] Tolstoy, *Death of Ivan Ilyich and Other Stories*, 101.
[77] Tarnas, *Cosmos and Psyche*, 126–134. This section on archetypal multivalence in relation to Mars is adapted from my essay "Astrology and the Modern Western Worldview," published in *Beyond a Disenchanted Cosmology. Archai: The Journal of Archetypal Cosmology*, issue 3 (2011).
[78] Wilhelm Reich had Mars in an exact 150-degree quincunx alignment to Saturn, recognizable in his theory of body armoring. See Reich, *Character Analysis*, third edition (New York: Farrar, Straus & Giroux Inc, 1980).

Chapter 17

Jupiter-Saturn Contrasts and Combinations

Although it has not been our main focus, we have already encountered the archetypal Jupiter in some of the charts explored earlier. To begin to appreciate more fully the qualities of the Jupiter, and to draw a contrast between the nature and style of Jupiter and Saturn, in this chapter let us now consider first, as an example, Jupiter in relationship to Venus.

The Good Life: Venus and Jupiter
Whereas Saturn is associated with experiences of contraction and limitation, Jupiter is associated with expansion and abundance. The nature of Saturn is restrained and conservative, often doubting and fearful, whereas Jupiter tends towards optimism, confidence, and sometimes extravagance and excess. Venus-Jupiter alignments, therefore, often correspond with experiences in which one is enriched by the overflow of beauty and pleasure, bringing high spirits and good feelings—we might imagine the glorious spring or summer day, with birds singing, flowers in bloom, and blue skies above. The flavor of the Venus-Jupiter combination is present in lavish settings, fine wine, rich food, the high life of social enjoyment, friends and parties, and abundant sensual, romantic, and sexual pleasures.

Many of these themes are evident in the work of the great Italian film director Federico Fellini, born with Venus in a trine aspect to Jupiter.[1] Fellini's aptly titled *La Dolce Vita*, for instance, depicts the indulgent, often hedonistic lifestyle of paparazzi journalist and aspiring writer Marcello Rubini in 1950s Rome, mixing with the wealthy and famous, often in opulent or glamorous surroundings and iconic locations and landmarks of the Eternal City, romantically involved with rich and beautiful women, and moving from one social scene and sexual encounter to another. Likewise, Fellini's later masterpiece *8½* provides another fine illustration of the Venus-Jupiter experience in the form of protagonist Guido Anselmi's "harem" daydream scene, in which his every whim is catered to by a house full of his deliriously happy mistresses and doting female housekeepers, pandering to him, dancing around, showering him with gifts, preparing his bath, and jostling for his attention. (Fellini's Venus and Jupiter are also in aspect to Neptune, which we will consider later).[2]

The Venus-Jupiter archetypal complex is associated with pleasurable experiences that can bring welcome respite from life's struggles and pressures, but that also, given Jupiter's tendency to excess, can become problematic themselves if overdone. The scope of this combination ranges from the tasteful to the tacky. The complex finds expression in a rich cultural life of art-gallery visits, operas and ballets, pleasurable expeditions to foreign lands and great cities, and the like, but it can also manifest as an attraction to the gaudy, cheesy, or crassly opulent—to kitsch as well as fine art. It is the archetypal complex of the lavish, indulgent, flamboyant, and the flowery.

These qualities are personified in the archetypal figures of "the showman" and "disco queen." A number of stars of popular music, known for their flamboyance and theatrical style, have major natal alignments between Venus and Jupiter, including Liberace, David Bowie, Freddie Mercury, Barry Manilow, and all three of the Gibb brothers in the Bee Gees—Barry, Robin, and Maurice. One thinks of the Bee Gees' music and disco attire in the mid-to-late 1970s or Bowie's larger-than-life personas of that decade, as well as the sheer glitz and glamour of the stage performances and visual presentation of all these figures. Venus pertains both to the costume or fashion and the musical performance, which take on an extravagant and exaggerated flair in each case. Manilow's song "Copacabana" well exemplifies this side of the Venus-Jupiter complex, bringing together the showgirl, music, romance, dance, and a party atmosphere: "Her name was Lola, she was a showgirl, with yellow feathers in her hair, and a dress cut down to there. . . Music and passion were always the fashion at the Copa."[3] Similarly, lyrics in Queen's songs reflect the influence of Freddie Mercury's Venus-Jupiter, as in "Don't stop me now, I'm having such a good time, I'm having a ball," as do his flamboyant, dramatic, and almost operatic stage performances.[4]

Similarly, major Venus-Jupiter alignments are also associated with the theme of the "high queen" of fashion, culture, and music, as well as the "disco diva" or the high-living socialite. Indeed, we find many of the most celebrated female disco and pop-music figures were born during major Venus-Jupiter alignments, including the globally popular Agnetha Fältskog of Swedish super-group Abba, who captures some of the blessings of the Venus-Jupiter archetypal complex in singing the lead on Abba's "Thank You for the Music": "I've been so lucky, I am the girl with golden hair, I want to sing it out to everybody, what a joy, what a life, what a chance!"[5] At its best, Venus-Jupiter is associated with overflowing good feeling in the heart, joy and romance, friendship and popularity—although, again, there is always the danger of too much of a good thing.

Chart 11

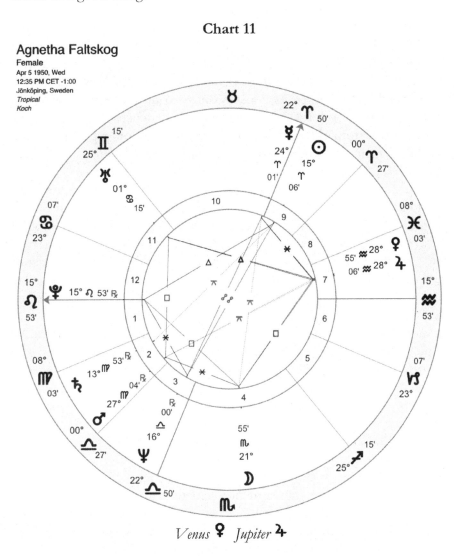

Venus ♀ *Jupiter* ♃

The same archetypal combination is present in the charts of Debbie Harry (of Blondie), Aretha Franklin, Beyoncé, and actress Nicole Kidman, who was able to give striking expression to aspects of the Venus-Jupiter experience in the 2001 film musical *Moulin Rouge!* with its memorable opening scenes of the garish and raucous dance show in the famous cabaret venue in Paris, with Kidman, as cabaret dancer Satine, hoisted high in the air on a trapeze. Scarlett Johansson, Penelope Cruz, Jennifer Lawrence, and Halle Berry also have this combination, as do celebrity figures in fashion Victoria Beckham and Kate Moss, and socialite personality Kim Kardashian.

The Jupiter principle underlies the impulse to move out into the world, to expand, to take in more. Venus encourages this move in search of pleasure, happiness, and beauty. Experiences associated with Venus, that is, serve the Jupiterian function of connecting one to the wider world, opening one's consciousness to different ways of living, different aspects of life—as in romantic experiences and friendships with people from different cultural backgrounds or exposure to the world through art and aesthetics. This dimension of Venus-Jupiter can be a pleasant distraction from one's central life focus.

The challenges this complex poses during individuation are obviously of a different order entirely to those associated with Saturn alignments. Venus-Jupiter is the archetypal signature of the biblical "wine, women, and song" motif, expressing, to put it in Jungian terms, the capacity of the anima to lure us into the world of sense experience and relationship entanglements in search of happiness and pleasure, and perhaps fame and celebrity. Under the influence of the Venus-Jupiter complex, one can be satiated by these anima experiences, but sometimes to the detriment of living a meaningful life of creative achievement, which invariably entails discipline, suffering, and sacrifice—qualities falling far outside of the thematic range of this combination. Venus, amplified by Jupiter, can promote a life of ignoble ease in which pleasure and comfort or superficial socializing take precedence over depth, authenticity, responsibility, and achievement, although the intervention of the other archetypal principles usually sees to it that one cannot live such a life indefinitely. Even if one does not actively seek out such Venus-Jupiter experiences, they can present themselves to us, sometimes in problematic ways, if one has a hard-aspect alignment between these planets—as in the party invitation one would rather not have, or an excess of friends and social engagements, which lend breadth to one's experience but can distract us or divert attention away from more serious or fulfilling activities.

The Archetypal Amplifier

Just as the Venus-Jupiter archetypal combination tends to accompany an expansion of experiences of love, beauty, and pleasure, so the Mercury-Jupiter combination, to give another example, can find expression in the big idea and sweeping breadth of intellectual vision, favoring broad strokes and universal themes rather than narrow specialisms and details. This complex can give rise to a rather dramatic style of communicating—long and rich sentences, as in the prose of Marcel Proust, or grandiose expressions in speech. Joseph Campbell and Donald Trump, both born with Mercury-Jupiter aspects, represent different dimensions of this complex, with Campbell's breadth of vision and erudite exaltation of world mythology and Trump's proclivity towards hyperbole, boasting, and sometimes brash language, but also humor and messages with popular appeal, as well as the sheer volume of communications, many delivered via social media during his time as US president, replete with capital letters and exclamation marks (the Jupiterian exaggeration).

The tendency towards amplification is equally apparent in examples of other Jupiter complexes. The Mars-Jupiter complex, for instance, can manifest in high spirits, vigor, and abundant physical energy, exuding cheery enthusiasm and active encouragement, but also on occasion manifesting as bravado, or as blundering insouciance, lacking subtlety and discretion. In concrete form, it finds expression in vigorous hikes or adventures, exploring the great outdoors or engaging in a wide range of physical activities. These traits and inclinations can take shape in the archetypal figure of the cowboy, with the martial tough, rugged, courageous warrior in combination with the Jupiterian themes of the outdoors, travel, wandering, journeying, and so forth. Such themes are illustrated by the music of Jon Bon Jovi (with a natal Mars-Jupiter conjunction) who, as a solo artist, recorded *Blaze of Glory*, the soundtrack for *Young Guns II*, a Western film about Billy the Kid, and, with rock band Bon Jovi, wrote and recorded tracks such as "Wanted Dead or Alive" and "Stick to Your Guns," explicitly referencing "Western" cowboy motifs.[6]

As well as taking shape as an upbeat, energizing, confident demeanor, this complex can express itself too in a free-flowing or laid-back effortless quality to exertion and an ease at expressing anger. The innate Jupiterian sense of confidence can give rise to public displays of anger—being assertive and forceful can come easily and perhaps too readily.

Chart 12

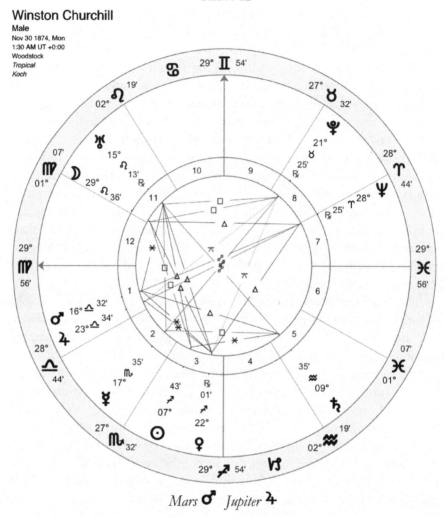

Mars ♂ Jupiter ♃

A number of these qualities are exemplified in the life and character of Winston Churchill, Britain's prime minister for much of the Second World War. Consider, for instance, his most famous speech, delivered to the British parliament in the House of Commons, serving to rouse the British in the face of the threat of Nazi Germany:

> We shall not flag or fail. We shall go on to the end, we shall fight in France, we shall fight on the seas and oceans, we shall fight with growing confidence and growing strength in the air, we shall defend our island, whatever the cost may be. We shall fight on the beaches,

we shall fight on the landing grounds, we shall fight in the fields and in the streets, we shall fight in the hills; we shall never surrender, and even if, which I do not for a moment believe, this island or a large part of it were subjugated and starving, then our Empire beyond the seas, armed and guarded by the British fleet, would carry on the struggle, until, in God's good time, the new world, with all its power and might, steps forth to the rescue and the liberation of the old.[7]

Note here the abundance of fights, all over the place, in every locale—with Jupiter expanding the scope of the Mars impulse for combat to every form of battle and in every terrain. Note too, crucially, the emboldened assurance, the positive expectation of success and indefatigable spirit—the "growing confidence" and "growing strength" as well as the reliance on the British naval fleet from far and wide ("our Empire beyond the seas").

The Jupiter principle manifests in comparable ways in other archetypal combinations. A Moon-Jupiter alignment, for instance, is associated with, among other things, dramatic or over-gushing emotional reactions, sometimes almost operatic in their quality, and with the opening of one's private emotional and domestic life to the wider world. It tends towards a buoyant or trusting emotional mood, the feeling that one is supported by family or by the bounty of life itself, symbolized by the fecundity and goodness of the Great Mother or Mother Nature. Sun-Jupiter aspects correlate with traits such as generosity of spirit, optimism, and a natural inclination towards growth and broadening of one's consciousness in the living of a full life, or an easygoing manner and way of being in the world that seems graced with success, happiness, or good fortune—although, in another inflection, also a smug satisfaction in one's life and achievements, or inflation sometimes bordering on arrogance. Although these few examples of the qualities and themes of each pairing do not do justice to the multivalence of these principles, they give a flavor of the character of Jupiter. As we can see, the common denominator of these Jupiter alignments and their associated archetypal complexes is not restriction, limitation, and pressure, as with Saturn, but ease, excess, expansion, and overflow. Not fear or self-protection but trust and optimism are evident here. The contrast is plainly apparent.

Magnification of the Problematic

With this context, we are better placed to consider the themes and expressions of the Saturn and Jupiter archetypes when they act in combination, as indicated by major alignments between the two planets.

We have already considered examples in which the archetypal Jupiter acts upon Saturn, in the rather dramatic overstatement of Schopenhauer's philosophy, as well as the translation of his experience of the sufferings of life into an entire worldview. Likewise, we considered the comical and magnified portrayal of Saturnian neuroses in the work of Woody Allen. With this alignment, Jupiterian supreme confidence, or the unconscious attempt to project it, can also serve to compensate for Saturnian inferiority. Allen, of course, portrays this side of the complex too, as in *Play It Again, Sam*, when he adopts a Humphrey Bogart persona as he tries to impress in romantic affairs.

The Jupiter-Saturn combination can also manifest as the big problem or as the positive development and opportunity that becomes problematic or burdensome. The experience of this archetypal combination can bring an overwhelming sense of the mountainous amount of work to be done and the long road ahead—the Jupiterian amplification of Saturnian labor. Yet it also gives rise to the aspiration to take on more work—the positive inflation, associated with Jupiter, which encourages one to strive towards success and greatness through one's efforts. A variant expression of this theme is the tendency of this complex towards producing a prodigious output, or working on a large scale. Equally, Saturn can impress upon us the moral obligation to grow, as one feels one must improve and overcome limitations and flaws, or one is painfully aware of the amount of work one still has to do, the improvements one has yet to make. In practical terms, and particularly evident during transits between these planets, the commitment to expansion can sometimes take form as entering into binding contracts that tie us to certain opportunities and make them possible but also restrict our sense of freedom—growth and restriction together.

However, while the Jupiter-Saturn experience can present us with projects that are problematic or feel overwhelming because of their size, scope, and potential, the complex also furnishes us with the capacity for careful logistical planning, taking form in the figure of the organizer and arranger, enabling us, or forcing us, to devise and implement plans in a systematic way. Jupiter is attuned to the holistic vision and the imagined success, Saturn to the working out of the details.

The Jupiter-Saturn complex may also manifest as taking a positive attitude in the face of obstacles and problems but conversely sometimes as encountering the problem in the opportunity. One example of the latter, and of a number of other Jupiter-Saturn themes, is the comedy television series *My Name Is Earl*, starring Jason Lee as Earl Hickey, a petty criminal and amiable waster whose life is transformed by the Jupiterian good fortune of a lottery win, followed immediately by the Saturnian misfortune of being injured in a road accident. Jason Lee has a natal configuration of Sun conjunct Saturn, both opposite Jupiter, and he draws on themes associated with his complex in assuming the role. With the winning lottery ticket in his hand, in his euphoria Earl walks blindly into the road and is promptly mowed down by a car. Recovering in his hospital bed, he comes to the realization that his misfortune has to do with karma, and he vows henceforth to do good deeds, making up for the numerous wrongs he has inflicted on people throughout his life. Thereafter, because of the Saturnian law-like commandment he imposes on himself, he is bound to his pledge to do good and thus to create positive karma, systematically working through a long list of every person he had previously wronged. Invariably, however, his attempts to do good result in further problems—the source of much of the humor in the show.

Perhaps especially with an opposition between Jupiter and Saturn, there can be an oscillation between faith and optimism, on the one hand, and negativity and pessimistic self-doubt, on the other, with a characteristic see-sawing between one pole and the other, until they can both be recognized, held in dynamic balance, and thereby integrated. Jupiter enables one to exude a cheery, upbeat energy or to present a carefree laid-back persona; Saturn tends to find expression as a fearful, negative countenance or at least as a serious way of meeting the world.

The Structured Ascent to the Summit

Another leitmotif of Jupiter-Saturn is structured growth or the large structure or the step-by-step path of ascent, with Jupiter as Zeus, so to speak, as the king of the gods on the mountaintop. We see elements of each of these motifs exemplified in the writings of mystic St. Teresa of Ávila, born with Jupiter and Saturn in an opposition, with her vision of the "interior castle" of the soul, through which one might come into closer union with God. She describes the many rooms or mansions of this inner structure. As we read in an introduction to the text: "I began to think of the soul as if it were a castle made of a single diamond or of very clear crystal, in which there are many rooms, just as in Heaven there are many mansions." "These mansions," she adds, "are not 'arranged in a row one behind another' but variously—'some above, others below, others at each side; and in the centre and midst of them all is the chiefest mansion, where the most secret things pass between God and the soul.'"[8]

In a related expression of this theme, the archetypal qualities of Jupiter and Saturn in combination were evident across the entire culture, in a world transit, when Led Zeppelin released the classic song "Stairway to Heaven" in November 1971, with Saturn in an opposition both to Jupiter and Neptune—the latter planetary archetype specifically associated with heaven.

We see the same motif of structured ascent in the life and work of famed martial artist and film star Bruce Lee (born November 27, 1940), who had a Jupiter-Saturn natal conjunction, in an incredibly potent T-square, with Jupiter-Saturn opposite the Moon, Mercury, Mars, and Venus, and both sets of planets square to Pluto—a configuration we will return to consider in Volume III. Restricting our attention to Saturn alignments for now, we can recognize immediately in Lee's life and personality the Mars-Saturn theme of disciplined physical training. Yet Lee also received early training in dance and ballet (reflecting the presence of Venus in the T-square), which came through in his graceful, almost catlike, movements.

The recovery of lost video footage of the closing scenes of Lee's final film, *The Game of Death* (recorded in 1972), illustrates multiple dimensions of Lee's expression of his Jupiter-Saturn complex. The film itself, which remained unfinished upon Lee's sudden death in 1973, was released posthumously in 1978 from a hotchpotch of recorded material, edited footage, and additional recording featuring stand-in actors. The recovered original ending of the film is set in a pagoda in South Korea, with each level of the pagoda guarded by a master of a different style of martial arts. Wearing his iconic yellow-and-black jumpsuit, Lee, playing retired martial arts champion Hai Tien (recast as Billy Lo in the 1978 version), moves from level to level engaging each guardian in combat, with successive victories demonstrating his superior skill and mastery of multiple styles. Finally, at the highest level, the diminutive combatant faces a giant opponent called Mantis, played by Kareem Abdul-Jabbar, 1970s American basketball star, who is over seven feet tall, with Bruce Lee again able to demonstrate the practical efficiency of his style of combat, finding a way to overcome his adversary by opportunistically exploiting his weakness—in this case a light-sensitivity condition in which Abdul-Jabbar's character is blinded by exposure to bright sunlight. Jupiter is the opportunism, and Saturn the weakness.

Chart 13

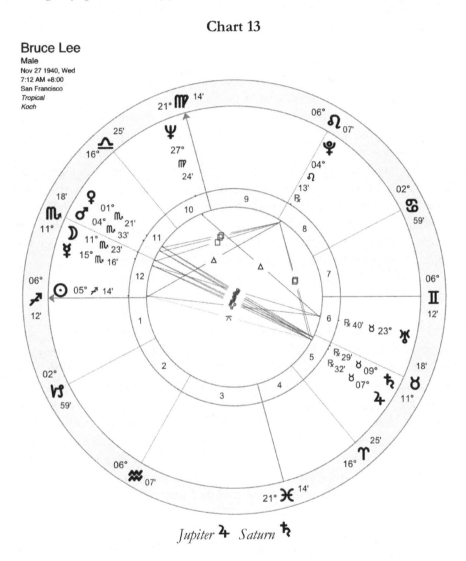

Jupiter ♃ Saturn ♄

Pragmatism and the Pressure to Grow

In addition to the structured ascent through levels, a number of other Jupiter-Saturn themes are suggested in this scene, themes also present in Lee's life. First, Lee worked to develop expertise in many forms of combat, from the Wing Chun style of kung fu and Japanese jujitsu to Western boxing and wrestling, which are integrated into Lee's own self-styled *Jeet Kune Do* ("the way of the intercepting fist"). Through a commitment to the study and practice of a wide range of styles, and through undertaking training in these multiple styles, Lee developed a kind of holistic mastery of the martial arts. We see here a Jupiterian expansion of Saturnian forms of practice, disciplines, and methods, with Lee ever willing to learn from any discipline, even outside of traditional martial arts, to improve. Lee was diligently committed to growth, both as a martial artist and as a human being, for ultimately, he realized, who one is as a person is inseparable from how one fights, moves, and lives. This commitment to self-improvement manifested in Lee's extensive studies of philosophy, psychology, spiritual teachings, self-help literature, and more, especially during a long period of forced inactivity after a back injury sustained by lifting weights—the Saturnian setback or problem met as a Jupiterian opportunity for growth. Note that Lee's Jupiter-Saturn is also aligned with Mercury, associated with reading and learning, and we also see this archetypal combination in Lee's careful documentation of principles and combat moves in his journals, and his concern with the philosophy behind it.

Again, we can discern the Jupiter-Saturn complex manifesting as the moral pressure or obligation to improve, the feeling that one should or must grow. And we also see, powerfully embodied in Bruce Lee's life and work, the Jupiter-Saturn theme of the elimination of the superfluous and a philosophy of employing whatever works, whatever is practical. Saturn trims Jupiterian excess—thus Lee's insistence that he do away with "flowery hands" of established martial arts practice, implementing instead more direct, efficient, and efficacious moves in combat. Lee encouraged his students to find whatever means they could to overcome an opponent rather than religiously adhering to the established codes of single forms of practice. As biographer Bruce Thomas noted: "In his teaching, Bruce [Lee] adopted a simple motto: 'Use only that which works, and take it from any place you can find it'."[9] Jupiter-Saturn tends to promote a pragmatic, realistic philosophy and outlook, with Jupiterian principles molded by the tests of Saturnian circumstance and the facts of the matter. Not least, the Jupiter-Saturn archetypal combination can be seen in Lee's capacity to sustain an astonishingly heavy workload of training and filming, a capacity that almost bordered on the supernatural, with the Jupiter principle magnifying the labor associated with Saturn. In Lee's case, with Pluto prominent in the T-square with Jupiter, Saturn, and Mars, all these expressions of Jupiter-Saturn were driven to an extreme, with characteristic Plutonic intensity and obsession, as he attained a degree of physical self-mastery that was perhaps unequalled, constantly overcoming his limits.

Notes

[1] I was led to an exploration of Fellini's chart from Richard Tarnas's 2004 "Archetypes, Art, and Culture" course at the California Institute of Integral Studies in which Tarnas examined a selection of Fellini's films in light of the Uranus-Pluto conjunction of the 1960s.

[2] Although the birth time is uncertain, in all likelihood Fellini also has a Moon-square-Mars aspect, with the Moon pertaining to the wife-mother dimension of the anima. In *La Dolce Vita*, we see this in Marcello fighting against what he experiences as the claustrophobic clinging and mothering of his fiancée (an expression of the maternal quality of the anima) and in the film's emotionally charged scenes and bitter arguments. The characters Marcello Rubini (in *La Dolce Vita*) and Guido Anselmi (in *8½*) were both played by Marcello Mastroianna who had a Venus-Neptune conjunction in a trine to Jupiter.

[3] Barry Manilow, "Copacabana," on *Even Now* (New York: Arista, 1978).

[4] Queen, "Don't Stop Me Now," on *Jazz* (EMI / Elektra, 1978).

[5] Abba, "Thank You for the Music," on *The Album* (Polar Music, 1977).

[6] "Wanted Dead or Alive" is on Bon Jovi, *Slippery When Wet* (Mercury Records,1986), and "Stick to Your Guns" is on Bon Jovi, *New Jersey* (Mercury Records, 1988).

[7] Winston Churchill, "We Shall Fight on the Beaches," International Churchill Society, accessed December 22, 2021, https://winstonchurchill.org/resources/speeches/1940-the-finest-hour/we-shall-fight-on-the-beaches/.

[8] St. Teresa of Ávila, "Interior Castle," accessed February 8, 2023, http://www. catholictreasury.info/books/interior_castle/ic2.php.

[9] Thomas, *Fighting Spirit*, 50.

Chapter 18

Case Studies of the Saturn Return: Joseph Campbell and Albert Schweitzer

For the most part, we have concentrated thus far on birth-chart alignments involving Saturn, but the same principles and themes associated with each of the archetypal combinations discussed above also apply to the study of personal transits—the relationship between the movements of the planets over time and the positions of the planets in a birth chart. Transits can be used to understand the archetypal qualities and themes that are accentuated during specific periods in one's life. Even if we do not have particular planetary aspects in our birth chart, we all experience transits in which the two planetary archetypes come into significant relationship. By studying personal transits, then, one can become aware of the specific archetypes that are currently active in one's experience and of the deeper life meanings that are manifesting through the particular circumstances that arise. An awareness of transits can inform and enhance our participation in both the individuation process and soul-making.

The most significant transit of Saturn is the "Saturn return," when the orbiting planet returns to its original position in a birth chart, indicated by its arrival at the same degree of the zodiac. In a typical human lifespan, the Saturn return occurs twice: the first at age 29 and the second at 58, with the transit spanning an overall period of about three years centered on those ages. The twenty-nine-year cycle is punctuated, every seven years, by other hard-aspect alignments between transiting Saturn in its orbit and the position of Saturn in the birth chart: the squares (90 degrees) occur at ages 7 and 21, 35 and 49, 65 and 79; and the oppositions (180 degrees) occur at 14, 43 and 72, approximately. These periods partake in the meanings and themes of the Saturn return, but are usually of somewhat lesser significance and of shorter duration.

Experiences arising at these seven-year intervals represent critical developmental transitions. Age seven accompanies the development of the child's ego and a nascent separation of the inner and outer personality. It can often bring a significant first encounter with a form of authority outside of the family—typically the authority of the teacher in the classroom. Age fourteen obviously pertains to the often awkward transition of adolescence, fuelled by the biological changes of this period, with the teenager subject to peer pressure and the desire to be accepted by the group, and thus developing a persona adequate to the task of social interaction while further screening the inner personality. The square of Saturn at age twenty-one or thereabouts often coincides with the end of college years or apprenticeships and the transition into the responsibilities of adulthood, working life, and professional ambition, sometimes curtailing the license and freedom of earlier periods, as the individual is pressured to commit to the reality of the world and continues to struggle to forge an ego and worldly identity. In all cases, these Saturn transits coincide with critical developmental pressure points and challenges of transition that mark the unfolding of the pattern of the Self into reality.

Themes of the Saturn Return

These developmental transitions reach a point of culmination and often of major crisis during the Saturn return itself, coinciding with a period in life when one's destiny or vocation, whatever that entails, decisively announces itself. Much has been written on this transit, which we might summarize in terms of a selection of typically occurring themes:

- Maturation and life endings and transitions
- A compression of time and the pressure to actualize oneself
- The discovery of and commitment to a life structure and vocation
- The assumption of responsibilities and duties that shape who one is and the work one is to do in the world
- Existential pressures and encounters with death
- The testing of conscience and exercising of moral judgments
- The necessity of standing in one's own authority, irrespective of the judgments of others
- The forging and fortification of the conscious ego as a separate entity

- The crystallization of the personality
- A shift in the existential gravity of one's life and a consolidation of one's energy levels[1]
- The experience of significant failures and setbacks as one comes up against the binding limitations of one's innate life pattern
- The discovery of mentors and authorities or the transition into this role oneself
- Settling into routines of living
- The completion of a major cycle in one's life.

These themes are in evidence during the other major hard-aspect Saturn transits to its own position in the birth chart but are especially prominent during the Saturn return, as the planet completes an entire cycle of the zodiac.

The experience of the Saturn return might be best illuminated with specific examples. For the first of two, I have chosen mythologist Joseph Campbell, whose life experiences—recorded in passages from his journals and letters—are detailed in *A Fire in the Mind*, the excellent biography written by Stephen and Robin Larsen. Campbell's long and full life gives us the opportunity to see both of his Saturn return transits, aged 28–31 and 57–60, in the context of his larger biography. As we will see, many of the aforementioned themes were constellated during the period of one or both of Campbell's Saturn returns.

Joseph Campbell's First Saturn Return: 1932–1935

In Campbell's birth chart, Saturn is positioned at 17 degrees 42 minutes Aquarius (see Chart 14). Looking in an ephemeris at the planetary positions at the time of the Saturn return, we find transiting Saturn first entered Aquarius in February 1932.[2] At that point, it was 17 degrees from the position of Saturn in Campbell's birth chart. It then left Aquarius, moving counterclockwise through the zodiac, and entered Pisces, the next sign, in February 1935. With a little latitude either side, we can take these two dates as marking the beginning and end of the three-year period of Campbell's Saturn return.[3] Transiting Saturn moved close to an exact conjunction with the position of Saturn in Campbell's birth chart in May–June 1933 (within about 1 degree 20 minutes) and fully exact on January 29, 1934—the exact alignment tending to coincide with the key phase of the transit and bringing important developments.

CASE STUDIES OF THE SATURN RETURN

Chart 14

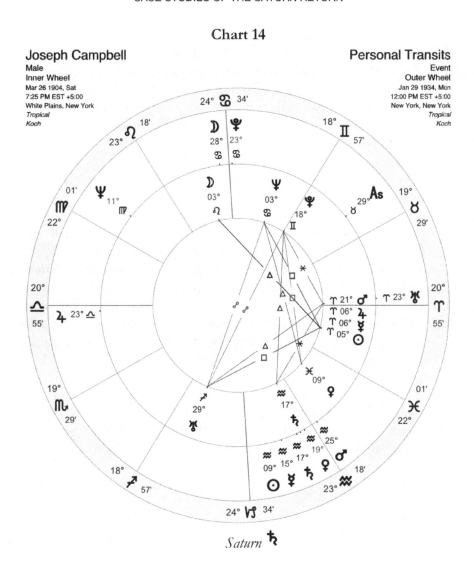

Joseph Campbell Personal Transits, January 29, 1934. Note the position of Saturn in the sky on that date was 17 degrees Aquarius—the same position as Saturn occupied at Campbell's birth.

In 1932, before he had turned 28, Campbell left the East coast of America and headed to the West, settling for a time in Monterey, California, where he entered a circle of creative artists and thinkers, including marine biologist Ed Rickets, author John Steinbeck, and Steinbeck's wife, Carol. In the midst of what was a remarkably stimulating period of Campbell's life, he found himself unexpectedly embroiled in a blossoming romantic relationship with Carol, whose marriage to John had become difficult and strained. Campbell wrestled with his moral conscience as to what to do: Should he act on his romantic desire for Carol? Or should he bring their relationship to an end? After much reasoned reflection on the dilemma, Campbell proclaimed in his journal: "'Life is not to be confused with emotional impulse."[4] "To hell with myself," Campbell had said to John as they tried to work through the complex situation that had arisen: "I guess I ought to be able to tell my emotions what to do."[5] And thus the resolution, declared in Campbell's journal: "In the light of these considerations I resolve to renounce this love—to smother it out."[6]

In terms of his birth-chart aspects, the capacity to restrain and negate the passions is related to Campbell's Saturn trine to Pluto, the moral conscience and reasoned judgment associated with Saturn coming to bear on the Plutonic instincts in a positive, supportive act of restraint. In Campbell's birth chart, Venus (associated, as we have seen, with the experience of romantic love) is in a sextile alignment with Pluto. With these planetary archetypes in combination, the tendency towards an intense and perhaps forbidden experience of romantic love is present, but as the planets are in a sextile alignment there is less compulsion associated with this experience than one would find with other aspects, such as the conjunction and square. As transiting Saturn came back to its own position in Campbell's birth chart, experiences associated with the natal configurations of Saturn trine Pluto and Venus sextile Pluto were accentuated in Campbell's life, with the characteristic tendency of Saturn to bring things to actualization through circumstantial pressure.

Campbell's solution to this situation, then, was an act of reasoned will taken against his feelings and desires. It is decisions of this kind—created by the binding pressure of circumstance—that can have the effect of further removing us from the womb of unconscious nature, launching us more fully on the road of individuation. During the first Saturn return (and to a lesser extent in other major alignments of Saturn to its own place in the chart) a psychological shift takes place that can decisively bring to end the mode of psychological functioning of youth and early adulthood. This transition might be understood as an increasing separation between the conscious will, centered on the ego, and how we would act if we simply followed our instincts and feelings—exemplified by Campbell's decision in accordance with reason and morality rather than his romantic longings. By consciously committing to a course of action in this way, there is, in effect, a renunciation of unconscious feeling as the primary determinant of life. As we have seen, Saturn pertains to the father principle, the representative of the spirit, whose interventions serve to separate us from the bosom of Mother Nature. The Saturn return transit, over its three-year period, incarnates us more fully into our existence as separate carriers of consciousness, responsible for actualizing a particular life destiny and assuming a role within the life of the community; we are pressed to realize ourselves as separate individuals in accordance with the *principium individuationis*.

During his twenties, Campbell had thrown himself into various pursuits: studies of Grail literature at Columbia University, travels in Europe to France and Germany, creative sojourns and periods of retreat in Woodstock and then in Monterey among artists and writers, reading widely and voraciously, learning languages, exploring a life philosophy, trying his hand at writing fiction, experiencing romantic dalliances and flirtations, and generally enjoying the freedom to experiment and explore outside of the pressures of conventional worldly life. By late 1931 and the turn of 1932, however, this period of youthful exploration had seemingly led to an impasse. The lack of a clear direction and life role was starting to weigh more and more heavily on Campbell—in coincidence with the onset of his Saturn return.

> I've been tied up in a sort of knot lately trying to decide which one of the roads stretching out before me I should take. The prospect of being simply professor of English at Columbia does not appeal to me. It gives me a case of goose-pimples and sometimes makes me sick. The prospect of being a magazine short-story writer does the same thing and I've been suffering from a pesky yearning to get back again to my Indians somehow. For an exceedingly awkward spell I've been trying to imagine myself first on one road, then on another, now a journalist, now an English prof., now a writer of cheap short stories, now a scientist in hot pursuit of an Indian or mummy.[7]

"What I miss," he wrote tellingly in his journal, "is the happy sense of getting somewhere. . . . I'm stuck. I'm milling about."[8] The feeling of being stuck and increasingly dissatisfied with one's situation is typical of the period of the Saturn return, as it first takes effect, as is the sense of being weighed down—Saturn is associated with gravity and weighty concerns. As the transit unfolds, the explorations and experiments of our twenties are curtailed and start to crystallize into a more specific and limited life structure. Decisions taken during the Saturn return can be binding, committing us for many years to come to a vocation, to a place, to significant people, and to guiding ideas.

Much of the period of Campbell's twenties could be characterized as the avoidance of a settled life in the community—as a flight from family life, domestic responsibilities, past religious conditioning, parental expectations, the intellectual straightjacket of academia, and so forth (directions influenced, it must be said, by the period of the Great Depression with its limited opportunities for employment).[9] The Saturn return transit brings youthful experiments to an end; indeed, it signals the end of an entire life phase, with the clearing away of the past and the assimilation of earlier life experiences as the foundation for the work and commitments of adult maturity. Saturn functions like the force of gravity in grounding the archetypal *puer* tendencies of earlier years with the solemn concerns and material pressures of *senex* reality.[10] In its relationship to the shadow archetype, Saturn forces us to face up to our inferior side at this time, to that which we have avoided and perhaps judged and rejected. For it is in the neglected parts of one's experience that, as we have seen, one might discover the foundation-stone of the structure of one's future life. Thus, from a life of the free-spirited explorer, Campbell was to become anchored in one place, in one job, for the next four decades. The contemplation of multiple fluctuating possibilities of different life paths became crystallized and consolidated into a particular life role. Such a shift during the Saturn return can be accompanied by a perceptible transformation in one's felt experience, with the center of existential gravity tangibly shifting, as Stephen Arroyo remarks: "What was just in the person's head before becomes a more integral part of the entire body, i.e., of his real life experience."[11] One's consciousness drops more fully into one's body, so to speak, and one's energies, Arroyo adds, become expressed more efficiently and consistently, even as one's overall energy levels tend to decrease.

As is the case for many of us, in Campbell's life at this time there were a number of false starts or attempts to move in directions that ultimately proved fruitless. During the Saturn return, we can have the sense of being constrained by the binding pattern and limits of our nature—the Self, in Jungian terms—with forays in other directions inevitably thwarted or unsuccessful. Having sent out over 70 applications to colleges looking for employment, Campbell initially accepted a position as a high-school teacher at Canterbury School, where he himself had studied, but soon found it frustrating, with onerous duties of pastoral care for his students alongside his class instruction—a role to which he did not feel at all suited.[12] In April 1933 he decided to leave the position at the end of that academic year, with transiting Saturn closely aligned with the position of Saturn in Campbell's birth chart.[13] At this point, he envisaged his future as a writer: "I've determined definitely to go back to my writing for keeps—or until I shatter completely. I shall have saved the enormous sum of $300 and I hope to make it last about ten months. If I don't sell a story by then (next March) I don't know what will become of me . . ."[14]

Looking back now, it is hard for us to imagine Campbell as a writer of short stories, living from hand to mouth, and not as the esteemed scholar of myth that he was to become. But, as is the case for many of us, we are moved to explore a range of paths and possibilities as we struggle to integrate our deeper nature with the demands of fitting in somehow to the established world order. Other pursuits might lead us astray but we can appreciate in retrospect that they serve to round out the character and give us a fuller experience of life in its variety before it crystallizes into a settled form.

Despite earning a little much-needed money from the publication of several short stories, Campbell also abandoned that particular life path. For finally, just after his Saturn return became exact, he received an invitation that was to resolve his vocational quandary and existential uneasiness. As the Larsens report: "It was in March 1934, and on the recommendation of his old Columbia professor W. W. Lawrence, that the fledgling experimental college for women, Sarah Lawrence, in Bronxville, New York, offered Joseph Campbell the faculty job that he would hold for the next thirty-eight years."[15] There, at Sarah Lawrence, Campbell was to meet his wife, the dancer-choreographer Jean Erdman.

These specific events in Campbell's life during his Saturn return illustrate the general rule: It is during the Saturn return that, as Arroyo explains,

> . . . one becomes aware to a greater extent than ever before of what one's destiny is and therefore what one *has* to do from here on out. No longer are there seemingly endless opportunities and alternatives; you now know that you've made your experiments and lived out your youthful illusions, but that from now on you have to work at

fulfilling your role in the vast drama, even if you have no idea how you have come to be assigned the part that you're now playing.[16]

Moving into this new teaching position and the regular routines of working life obviously marked quite a significant point of transition for Campbell, which he captured well in a letter at the time. "Having an income and a set of limited working hours takes a good deal of the adventure out of the picture, but it is a pleasant rest for a change. So I am now a recognized member of the community with at least nine months of future ahead of me. . . ."[17] As Arroyo stresses, although changes occurring during the Saturn return can bring a sense of limitation and the heavy weight of responsibility, they can also bring a sense of freedom from the past and from endless deliberation. The die is now cast, as it were, and much of the uncertainty about what one is to do with one's life is removed.

Another element of Campbell's first Saturn return, one less overt but nonetheless significant in terms of his future life focus and contribution to society, was the discovery of the work of two figures who thereafter became pole stars for Campbell: Oswald Spengler, whose book *The Decline of the West* Campbell first encountered in 1932 and then read seven times over the next decade, and Leo Frobenius, whose work Campbell came into contact with in September 1933.[18] Frobenius's ideas shaped Campbell's understanding of mythic cycles, particularly that of the hero, which was to become so central to his entire body of work. Reflecting later on the significance of this period of his life, Campbell observed: "The whole range of my studies became now coordinated under the sign of an as yet only dimly foreseen meaning of the magic word: Mythos."[19] Thus, the Saturn return coincided with a consolidation of his intellectual breakthroughs and intuitive epiphanies from his youth into a settled position and a consistent view of myth and the world, which was to sustain his thinking and writing for the rest of his life.

Campbell's Second Saturn Return: 1962–1964

Some 29 years later, during 1963, Saturn had completed another cycle around the zodiac, returning to its own original position of 17 degrees 42 minutes Aquarius in Campbell's birth chart. On this occasion, Saturn entered Aquarius in January 1962 and left this sign, moving into Pisces, in December 1964—dates which, again, might be viewed as approximate symbolic markers of the overall period of the Saturn return transit. Saturn was exactly aligned with Campbell's natal Saturn

CASE STUDIES OF THE SATURN RETURN

three times during 1963: in March, September, and November. These multiple exact alignments are created by the phenomenon of retrograde motion, when a planet appears to move backwards in its course because of the relative speed of the moving Earth.[20]

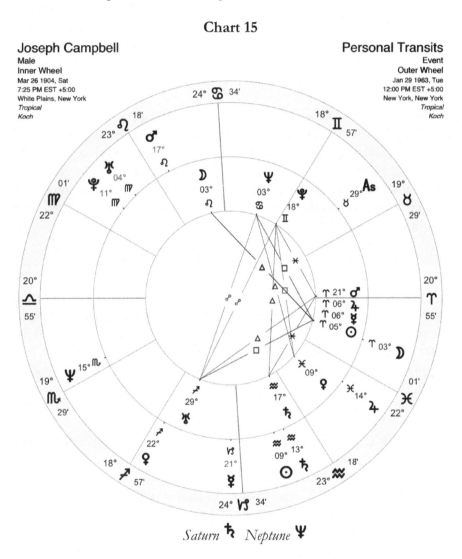

Chart 15

The above shows Joseph Campbell's personal transits on January 29, 1963, during Campbell's second Saturn Return. Note that the position of Saturn in the sky had moved close—within 4 degrees—to the position of Saturn in Campbell's birth chart. Note also in the outer wheel the square aspect between transiting Neptune and transiting Saturn, within two degrees of exact.

Unlike Campbell's first Saturn return, perhaps the major theme of the completion of the second Saturn cycle was an encounter with death. The assassination of President John F. Kennedy in November 1963 was to have a potent impact on Campbell, informing his teaching for long afterwards. Witnessing Kennedy's funeral on television, Campbell was struck by its psychological import as "a ritualized occasion of the greatest social necessity" and "a compensatory rite to re-establish the sense of solidarity of the nation."[21] Campbell was also struck by the mythic significance of the funeral precession,

> particularly to the symbolism of the gun carriage bearing the flag-draped coffin, drawn by seven clattering gray steeds with blackened hoofs, another horse prancing slowly at their side bearing an empty saddle with stirrups reversed, also with blackened hoofs and conducted by a military groom. I saw before me, it seemed, the seven ghostly steeds of the gray Lord Death, here come to conduct the fallen hero youth on his last celestial journey.[22]

The Saturn return transit does not occur in isolation, but alongside numerous other transits taking place at the time. In this case, not only was Saturn conjunct its own position in Campbell's chart, but transiting Neptune had moved into a square alignment with Saturn. The Saturn-Neptune complex, as we will later consider, has been associated by Tarnas with themes such as "the sanctification of death," and "the loss of an idealized figure" with the expression of the Neptune archetype, in Campbell's case, leading him to construe the Saturnian experience of death in symbolic terms, as well as to participate in the collective experience of loss and mourning.[23]

Campbell also experienced death within his family during this Saturn return, with the passing of his brother, Charlie, on July 25, 1964, after a battle with alcoholism and illness. Later the same year, in October 1964 and still during the Saturn return, Campbell's former editor Pascal Covici died. Such encounters with death tend to lead inevitably to reflections on one's own mortality, which are tied in, during this second Saturn return, with an awareness of what one needs to do with the time one has left, including making provisions for one's security in older age, entering into a new life pattern and structure that will serve one during the ensuing years. One might reflect too on the lasting contribution that one might bequeath to future generations (whether one's family or the wider culture), on one's legacy and concrete achievements over the course of one's life.

This period of Campbell's life was characterized by a heavy workload, as is often the case during major Saturn transits, but also the ripening, culmination, and fruition of many streams of his work.[24] With many years of teaching, editing, and writing behind him, Campbell was poised, within the space of a few years, to step into the role of a kind of cultural elder, mediated by his association with Esalen Institute in Big Sur, California, and especially through television broadcasts of his lectures. During the Saturn return in 1963, he made "his television debut before the American public," when he recorded a series of thirty-four episodes on myth for Channel 13.[25] It was through this medium, of course, that he was to later come to the attention of a global audience with the PBS *Power of Myth* interviews with Bill Moyers broadcast in the late 1980s.

In his creative work, Campbell was absorbed in the writing of the fourth and final volume of *The Masks of God* series, entitled *Creative Mythology*—in many respects the defining contribution to this series. His reflections in the opening to this book were of a distinctly Saturnian flavor, for it was here he noted the dangers of a crystallization of life such that, "coerced by social patterns," one might "harden to some figure of living death" rather than, guided by a living myth, willingly consent to life's necessary endings and transitions.[26]

While initiating a new life phase, the Saturn return also often signals the completion of a cycle, bringing the possibility of actualization and fulfillment. One aspect of this development for Campbell was a return to the Grail literature that had so inspired him as a younger man. As the Larsens note: "Thus, in his sixtieth year, Joseph Campbell had returned to the world to which he was first introduced in his twenties, the marvelous landscape of the Grail romances and the lore of the Arthurian Middle Ages."[27]

Fittingly, too, in another expression of this theme, it was at Covici's funeral that Campbell was to come into contact again with John Steinbeck, their first meeting since the parting in Monterey during Campbell's first Saturn return. Reflections on death and the passing of time, further prompted by the reading of Schopenhauer's essay "On an Apparent Intention in the Fate of the Individual," gave Campbell an increasingly clear awareness of life as conforming to an innate pattern or form, coherently unfolding over time. As the Larsens report:

As we researched Campbell's biography, this was the first time we had seen him articulate this philosophy in the style of his later enunciation of it. Though he had probably read Schopenhauer's essay in his late twenties [first Saturn return], now it was speaking to him of the ways in which life creatively may unfold . . . if one held to the true form within one's life—form, in the highest Platonic sense—one's life would reveal its essential coherence. He expressed this elegantly—indeed, quintessentially—in his tribute to Covici.[28]

Saturn transits to its own position are closely connected to what Tarnas has called the "structural unfolding of life" and thus Schopenhauer's essay, describing the realization of the innate potential of the "intelligible character" in the "empirical character" or ego personality, is especially relevant to the understanding of this unfolding and to themes central to the Saturn return.[29]

Albert Schweitzer

Born in January 1875, the same year as Jung, and almost exactly one Saturn cycle before Campbell, Albert Schweitzer, our second example, presents a helpful comparison and contrast. The winner of the Nobel Peace Prize in 1952 for his service to the peoples of Africa and his campaign for a nuclear-free world, Schweitzer first became known for his studies of Christianity, focused on the gospels and the life of Jesus, and later for his philosophy of the "reverence for life," inspired in part by the Indian religion of Jainism.

Whereas Campbell's chart is dominated by a prominent Jupiter, in major alignments to the Sun, Mercury, Mars, Uranus, and Neptune, Schweitzer's chart features a prominent Saturn, in a grand cross with Mars, Uranus, and Pluto, alongside a T-square involving the Sun, Mercury, Jupiter, and Neptune. While both men lived lives blessed with Jupiterian achievement and success, and while both exhibited high idealism and a generosity of spirit, the far greater emphasis on Saturn in Schweitzer's chart is reflected in the accentuated struggle and resistance he encountered during and after his first Saturn return, as well as the hardship of the life he chose to live.

Schweitzer's natal Saturn is positioned at just after 14 degrees Aquarius. His first Saturn return became exact in February 1904 and again in October–November 1904, with Saturn leaving Aquarius for the final time in January 1906, as Schweitzer turned 31. Examining the details of his life, recorded in his autobiography *Out of My Life and*

Thought, we discover that this period saw the completion and publication (in 1906) of the first edition of *The Quest of the Historical Jesus*, the book for which he became widely known, which seeks to determine the extent to which the life and teaching of Jesus, as recorded in the synoptic gospels, were influenced by eschatology, especially by the belief that Jesus saw himself in Messianic terms—that is, as a Messiah. The book grew out of research Schweitzer undertook for a lecture series given to the Theological Faculty at Strasbourg during the summer of 1905. In many respects, it marked the fruition and climax of the first Saturn cycle of his life, which was then to take an unexpected direction.

Having spent years studying for a degree in philosophy and for theological licensure, and then having published significant books on theology and also on the music of Bach, and having attained to the position of principal of the Theological College at St. Thomas in Strasbourg, during his Saturn return Schweitzer took the conscious decision to radically reorient his life. As the chapter title of his autobiography declares: "I Resolve to Become a Jungle Doctor."

Schweitzer initially endeavored to serve the needy in Europe, including "tramps and discharged prisoners," but his efforts in this direction met with only partial success, and he soon reached the conclusion this would not provide the means of service he was looking for.[30] The situation resolved itself during the time of his exact Saturn return in the synchronistic discovery of his calling, as Schweitzer reports:

> One morning in the autumn of 1904 I found on my writing table in the college one of the green-covered magazines in which the Paris Missionary Society reported every month on its activities. . . . That evening, in the very act of putting it aside that I might go on with my work, I mechanically opened this magazine, which had been laid on the table in my absence. As I did so, my eye caught the title of an article: *Les besoins de la Mission du Congoi* ("The needs of the Congo Mission.")[31]

The article drew attention to the shortage of missionary workers in Gaboon, Northern Congo, and with it was an appeal for help. "Having finished the article," Schweitzer reports, "I quietly began my work. My search was over."[32] In committing to a life as a doctor dedicated to the service of the sick in Congo, Schweitzer found the calling that was to occupy him throughout the rest of his days, and from which sprang his philosophy of "reverence for life"—his lasting legacy to humanity.

Chart 16

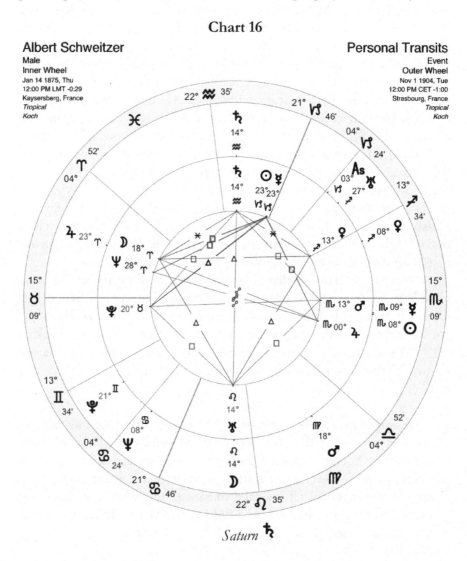

Albert Schweitzer's Personal Transits, November 1, 1904. Note the position of Saturn in the sky on that date was 14 degrees Aquarius—the same position as Saturn occupied at Schweitzer's birth. Schweitzer was born with Saturn opposite Uranus (at 14 degrees Leo), an aspect associated with the theme of the sudden break or change in the structure of one's life. Both Saturn and Uranus archetypes were therefore being activated during Schweitzer's Saturn return.

With the decision set in his mind, Schweitzer informed those closest to him:

> On October 13th, 1905, a Friday, I dropped into a letter box in the Avenue de la Grande Armée in Paris, letters to my parents and to some of my most intimate acquaintances, telling them that at the beginning of the winter term I should enter myself as a medical student, in order to go later to Equatorial Africa as a doctor.[33]

The major challenge of his Saturn return, however, took the form of the judgments and criticism of what seemed to those around him to be a quite incomprehensible choice of life direction, especially given the additional training and labor it would entail.

> What seemed to my friends the most irrational thing in my plan was that I wanted to go to Africa, not as a missionary, but as a doctor, and thus when already thirty years of age burdened myself as a beginning with a long period of laborious study. And that this study would mean for me a tremendous effort, I had no manner of doubt. I did, in truth, look forward to the next few years with dread. But the reasons which determined me to follow the way of service I had chosen, as a doctor, weighed so heavily that other considerations were as dust in the balance.[34]

We recognize here familiar Saturnian traits, accentuated during this period of the planet's transit to its own position: the burden, the labor, the effort, the foreboding, and not least the heavy weightiness of the decision, experienced as a moral imperative—something we simply must do in spite of the upset and disturbance it will cause.

By his own account, Schweitzer suffered acutely at the hands of incredulous and misunderstanding friends and relatives, who, he recalls, "all joined in expostulating with me on the folly of my enterprise. I was a man, they said, who was burying the talent entrusted to him and wanted to trade with false currency."[35] The fiercest critiques and challenges came from his Christian associates, in spite of Schweitzer's argument that he was obeying the directives of Jesus. Taking this line, he reports, "brought upon me an accusation of conceit, although I had, in fact, been obliged to do violence to my feelings to employ this argument at all. In general, how much I suffered through so many people assuming a right to tear open all the doors and shutters of my inner self!"[36] But Schweitzer came to view this criticism in a positive light for it forced him to be clear in his reasons and motives for the decision, and to reflect on the possibility that the project may fail.

There are resonances here with Campbell's moral decision with respect to the Carol Steinbeck affair in that both episodes in the two men's lives caused them to stand firmly behind their own choices. Schweitzer especially, in enduring painful criticism, had to find it within himself to stand alone in affirming his decision and to disregard the opinions of others in favor of his own sense of what he must do with his life. Needless to say, this can be very difficult, especially since Saturn pertains to those areas of life in which we tend to be unsure of ourselves and very sensitive to the judgments of others. But this is precisely the challenge many of us face during the Saturn return. We are called upon at this time to take responsibility for our own life and to develop moral backbone, trusting our own judgment above all else. The avoidance of this challenge can leave us trapped in a life structure that does not reflect our authentic nature, which is a recipe for an unsatisfying empty existence.

With the approach of his second Saturn return (starting in February 1932, when Saturn entered Aquarius, and ending, roughly, as Saturn left Aquarius in February 1935), Schweitzer, like Campbell, transitioned into the role of something like a cultural elder, as he undertook a series of lectures across Europe, including the Hibbert Lectures at Manchester College, Oxford and at London University, and the prestigious Gifford Lectures in Edinburgh (in 1934 and 1935, aged 59–60), an honor reserved for eminent figures in the field of theology.[37] In combination with these lectures, which led to several further publications, the period of his Saturn return was largely consumed by his treatment of patients in his hospital in Africa. In certain respects, these years brought the full flowering of Schweitzer's life and personality, with heavy burdens of work, gladly borne. "During these years," Schweitzer recorded, "the hospital has usually been filled to capacity largely on account of the influenza epidemic. In this period also, as many as thirty patients might be waiting at one time for their turns on the operating table."[38] But, as is typical of this transit, this period also saw important structural changes as Schweitzer and his family, in response to the pressure of circumstance, relocated from Königsfeld, Germany to Lausanne, Switzerland, a location "chosen . . . for the climate and for the resources offered by the city for their daughter's education."[39] Chiefly, however, the move was a response to the rising force of Nazism in Germany, with increasing acts of persecution against Jews, and thus a sense of an imminent threat to the Schweitzer family. Confronting the rise to power of Hitler, both in terms of his own situation and its threat to Germany, was one aspect of Schweitzer's second Saturn return. The political situation weighed heavily on his mind at the time, as Nils Oermann's biography reports. In a letter to his wife, Helene, in early 1933, Schweitzer reflects:

> Oh, I suffer terribly from these times. I am completely without hope. What will all this lead to . . . . The situation in France. . . God help us out of this. And this terrible pressure that rests on me numbs me in my work. Every day I have to tear myself out of this sadness in order to get to work.[40]

As we can see, Saturnian themes of entrapment, suffering, pressure, and work were creating an oppressive situation, a contraction of circumstance, characteristic of the Saturn return.

Finally, and on a more positive note, as if to justify and confirm the rightness of his decision during his first Saturn return to put to one side his theological vocation and retrain as a doctor, Schweitzer received widespread public recognition and awards. To commemorate his sixtieth birthday, the city of Strasbourg, where Schweitzer obtained his doctorate and was ordained, named one its parks after him.

Although it differed in form from the anguish of the first Saturn return period, the second return was defined by characteristic themes of this transit: the restructuring of the practical arrangements of life (often in preparation for one's later years), encounters with suffering and death, a culmination or consolidation of one's life work (sometimes with public recognition), heavy burdens, deep concerns with ethical matters, and the completion of major projects bringing to a close periods of one's life. Always, when transiting Saturn forms major hard-aspect alignments to natal Saturn, one is subject to a concentrated and sometimes prolonged exposure to Saturnian themes of many kinds.

Notes

[1] See Arroyo, *Astrology, Karma, and Transformation*, 84–85.
[2] An ephemeris is a book or table of data showing the positions of the planets in degrees of celestial longitude (including minutes) in the signs of the zodiac. For use in astrology, they often contain data for periods of 50 or 100 years,

such as an ephemeris for the twentieth century. Such data is now readily available in astrology software.

3 Experience suggests that a much larger orb applies to the Saturn return than to other personal transits. Rather than measure specific degrees before and after exact, it is often better to focus on a three-year period centered on the date of exacts Saturn return transits.

4 Larsen & Larsen, *Fire in the Mind*, 192.

5 Larsen & Larsen, *Fire in the Mind*, 193.

6 Larsen & Larsen, *Fire in the Mind*, 192.

7 Larsen & Larsen, *Fire in the Mind*, 160.

8 Larsen & Larsen, *Fire in the Mind*, 160.

9 Note that Campbell's Saturn return was focused on the 4th house, pertaining to home, family, past, one's anchoring in the world, domestic life, and so forth.

10 The *puer* or *puella aeturnus* is the archetypal figure of the eternal youth.

11 Arroyo, *Astrology, Karma, & Transformation*, 85.

12 Larsen & Larsen, *Fire in the Mind*, 214.

13 Larsen & Larsen, *Fire in the Mind*, 218.

14 Larsen & Larsen, *Fire in the Mind*, 192.

15 Larsen & Larsen, *Fire in the Mind*, 228.

16 Arroyo, *Astrology, Karma, & Transformation*, 83.

17 Larsen & Larsen, *Fire in the Mind*, 230.

18 Larsen & Larsen, *Fire in the Mind*, 224.

19 Larsen & Larsen, *Fire in the Mind*, 227–228.

20 In cases of multiple exact transits (not only the Saturn return but for all transits), I have found that these tend to correlate with specific "acts" or stages in the working through of particular challenges. The first exact pass is like the first act, which introduces the theme and the challenge; the second one often brings some kind of critical development or turning point; and the third brings a resolution. In some planetary transits, there can be five exact alignments, in which case the third exact transit marks the turning point.

21 Campbell, *Myths to Live By*, 53.

22 Campbell, *Myths to Live By*, 54.

23 Tarnas, "The Ideal and the Real (Part Two)," 105–106 & 118 in *Cultural Crisis and Transformation*, 105–127.

24 Larsen & Larsen, *Fire in the Mind*, 457.

25 Larsen & Larsen, *Fire in the Mind*, 455.

26 Campbell, *The Masks of God, Volume IV: Creative Mythology*, 5

27 Larsen & Larsen, *Fire in the Mind*, 459–460.

28 Larsen & Larsen, *Fire in the Mind*, 612, note 5 to Chapter 22.

29 Tarnas, *Cosmos and Psyche*, 119.

30 Schweitzer, *Out of My Life and Thought*, 86.

31 Schweitzer, *Out of My Life and Thought*, 88.

[32] Schweitzer, *Out of My Life and Thought*, 88.
[33] Schweitzer, *Out of My Life and Thought*, 84.
[34] Schweitzer, *Out of My Life and Thought*, 94.
[35] Schweitzer, *Out of My Life and Thought*, 89.
[36] Schweitzer, *Out of My Life and Thought*, 90.
[37] See Nils Ole Oermann, *Albert Schweitzer: A Biography*, 157–158.
[38] Schweitzer, *Out of My Life and Thought*, 250–251.
[39] Schweitzer, *Out of My Life and Thought*, 250.
[40] Oermann, *Albert Schweitzer: A Biography*, 156.

Chapter 19

Idealism and Imagination: The Spiritual Realm of Neptune

As we turn now to contemplate the planetary archetype Neptune, we enter into a wholly different order of reality—a different archetypal world, one might say. The Neptunian experience encompasses the world-dream and illusion of *maya*, the rapture of divine bliss and paradise, the eternal realm of the ideal, and the magical allure of visions and fantasies. Neptune is the archetypal principle that leads us into transpersonal experience and transcendent insight, and that dissolves and disintegrates all stable structures, leading back into the undifferentiated and unformed primal world—perhaps into escape, madness, delusion, and regression. All these Neptunian experiences must be understood in the context of Saturn, as a response to the basic Saturnian facts of existence.

Over time, the experience of the Saturn archetype exposes us to something like the biblical Fall of Man into exile and alienation, bringing suffering, labor, loss, aging, and ultimately death, even as it moves us towards the actualization of our innate potential. Saturn pertains to the temporal, space-bound flesh-and-blood reality of incarnate existence, with all its limitations and pressures that constitute the fundamental experience of what it is to be alive. We are naturally motivated to seek release from such limiting conditions—release into the beatific experience of infancy now lost to us, release into an enchanted world now faded from memory and seemingly out of reach, and perhaps release into mystical rapture and transcendent realization. From within these motivations lies every human aspiration for a more perfect world, a more ideal life, and the pursuit of every dream and vision, every wish and every alluring fantasy.

Idealistic and Altruistic Heroism: Sun-Neptune

When the Sun and Neptune form major geometric alignments in a birth chart, this indicates that Neptunian themes will in one way or another be central to the individual's life experience, identity, and forms of heroism and creative self-expression—dimensions of the psyche associated with the Sun.

We can see the Sun-Neptune archetypal combination, first, in the idealistic hero, sacrificing his or her life to an ideal, championing and illuminating a cause, or using celebrity to promote a cause, perhaps becoming its figurehead or spokesperson. We see it too in the altruist, living and acting out of empathy, compassion, and sense of unity with others, in touch with our universal humanity and motivated by the urge to alleviate suffering. The Sun-Neptune complex can allow one to participate in the universal love and compassion of Buddha consciousness or Christ consciousness, and to embody this in one's life and one's personality.

Bob Geldof is a fine example of the altruistic and idealistic dimension of the Sun-Neptune complex. He was born in 1951 during a Sun-Mercury-Saturn-Neptune conjunction, all opposite Jupiter and square to Uranus—these planets forming a T-square alignment. As one can imagine, with so many major aspects to the planet Neptune the corresponding archetype assumes a prominent place in Geldof's life. Taking up the plight of the millions of people afflicted by famine and starvation in Ethiopia in the 1980s, Geldof became the figurehead and pioneer of Band Aid and Live Aid, raising vast sums of money in a famine-relief movement of unprecedented scale (the Jupiterian flavor of the complex), with the Live Aid concerts becoming one of the iconic moments and movements of the decade (a theme associated with the Jupiter-Uranus combination, which we will consider in Volume III). Although well known before as the lead singer of The Boomtown Rats, thereafter Geldof's name became synonymous with Band Aid and the promotion of idealistic causes and charitable works, which have become something of the signature of his life and personality.

Midge Ure, of the band Ultravox, who co-wrote the British Band-Aid single "Do They Know It's Christmas?" with Geldof, and helped him organize the Live Aid concerts, also has the Sun-Neptune pairing (in a five-planet conjunction with Saturn, the Moon, and Venus), with the Sun, Neptune, and Saturn also square to Uranus at the time of his birth in 1953. The Neptunian sensibility that enables one to identify with the plight of another, feel sympathy and compassion, and seek to alleviate suffering are combined in both these cases with the Saturnian capacity for practical action in the world—the theme of spirit in the world, or "this-worldly religiosity," as Tarnas has called it.[1] The Sun-Neptune alignment often indicates the centrality in one's life experience of the Neptunian acts of compassion and altruistic service, and the tendency for a person to identify with such acts and derive esteem from them. Through Neptune's influence on the Sun, one's focus and the sphere of one's consciousness become universalized, in a sense, with the relinquishing or setting aside of exclusively personal interests in the service of an ideal. Neptune opens the individual consciousness and intentional focus of the Sun to the unity and common bonds of sympathy that we can often overlook in our pursuit of individualistic concerns and in facing up to the demands and necessities of life.

This is true not only of natal Sun-Neptune aspects, but also during Neptune transits to the Sun—periods of up to five years in which the orbiting Neptune makes significant geometric alignments with the Sun's position at the time of an individual's birth. During these transits, one can more readily express and act on one's compassion and empathy, moving beyond one's personal interests and close-minded egoic concerns to help others and give of oneself to the greater good. Such a response might be elicited by circumstance if it is not consciously chosen. Under the influence of Neptune, we can move into a transcendent field of awareness and realization in which life is not just the conflict and collision of wills, born of the Saturnian *principium individuationis*. For behind the apparent separateness and strife lies a unity, from which acts of compassion and sympathy emerge. The Sun-Neptune combination gives us, or moves us towards, an innate attunement to this unity.

Another example of a widely known celebrity musician who became identified with a compassionate cause is Linda McCartney. Together with her husband, Paul, she worked tirelessly up to her death in 1998 to champion animal welfare (through organizations such as PETA) and to bring to light the suffering involved in the inhumane farming and slaughter of animals for meat production. She was a passionate advocate for a vegetarian diet and even established a vegetarian frozen-food range emblazoned with her name—another instance of the use of celebrity personality (the Sun) in service of a cause (Neptune) and concern for other beings.

She was born with the Sun conjunct Neptune in a close-to-exact trine to Saturn and Uranus. Her motivation for vegetarianism was captured in two well-known remarks: she does not eat anything with a face, and if slaughterhouses had glass walls everyone would be vegetarian—exposing the human tendency to live in delusional ignorance of the suffering inflicted on our fellow creatures. We see again in her stance, taken up and furthered by her husband, an active expression of Neptunian compassion and sympathy, exemplifying the power of the solar archetype to shine a light on and radiate the qualities of the planetary archetypes in aspect with the Sun. Paul McCartney, incidentally, has the Sun conjunct Jupiter, square to Neptune.

Chart 17

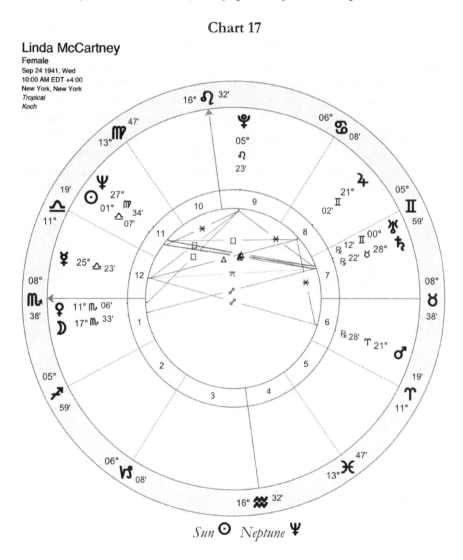

Sun ☉ *Neptune* ♆

Of course, regardless of planetary placements, each of us has access to and expresses some form of Neptunian idealism, compassion, empathy, and the desire to alleviate suffering. The particular alignments involving Neptune, however, in birth charts and in transits, give specific indications as to the ways in which these qualities and motivations are experienced. As in the above examples, Sun-Neptune symbolizes the tendency to identify with a cause, such that the living out an ideal is central to one's identity, perhaps even to the degree that one's name becomes closely associated with it.

One figure most immediately associated with living a life in accordance with universal ideals is Mahatma Gandhi. Born with the Sun opposite Neptune, Gandhi is the very paragon of an individual existence sacrificed to a greater cause, held up as a shining example of a life dedicated to the promotion of peace even in the face of great hostility. His was a life molded around religious values, illustrating well the centrality of Neptunian idealism and spirituality for many of those with Sun-Neptune alignments. As Einstein remarked, in an oft-quoted statement, on the occasion of Gandhi's seventieth birthday: "Generations to come, it may well be, will scarce believe that such a man as this one ever in flesh and blood walked upon this Earth."[2] Gandhi's life assumed the character and stature of that of a saint, and has come to represent a type of socially engaged spiritual path in the modern world—an ideal to which many people today now aspire. In Gandhi, we see an exemplary expression of the Sun-Neptune capacity to live one's ideal, to become the ideal, embodying it in one's very way of being in the world. (His worldly, socially engaged form of spirituality also reflects his natal trine between Saturn and Neptune, a combination we will later consider.)

Another prominent figure identified with the promotion of peace was Alfred Nobel, giving his name to the prestigious annual awards in the sciences and literature and to the Nobel Peace Prize, for which he is best-known. During his lifetime, however, Nobel was dubbed the "merchant of death," for he built a business empire that developed various kinds of explosives.[3] Concerned with his legacy, and the image of him that would remain after his death, he bequeathed most of his vast fortune to the establishment of the Nobel prizes. He was born with the Sun and Mars square to Neptune, all opposite Jupiter, which we see in the concern with image and in the benevolent generosity of his donation and vision, which totally eclipsed his earlier life aims and endeavors. Bertha von Suttner (born June 9, 1843), who was influential persuading Nobel to set up the peace prize, had Sun trine Neptune, and was herself awarded the prize in 1905—the first woman to receive it. Albert Schweitzer, too, born with the Sun square Neptune, received the Nobel Peace Prize in 1952 for his "reverence for life" and altruistic service to mankind, and, as we saw earlier, his name is closely associated with his studies of Christian eschatology and mysticism, conveying multiple dimensions of the Sun-Neptune complex in living a life modeled on the ways of Jesus and Jain philosophy. Finally, Louis Pasteur and Alexander Fleming, the two prominent chemists, whose work did so much to treat, prevent, and alleviate illness through the development of vaccines, pasteurization, and antibiotics, also had Sun-Neptune square alignments. Traditionally, all forms of drugs and medication fall under the archetypal jurisdiction of Neptune, both in their association with the alleviation of suffering and the altered states of consciousness they can induce.

Gandhi is also an example of another characteristic form of expression of the Sun-Neptune combination, that of the idealized figure, the figure who becomes a carrier for the spiritual projections and ideals of the people, and whose person and personality become a vehicle for the ideal. The same is true of Eva Peron, the Argentinean politician and wife of President Juan Peron. Born with the Sun square to Neptune, she was adulated by the Argentine people during her time in power (1946–1952), and she sacrificed herself to her country, acting to help those in need, working selflessly for charitable causes and women's suffrage. She was proclaimed, by decree of the Argentine Congress, the "Spiritual Leader of the Nation" and her name remains synonymous with Argentina even today. We see elements of such themes, too, in the British Royal Family: both Prince William and Prince Harry have Sun-Neptune hard aspects, and their mother Diana, Princess of Wales, had Sun trine Neptune. Each is associated with compassionate works on behalf of the less fortunate, championing their chosen causes, and each in different ways came to be idealized and projected onto by people around the world.

The Savior and the Prophet
Undertaking an altruistic mission can provide an outlet for the Neptunian impulses towards charity, the love of one's neighbor, sympathy, and the alleviation of suffering, supporting a sense of identity as a compassionate and sensitive individual. Neptune elicits a genuine sacrifice and inspires us to authentic altruism, born of the recognition of the unity of all life, and perhaps inspired by spiritual

experiences and religious values. However, the Sun-Neptune archetypal combination can also give rise to pride in one's altruism and sacrifice—recall the Sun's association with egoic identity, self-esteem, and pride. The solar principle, manifest through the ego, identifies with, and derives its identity and esteem from, the Neptunian sacrifice and altruism. In acting on behalf of others, one can also be subtly serving one's own ego.

Indeed, in acting out of the Sun-Neptune complex, one might unwittingly assume the role of savior, even to the extent that one actually believes oneself to be some kind of exalted messianic figure, singled out for a divine mission and identifying with this archetype above all else, to the detriment of the realization of one's wholeness and the cultivation of one's individual essence and soul spark. Identifying with the savior archetype in this way, one is effectively freed from the existential burden of forging one's own life, deciding for oneself, and finding one's own unique path, for one's entire reality is molded around the fulfillment of the archetypal role—a pattern carved out over time and deposited within the collective unconscious as part of our living inheritance of psychic forms.

In terms of individuation, the exclusive identification with a Neptunian archetypal role—such as savior, guru, martyr, or prophet—invariably entails self-loss. Even if well intentioned, a life committed to religious practice, charitable works, and altruism can sometimes be an escape from oneself, a flight from the struggle of individuation. For it is often easier to sacrifice oneself to a religious path or to think only of others, with no concern for oneself, than it is to endure the creative risk, uncertainty, and suffering of truly being an individual. Living altruistically in this manner might well entail an heroic sacrifice of oneself, but to what end? Altruistic deeds, as Nietzsche recognized, can offer a form of escape into a way of being that wins the nodding approval, even the high praise, of society and all those that conform to its values; and that approval feeds one's needs for ego gratification (associated with the Sun) and provides justification for one's life, vanquishing ambiguity and uncertainty about who one is and how one should live one's life. Nietzsche himself had the Sun trine to Neptune.

A similar danger is evident with any archetypal figure, such as that of the prophet, with the Neptunian abilities for prescience and visionary attunement to some spiritual truth or coming revelation taking over the conscious personality and the promulgation of the prophecy becoming the central mission of life. The role furnishes us with a sense of high purpose, seemingly offering a romanticized life of spiritual meaning, which can be especially alluring in the midst of psychological turbulence and suffering, when one is searching for a deeper identity beyond that of the persona. The Neptune principle, like all archetypes, is a double-edged sword, for it inspires in us the capacity for selflessness and transcendence, to which all spiritual paths aspire, and yet it also associated with the regressive self-loss and delusion that can rob us of our authentic selfhood. One often has to run the risk of the latter in the quest for the former.

Even if one cannot become a prophet oneself, another prospect presents itself: to become a disciple or devotee, which brings its own dangers, as Jung describes:

But besides the possibility of becoming a prophet, there is another alluring joy, subtler and apparently more legitimate: the joy of becoming a prophet's disciple. This, for the vast majority of people, is an altogether ideal technique. . . . The disciple is unworthy; modestly he sits at the Master's feet and guards against having ideas of his own. Mental laziness becomes a virtue; one can at least bask in the sun of a semi-divine being. He can enjoy the archaism and infantalism of his unconscious fantasies without loss to himself, for all responsibility is laid at the Master's door. Through his deification of the Master, the disciple, apparently without noticing it, waxes in stature; moreover, does he not possess the great truth—not his discovery, of course, but received straight from the Master's hands? Naturally the disciples all stick together, not out of love, but for the very understandable purpose of effortlessly confirming their own convictions by engendering an air of collective agreement. . . . One feels the full dignity and burden of such a position, deeming it a solemn duty and a moral necessity to revile others not of a like mind, to enrol proselytes and to hold up a light to the Gentiles, exactly as though one were the prophet oneself.[4]

With a natal Sun-square-Neptune aspect (see Chart 20), Jung was exceptionally attuned to the dangers the associated archetypal complex can pose during individuation: self-loss or flight from the self and from the living of one's own individual life; the relinquishing of responsibilities; the attraction to a charismatic personality; idolatry and deification of the guru, and the service and devotion to such a figure; delusion and absorption in fantasy; and the common bond of collective belief in the cause and ideology. Sun-Neptune complexes can manifest in hero worship of an idealized figure, promoting the imitation of the life of another, rather than the living of one's own life. One's own capacity for individual heroism and creative self-expression, associated with the Sun, can be effectively dissolved or suspended by the hypnotic power of an image or ideal. Forsaking the hero in oneself, one can only wait passively in hope and expectation that salvation will come from without. Solar qualities—autonomy, purposive intentionality, individual self-expression, directed will—can remain undeveloped, as one's own innate capacity for heroism is projected onto figures of religious devotion, powerful leaders, culture heroes, or one's partner or parents. When this happens, the autonomous ego invariably remains passive, at the mercy of projections.

In Christian terms, we can see this tendency in the aspiration to follow and imitate the ways of Jesus—the *imitatio Christi*. Such imitation, even if it moves us away from the worldly aims of the ego in the living of a religious life and leads to certain moral improvements of character, can rarely deliver unique spiritual insight for one is merely copying the prescribed ways of another. More broadly, the patterns of the Sun-Neptune archetypal complex can lead one to sacrifice one's identity and one's life to a formal spiritual path or to get involved in a spiritual movement or cult. I have seen cases of Sun-Neptune alignments, both hard and soft aspects, in which, through participation in such spiritual groups, it is as if the individual has not truly begun to exist as a person in his or her own right. While following an established spiritual path offers the possibility of genuine realization, it also brings the danger of self-loss and the failure to adequately develop one's egoic identity and individual will. Neptune can inspire, but also weaken and dissolve, the individual ego, associated with the Sun.

As much as it can elicit spiritual experience and insight, then, the Neptune principle can seduce us into a false existence based on the living out of an image of ourselves—another example of "self-image actualization" and possession by an archetype, rather than the realization of our unique deeper nature. While individuation entails sacrifice to the spiritual authority of the Self, and thus leads us beyond a life of narrow self-interest dictated by exclusively personal concerns, individuation also entails reckoning with one's inner daimon, the demonic compulsion of the instincts, and the morally ambiguous imperatives of the Self, which are not always aligned with conventional religious conceptions of goodness and altruistic love of one's neighbor. Individuation is not synonymous with doing good deeds and living the life of a saint, even if individuation constitutes a spiritual path. We will address such considerations more fully when we consider the Neptune-Pluto complex in Volume IV.

Idolization and Disintegration: Diego Maradona

One compelling example of a range of expressions of the Sun-Neptune pairing is another famous Argentinean, the 1980s football genius Diego Maradona (born October 30, 1960), widely revered as one of the greatest players of all time, due in no small part to his astonishing performances at the 1986 World Cup in Mexico. After that tournament, sports journalist Daniel Arcucci notes in a documentary on Maradona's life, "it was as if Argentina was celebrating its saviour."[5] Leading Argentina to victory brought upon him the adulation of his countrymen, who saw him as a kind of god—a fine example of the tendency to idealize figures with Sun-Neptune natal alignments. Maradona was born with a close conjunction of the two planets in Scorpio (see Chart 18).

If it were possible, Maradona was even more idolized, even worshipped and deified, by the supporters of his domestic club, Napoli, in Italy, which he joined in a surprise transfer from Barcelona in 1984. In the 1986–1987 season, Maradona led the unfashionable club from the south of Italy, often subject to the derision and prejudices of the more affluent north, to the top of the Italian *Serie A* and on to claim the club's first *Scudetto* (the league championship) in the history of the city. The team, inspired by Maradona, then also won the Italian Cup in the same season. Maradona duly came to carry the projections of the people associated with the club and city—as savior, hero, and god. One story from the 2019 documentary on Maradona's life gives a sense of the degree to which he was idolized and revered: "After he underwent a blood test, the nurse took the phial of Diego's blood and placed it in the church of San Gennaro like he was a demigod."[6] The *Football Italia* website, for Channel 4 television in the UK, gives a fuller account of Maradona's significance to the city:

> What Diego meant to football in Naples is something almost too complex to explain. He was the symbol of the 80s. Without ever seeing him, or knowing a Neapolitan at that time, it is impossible to conceive what he meant for the inhabitants of that sprawling, almost third world city.
>
> He was loved immediately on his arrival. He was every mother's son, everyone's brother, every girl's boyfriend. He was the man who

would show the rest of the world that Napoli could and would teach everyone else how to play football. Apart from his *calcio* [soccer] skills, his social importance was of enormous benefit to people's self esteem and he soon became the idol of the people.

Naples is not a rich city and the slums, where he was put on the same pedestal as the Virgin Mary, were atrociously poor. However Diego, unlike so many of the greats, helped people forget their problems. He alleviated the pain and misery that walked hand in hand down the flapping, washing line-strewn back streets.[7]

Maradona became, the article continues, "a cultural, social and borderline religious icon for Neapolitans." In his outward worldly identity, associated with the Sun, Maradona was thus fulfilling a Neptunian role: carrying religious projections, alleviating suffering, and offering escapism and transcendence of the mundane reality of life.

Understandably, this degree of worship from supporters of his domestic club and his country eventually took its toll on him—"it disturbed him psychologically," Arcucci notes.[8] At this point, having risen to the pinnacle of world football and superstar status, Maradona fell victim to a cocaine addiction, and thus began his transition into a different dimension of the Sun-Neptune archetypal combination, through which an individual becomes enveloped by the mythic power of the projection he or she is carrying and becomes lost in it—a problem exacerbated in Maradona's case by the cocaine use. Under the influence of the drug, "I felt like Superman," Maradona recalls, and he was regularly supplied by the local Naples mafia, eager to ensure he would not seek a transfer away to another club. Despite winning a second *Scudetto* in 1990, Diego Maradona the person, the documentary explains, was lost in the myth of Maradona, which consumed his personality.

What happened to Maradona during his time at Naples has been compared to a kind of crucifixion. From being worshipped as savior and even having a church established in his name, Maradona was subsequently vilified and reviled, even loathed, by the Neapolitans and by people across Italy. "Maradona is the devil," was one magazine headline after his penalty for Argentina helped to knock Italy, the host nation, out of the 1990 World Cup, in a game played, as fate would have it, in Napoli's own stadium. A survey afterwards found that Maradona had become "the most hated person in Italy" and another headline declared that "Lucifer lives in Naples."[9] The radical switch from loving to loathing reflects in part the extremes of feeling judgment associated with the Venus-Pluto and Moon-Pluto alignments in Maradona's chart—archetypal pairings we will consider later. But the religious projections onto Maradona and the mythic quality of his life are an expression of the Sun-Neptune complex.

Chart 18

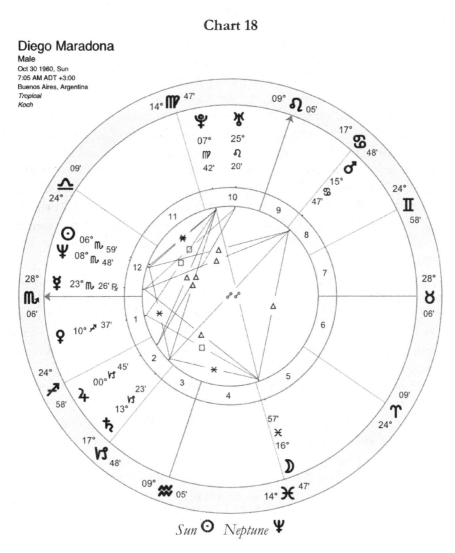

Sun ☉ *Neptune* ♆

His fall from grace and his drug abuse led, perhaps inevitably, to the catastrophic disintegration of Maradona's public image, to personal despair, and then to his flight from Italy. Having already failed a drugs test, for which he was banned from football for a year, the wire-tapping of Maradona's phone exposed his connections to drug and prostitution rings in Naples. He fled to Buenos Aries where he was subsequently arrested for drug possession. The tragic course of events finally forced him to enter a psychiatric hospital.

In this sad account we see multiple dimensions of the Sun-Neptune complex—from the godlike worship and idealization as a savior, carrying the projections of the people and providing inspiration to raise them out of the struggle of their lives, Maradona suffered at the hands of his once-devoted followers and took flight from his fame and misfortune through drugs. As we have seen, the Neptunian archetype can inspire and idealize but it can also lead a person to pursue transcendence and escape through drugs, alcohol, and other addictions, sometimes leading in turn to a dissolution of the individual personality.

Maradona ultimately became a carrier of the religious archetypal projections of the people. As we read in Daniel Arcucci's summary: "Rebel. Cheat. Hero. God. . . . Perhaps the best football player in history . . . . Maradona the footballer was finished and all that survived was the myth."[10] Above all, we see in the events of Maradona's career the tendency, associated with Sun-Neptune complexes, to live and suffer a kind of mythic life.

This became even more apparent on the event of Maradona's death from a heart attack on November 25, 2020, as newspapers around the world captured the idolization of the man, his myth, and his divinization. *L'Équipe* ran the headline "Dieu est mort." *The Guardian* featured headlines describing Maradona as "the Messiah" and "the prodigy who fulfilled the prophecy." With reference to his infamous "hand of God" goal against England in 1986, others noted, with gentle irony, that Maradona was now "in the hands of God."[11] As fellow Argentine soccer superstar Lionel Messi put it: "Diego is eternal."

For the BBC, Tim Vickery described Maradona as an "Argentine deity" due to his "tormenting of England" in the World Cup finals of 1986 in the wake of Argentina's military humiliation in the Falklands War of 1984.[12] Guillem Balague, also writing for the BBC, after doing research for a book on Maradona, remarked that he realized he did not know him at all:

> And the reason for that is because there were 100 different Maradonas. The magician, the cheat, the god, the flawed genius, the loving father, the serially unfaithful husband, the generous benefactor, the foul-mouthed oaf, the boy from the barrio with

magic in his boots and the man who made it to the top of the mountain and fell down it, his body broken by cocaine.[13]

Balague concludes: "He was unable to cope with the god-like status bestowed upon him, yet was seemingly incapable of surviving without it."[14]

We might mention here other comparable examples of similar themes and similar fates from the world of rock music. Elvis Presley, perhaps idealized more than any other celebrity figure on the planet, had a trine between the Sun and Neptune. He too, of course, was consumed by the myth and worship that surrounded him, succumbing to drink, drug, and food addictions, as he disintegrated under the glare of public adulation and celebrity. His death in 1977 confirmed his almost divinized status. The same is true of other idolized musicians, including Jim Morrison (Sun quintile Neptune), Kurt Cobain (Sun square Neptune), and Amy Winehouse (Sun square Neptune) each members of the mythologized "27 club," reflecting the age of their deaths and their immortalization in the eyes of their devoted fans.[15]

Identity Confusion

As we can see in the case of Maradona, the Sun-Neptune combination is also associated with the theme of identity confusion. At the level of the persona and self-image, the Sun-Neptune complex can manifest as an attraction to idealized, romanticized, glamorous life roles or ways of seeing oneself—a tendency reinforced by the capacity of Sun-Neptune to elicit and carry the idealistic projections of others. The innate capacity to imagine one's self into a variety of such roles and personalities, and to act and pretend, often goes hand in hand with a fluid or porous sense of identity, in which one is not sure of who one really is. There is no firm ego identity and thus it is as if one can "try on" different identities. This can be a blessing and gift in acting, of course, and it can be helpful too in life, for Neptune in alignment with the Sun grants the capacity for imitation, and the channeling of other selves, other identities, other personas. But it is sometimes the case that one does not always know that one is pretending, and one becomes identified with the role, and loses oneself in the process.

The Neptunian quality of dissolution can render the boundaries between self and world, and between ego and unconscious, porous and diffused—on the one hand, opening us to experiences of compassion and mystical unity with the environment, but, on the other hand, giving rise to a confused or undeveloped sense of selfhood and personal identity. Neptune moves us to seek escape from conditions of life that are limiting, painful, burdensome, crude, or oppressive. Thus Sun-Neptune can manifest in the form of the escapist, dropping out and running away from hardships, for it is associated with tendencies towards retreat, surrender, and avoidance. In some instances there can be an attraction to drugs in search of the needed experiences of transcendence, flow, and escape. There can be a generalized weakness of the will, associated with the absence of a developed self sense with a distinct individual identity and will. Without a stable ego-structure, there is, therefore, susceptibility towards the disintegration of ego boundaries, opening the individual to the fantasy world of the unconscious, with its plurality of numinous archetypal figures. Accordingly, the Sun-Neptune character is often permeable, with a fluid sense of identity.

David Bowie provides a helpful example of this dimension of the Sun-Neptune complex. He was born with the Sun square to Neptune, and the Sun in the 12th house, ruled by Neptune, thereby reinforcing the relationship between the two archetypes. Both the Sun and Neptune were also in alignment to the planet Uranus—Neptune in a trine and the Sun in a quincunx (150-degree alignment)—a configuration of planetary archetypes that is associated with the endlessly creative changes in artistic direction and innovations in style that defined his career. Bowie was described as an "artistic chameleon," which reflects well both the Sun-Neptune capacity to take on different identities and the Uranus-Neptune theme of suddenly shifting images—a topic to which we will return in Volume III.

Bowie was well known for his on-stage alter-egos, of course—most notably Ziggy Stardust, the "androgynous alien." Adopting these personas enabled him to serve as a channel for something beyond himself. "I was not a natural performer," he confessed in an interview. "I didn't feel at easy on stage—ever—and I had created this one character, Ziggy Stardust . . . . I liked the idea and I feel really comfortable going on stage as somebody else."[16] The capacity to take on different identities was not only a performance device, but something intrinsic to the indefiniteness and permeability of Bowie himself. "[I] didn't try and identify myself or try and try and ask myself who I was. The less questioning I did about myself as to who I was the more comfortable I felt. So now I have absolutely no knowledge of who I am."[17] Bowie's stage performance presented a pluralistic vision of selfhood, at least at the level of the persona, appealing to all those

IDEALISM AND IMAGINATION: THE SPIRITUAL REALM OF NEPTUNE

people in search of their own identities within a rapidly changing culture. Indeed, Bowie remarked that he was pleased with the idea that he "was at all responsible for helping people find more characters in themselves than they originally thought they had."[18]

Chart 19

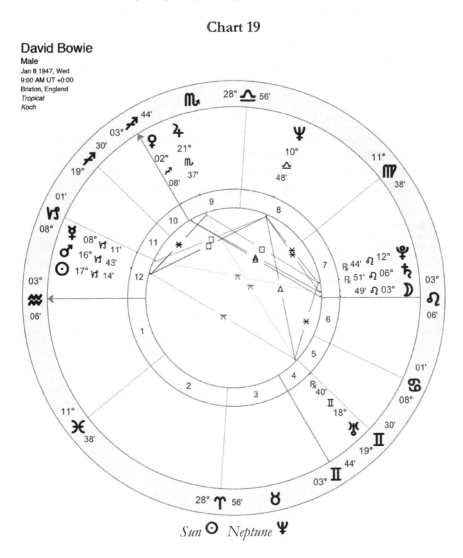

Sun ☉ Neptune ♆

One Bowie character we might readily call to mind is Major Tom, who features in "Space Oddity" (1969) and "Ashes to Ashes" (1980). In Bowie's early recording, Major Tom is the floating starman, the astronaut who has "made the grade" and is idealized by the people below and celebrated by the media ("the papers want to know whose shirts you wear").[19] Eleven years later, he reappears as the drug addict of the second song: "Ashes to ashes, funk to funky. We know Major Tom's a junkie, strung out on heavens high, reaching an all-time low").[20] Both depictions convey something of the qualities of Sun-Neptune: the floating, spaced-out quality, the "space cadet" out of touch with reality, and then the junkie in the depths of despair and disintegration, mirroring Bowie's own drug addiction and alcoholism.[21] These kinds of experience can, for any of us, often be activated during Neptune transits to the Sun, which can signal the experience of being incapacitated or held in suspended animation, and of losing one's focus and direction, even losing a sure sense of who and what one is. Neptune opens the heroic individual consciousness associated with the Sun (the "action man," in the words of Bowie's "Ashes to Ashes"—Bowie had a Sun-Mars conjunction) to the reality of the spirit. Often, this initially takes the form of disintegration, a humbling defeat, reaching an "all-time low." During Neptune's transit to the Sun, one can become disillusioned with all worldly goals and aspirations, which can seem pointless or unfulfilling, as if there is no place for one in the world, and one must find one's place and purpose in a source not of this world, or in service to others, with one's own life appearing of little worth and significance.

Another of Bowie's best-known tracks "Starman" conveys this otherworldly quality of Sun-Neptune, especially given the relationship to Uranus in Bowie' chart. The Starman is the prophet from outer space delivering a message of hope to the people: "he told us not to blow it, 'cos he thinks it all worthwhile."[22] Neptune universalizes the focus of the Sun, opening one's consciousness to transcendent and cosmic realms.[23]

Portraits of a Psychologist

A similar pluralism of selfhood, at a deeper level, was evident in Jung, as we have seen. His theory of archetypes was the formalization of his own experience of engaging in dialogue with multiple imaginal figures or spirits, including Philemon, Salome, and Elijah—dialogues detailed in the dramatic episodes of *The Red Book* based on Jung's original *Black Books*. Jung had the Sun in a square alignment to Neptune, an archetypal combination that granted him direct access to the invisible realm of the spirit behind the phenomenal world of sense experience. For Jung, as he remarks in his autobiography, the inner world of dreams, fantasies, spirits, ancestors, God, and gods was his primary reality—with the solar light of consciousness illuminating the spiritual background of the psyche, normally hidden from our awareness. The "dividing walls" between the known world of ordinary experience and the one beyond the veil, Jung remarked, were for him "transparent."[24]

Chart 20

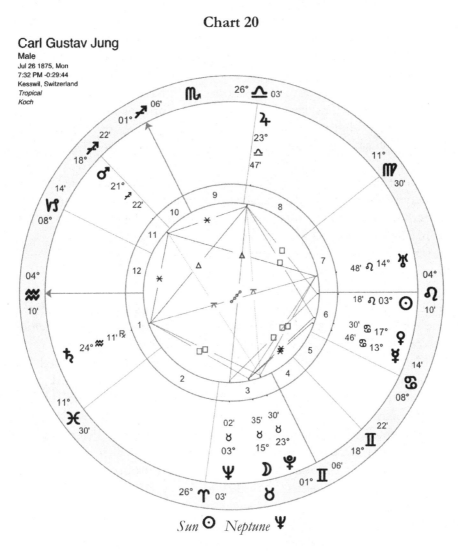

Sun ☉ Neptune ♆

The Sun-Neptune complex also manifested in Jung's experience of identity confusion, bringing with it the specter of insanity, as he struggled, especially during his midlife "confrontation with the unconscious," to come to terms with the unseen factors and multiplicity of sub-personalities within his psyche. Neptune acts to open one's consciousness to the influx of fantasies from the unconscious, and to render the ego permeable and unstable, at least until such time that it becomes adjusted to a fluid self-sense or becomes anchored in the immutable core of the Self. Particularly with hard aspects between these planets, there can be a tension between the need to be someone in one's own right, a defined human personality, and allowing oneself to be a channel for the expression of the divine or archetypal-mythic energies seeking to find expression. One has to come to terms with what the unseen power of the spirit would have us be and do. As in Jung's own case, though, one might have to assert one's solar self, one's ego, to awaken from the dream-world of non-existence, as consciousness heroically struggles to become free of the blinding hypnotic illusion of the archetypal images and move into the clear light of day.

Above all, what is needed when facing the challenges posed by the archetypal Neptune is the capacity for honest self-analysis and clear discernment, but often this capacity is precisely what is lacking or out of reach when Neptune is activated. The trajectory of moving through the Sun-Neptune complex thus often consists in developing one's consciousness through the progressive shedding of the various images and illusions that can enchant but also distort one's experience of reality. One must endeavor to withdraw projections from one's self and one's life, so that one might progressively differentiate the conscious personality from the veil of *maya* in which life is lived.

Many of the various characterizations of Jung, proffered by numerous commentators and interpreters of his life and work, also disclose the influence of Neptunian themes on his solar identity. He has been portrayed as a mystic (by Gary Lachman in *Jung the Mystic*), a Gnostic (Stephan Hoeller in multiple books), a prophet (Peter Kingsley in *Catafalque*), a charismatic cult leader (Richard Noll in his *The Jung Cult: Origins of a Charismatic Movement*), a figure appropriated by the New Age movement (as discussed by David Tacey in his *Jung and the New Age*), a phenomenologist (in Roger Brooke's *Jung and Phenomenology*), a pioneer of a new religion or "new dispensation" (Edward Edinger, especially in *The Creation of Consciousness*), a Christian in many publications, a Taoist (in David Rosen's *The Tao of Jung*), and also as a racist and Nazi sympathizer, a mythmaker, an alchemist, an astrologer, a shaman, a spiritualist involved in mediumistic séances with his cousin, an investigator of the paranormal, and more. All these roles have a Neptunian element: from the spiritual, mythic, and mystic to the symbolic, ideological, and the psychic. The Sun-Neptune complex can take the form of the mystique and charismatic influence of what Jung called the "mana-personality"—with a susceptibility to godlike inflation, on the one hand, and loss of self or identity confusion, on the other. A key challenge of the Sun-Neptune combination, then, is to find a way to integrate one's personal identity with the transpersonal dimension of experience. Just as Sun-Saturn alignments correlate with the act of bringing to consciousness the dimension of experience associated with Saturn—problems, suffering, toil, duty, time, death, the world of practical concerns and daily business, and so forth—so Sun-Neptune alignments correlate with the bringing to our awareness the experience of and reality of the Neptunian dimension of life, perhaps especially the experience of the spirit through mysticism, religious practice, spiritual psychology, mythology, and enchanted modes of being in the world. The Sun-Saturn complex is associated with experiences of limitation and entrapment, Sun-Neptune with experiences of dissolution and escapism or transcendence. Such experiences are usually more potent and challenging with hard aspects between the two planets, whereas the trine and sextile alignments between the Sun and Neptune often imply a relative ease in refocusing one's life in a more spiritual direction, expressing compassion, universal concern, or attuning to a spiritual mission, with these spiritual concerns supporting one's sense of selfhood and identity.

Varieties of the Neptunian Identity

As in our treatment of Saturn, we can turn to film and comedy for further illustrative examples of the different expressions of the planetary archetypes. We considered earlier Ben Stiller's film roles, which tend to convey well the Sun-Saturn and Moon-Saturn complexes, indicated by major alignments between these planets in his chart. Owen Wilson, a friend of Stiller's, starred alongside him in a number of films. Born with the Sun conjunct Neptune, Wilson often takes on roles that enable him to express various sides of the Sun-Neptune complex, forming a clear contrast with Stiller's Sun-Saturn. Wilson is variously cast as a spiritual and sensitive guy, a romantic dreamer, and a drug-taking escapist.

In the *Meet the Parents* trilogy of films, Wilson plays Pam Byrnes's wealthy ex-fiancé, the too-good-to-be-true Kevin Rawley, whose effortless perfection, grace, and seeming selflessness are matched only by his generosity and humility. Kevin exudes an aura of spiritual sensitivity and perfection—indeed, he makes his introduction in the film to the strains of Bach's *Jesu Joy of Man's Desiring* and he soon unveils a resplendent, elaborate hand-carved wedding altar that he created as a wedding gift for Pam's sister.

Chart 21

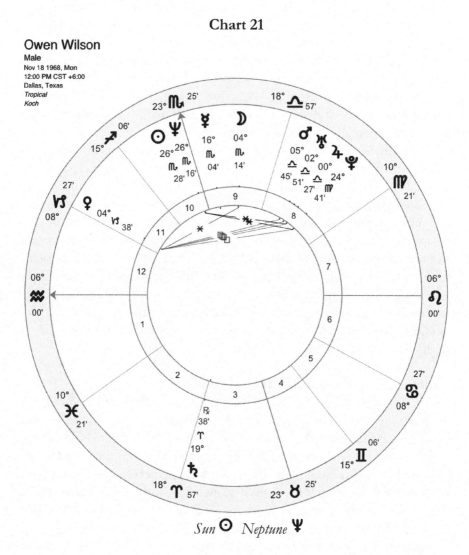

Sun ☉ Neptune ♆

In dialogue with Greg Focker, we hear of Kevin's version of the *imitatio Christi*:

> Greg: So what got you into carpen . . . tering?
> Kevin: Carpentry? I guess I'd have to say Jesus. He was a carpenter and I just figured if you're gonna follow in someone's footsteps, who better than Christ.[25]

His perfection stands in stark contrast to the blunders and insecurities of Stiller's Greg Focker. Similarly, in *Starsky & Hutch*, Wilson's character, Hutch—morally questionable, drug-taking, and laid-back—is the polar opposite of Stiller's often uptight, rule-following Starsky. The two actors portray, with vivid contrast, traits associated with the archetypal complexes associated with Sun-Neptune and Sun-Saturn.

In Woody Allen's *Midnight in Paris*, Wilson plays American screenwriter and novelist Gil Pender, who, on the stroke of midnight, finds himself mysteriously transported to Paris of the 1920s, in the circle of Gertrude Stein's salon. Pender is an unapologetic nostalgic dreamer whose romantic vision of that era, and the great artists in it, is more real for him than the present-day world, for here, in the romanticized past, he encounters the figures of his imagination as real people, much as Jung had dialogues with psychologically real spirit figures. Neptune tends to romanticize and glamorize certain aspects of our experience, which then become alluring and exude magic and mystery. Woody Allen himself has a Sun-Neptune alignment (as well as Sun-Saturn), and this archetypal combination is evident in his belief that "one must have one's delusions to live"—for without these delusions the painful Sun-Saturn reality would be too unbearable. Neptune is the archetypal principle behind the delusions and illusions of life, unconsciously projected onto reality, at once enticing us into participation with the world and blinding us to the true nature of things, as we become ensnared in *maya*—this is the Neptunian dimension of the anima. The character of Gil Pender experiences such illusions, if that is what they are, as very real, and they provide for him a source of creative inspiration and a means to transcend the limiting reality of his life.

The Mythic and the Mystic

With Sun-Neptune aspects specifically, then, there can be an attraction to roles and ways of being that have a certain mystique or are perceived as romantic, inspiring one's imagination, and thus enabling one to transcend the mundane reality of day-to-day life, as if one were living in a dream or a great cosmic drama. We are reminded here of Jung's call to reclaim the symbolic life and thus to re-enter the mythic world now lost to us—a motivation coming out of his own Sun-Neptune archetypal complex. A central aim of Jung's life was the discovery of his personal myth, while also emphasizing the critical significance of the hero myth in the process of psychospiritual transformation, and championing the value of Christianity, the precious "life-preserving myth of the inner man."[26] Each of these express elements of Jung's Sun-Neptune archetypal complex, recalling the Sun's association with the hero and the individual self, and Neptune's connection to myth, religion, and the Christ pattern.

The living of a mythic life is a theme also emphasized by Joseph Campbell, who, as we have seen, was extremely influential in promoting and articulating an individual form of mythology, based on the living out of the heroic pattern of one's own life. Born with the Sun square to Neptune, Campbell articulates a key dimension of the archetypal combination of Sun-Neptune in his correlation of heroism with sacrifice and submission to a higher will. "The hero," Campbell proclaimed, "is the man of self-achieved submission."[27] The hero gives his or her life in sacrifice to mystical realization—a theme prominent throughout *The Hero with a Thousand Faces*. Years earlier, these themes had been treated by Jung in his *Symbols of Transformation*, first published in 1912, which is concerned with the dissolution of the conscious personality in the "prelude to a case of schizophrenia," based on the fantasies of a Miss Miller. Jung explores the individual personality's dissolution in the maternal ground of the unconscious as portrayed in the symbolism of "the myth of the hero" and "the sacrifice"—two chapter titles of that book. As we will later consider, the influence of the Uranus archetype is also in evidence in Jung and Campbell, especially in their emphasis on going one's own way, finding one's own unique path. Both men were born with major configurations involving Uranus with the Sun and Neptune.

In literature and poetry, similarly, James Joyce and Dylan Thomas, known for their mythologization of modern life, in Ireland and Wales respectively, each had Sun in a square aspect to Neptune. Joyce's "Ulysses" and "Finnegan's Wake" attempt to reveal the universal motifs and experiences of human life, weaving intricate mythic connections into the personal, everyday worlds of characters in early twentieth-century Dublin. Dylan Thomas's "Under Milk Wood" occupies a similarly exalted place in the mythology of Welsh culture. Recalling here too other sides of the Sun-Neptune complex discussed above, Thomas was the quintessential tragic poet, inspired and later idealized, but alcoholic and escapist, sometimes destitute and homeless, ill-suited to the practical demands of living. We might also mention here T. S. Eliot's mythologization of English life in the *Four Quartets* through developing what he called the "mythical method," with references to Sanskrit, Christian symbolism, and theology. Eliot had the

Sun in a trine to Neptune. And, in a similar vein, in painting, the work of Georgia O'Keeffe did much to communicate the mythic spirit of the high-desert landscape of New Mexico. She also had a major Sun-Neptune natal aspect—an opposition. It is often the case that the presence of major Sun-Neptune alignments at birth indicates a need to inhabit a dimension of reality beyond that of the mundane world of facts, necessities, duties, and so forth—to attune to a primary mode of reality that permits a transcendence of the everyday, whether through myth, through mysticism, or through art (especially when Venus is also in relationship to Neptune).

In many cases, as Richard Tarnas has noted, the combination of the Sun and Neptune principles takes form in the character of the mystic, when the solar identity and basic sense of reality are pervasively shaped and defined by the Neptunian experience of the spirit, in whatever form that is conceived. At one level of expression, Neptune can act on the solar identity to promote a transcendence of the ego, such that the individual serves as a conduit for some divine source of inspiration beyond the personal sphere of life. A survey of major figures of the twentieth century who have shaped the modern understanding of the spiritual life gives a sense for the mystical character of Sun-Neptune: Pierre Teilhard de Chardin (conjunction), Paul Tillich (square), Carl Jung (square), Albert Schweitzer (square), Joseph Campbell (square), scholar of Jewish mysticism Gershom Scholem (opposition), Viktor Frankl (square), Marion Woodman (conjunction), Indologist Heinrich Zimmer (opposition, also Sun conjunct Venus opposite Neptune—apparent in his focus on Indian art), Friedrich Nietzsche (trine), and Sri Aurobindo (trine). In each of these figures, in one way or another the solar identity gives expression to the Neptune archetype, whether through mysticism, symbology, the living of a religious life, idealistic heroism, or in sacrifice to some inspiring vision.

Neptunian idealism does not always tend in the mystical direction, however. B. F. Skinner, the famed behaviorist and arch exponent of stimulus-response conditioning, had natal Sun square to Neptune, an archetypal combination evident in the idealism behind his disturbing utopian vision, described in *Beyond Freedom and Dignity*, of the conditioning of human beings to produce the perfect society—the conditioning itself, and what many perceive to be a dark view of human nature and society, can be understood in terms of his natal trine alignment between Saturn and Pluto, a pairing that we will consider in the next volume.

Dissolution and the Night-Sea Journey: Neptune-Sun Transits

The range of experiences associated with the archetypal Neptune is well represented by the symbolism of water in all its forms: oceanic depths, tranquil lakes, clouds and fog, fountains and springs, morning dew and moisture, the flood and deluge, baths and pools, the oasis, the whirlpool, and more. Watery metaphors thus prove to be especially helpful for describing the experience of Neptune in our lives. When Neptune is activated, one can feel as if one has entered a dense fog or has been pulled into the ocean depths, or one can access a renewing flow of inspirations and idealism, as if one has tapped into the eternal wellsprings of life. Similarly, the transforming power of Neptune in our experience can be understood in terms of metaphors of flow, dissolution, drowning, thirst, washing and cleaning, soaking, erosion, leaking, and permeating. Neptune acts to permeate all structures, dissolve all boundaries, stirring within us a thirst for spiritual experience and transcendence, moving us towards pristine clarity and purity, removing the stain of the world. The naming of the planet after the Roman god of the sea was thus most appropriate in this respect.

During transits of Neptune to the Sun, many of the themes discussed above manifest within a particular period of one's life coinciding with the duration of the transit, from the time Neptune moves within five degrees of the Sun in one's birth chart to around four degrees after the position of the Sun. Among the most consequential of these experiences is the dissolution of the boundaries of one's conscious identity and its established way of engaging with life. Neptune transits to the Sun (or other transits that activate a natal Sun-Neptune complex) can coincide with what Jung called the "dissolution of the persona," a key precipitating experience of the individuation process, which can leave one all adrift, rudderless, as if lost at sea, or give rise to the very real sense that one is sinking and drowning—an experience suggested by the mythic motif of the "night-sea journey."[28] There can be a demoralizing sense that one is disintegrating, or even that one's entire self is gone, which can naturally thrust one into confusion and perhaps even despondency and despair.

Especially during hard-aspect transits, there can be a dissolution of egoic pride and self-esteem, and the impairing of one's capacity for effective, intentional functioning. All those elements of our life and character that were the source of feelings of self-worth and pride can appear to vanish. As the dissolving power of Neptune takes effect, one can feel weak and defeated, depressed and disillusioned with everything life seems to offer, with circumstances refusing to respond to one's attempts to change the situation for the better, even if one can muster the will to try to change things. In some cases, Neptune transits to the Sun correspond with a weakness of the will—this is particularly problematic with hard aspects.

Neptune transits to the Sun also tend to increase one's desire for escape from limiting or painful circumstance, and thus from the world itself, and for transcendence of the limitations of one's ego personality. This can prompt the deepest of spiritual feelings, such as the yearning for heaven or nirvana; indeed, the transit might coincide with among the most spiritual periods of one's life, although the particular direction of spiritual interest is not indicated astrologically, of course—one person might be attracted to Hinduism, another to Western esotericism, another to the Native American tradition, and so forth. Yet the transit also brings with it certain challenges and dangers, for the yearning for transcendence and enchantment can, in the midst of confusing emotions, lead one into flight and escape through drugs and alcohol, which offer more immediate avenues of release. As we have seen, lacking a clear sense of individual identity at these times, one can become susceptible to the hypnotic allure of various archetypal roles and life paths, seduced into giving oneself away to some seemingly special calling for which one has been singled out. Succumbing to illness as an act of surrender also frees one from the burden of individual selfhood, simultaneously providing a way of escape and evoking the sympathy of others.

Neptune moves us out of the scope of the ego, with its rationality and intentional will, but the direction of this movement can be towards the prepersonal as much as the transpersonal. That is, the influence of Neptune—the yearning for release from the pressures and sufferings of life—can easily lead us to forsake individual rational consciousness and to abandon selfhood and responsibility in a kind of regressive turning back or collapse, unconsciously motivated by the search for paradise lost. In Grofian terms it can effect a regression from the struggle and limitation of BPM II, the Saturnian perinatal matrix, back to the Neptunian realm of BPM I, back to the state of non-differentiation and helplessness of the womb, rather than following the progressive trajectory into and through the transformative rebirth process (the Plutonic BPM III) towards the release and liberation of BPM IV (Uranus). Jung characterizes the possibility of such a turning back as a "regressive restoration of the persona," when, facing the crisis of transformation of individuation, one takes refuge from the painful ordeal by the resurrection of an older, simpler persona.[29] The response is, of course, a pretense, although often not recognized as such. More broadly, we can think of this occurrence as the regression to an earlier stage of one's life or the nostalgic longing for times past or more glamorous eras. These possibilities might manifest during a number of Neptune transits, but they tend to be especially prominent during Neptune-Sun transits, given that the Sun is associated with conscious selfhood, one's identity, and one's will.

In terms of the larger trajectory of individuation, then, this transit can correspond with a significant part of the process of letting go of the old life of the personal ego and coming into relationship with the spiritual authority of the Self, the universal being within us. One might find oneself pulled away from worldly concerns and interests into a kind of hermetic pedagogy or isolation in which the focus of one's attentions moves towards spiritual or artistic concerns, often of less obvious tangible and practical value. Within these transits, often one is called to cultivate humility and to surrender to what is unfolding. One is made as naught that one might experience oneself as part of everything, an expression of a universal consciousness and a unitary being.

Ultimately, despite the risks of pathology, escapism, and even disintegration, the purpose of the Neptune transit is a positive one, especially viewed from the perspective of one's spiritual life, for it opens us to the reality of spirit beyond the limitations and usual scope of awareness of consciousness. At its higher levels, it pertains to the mystical path of the absorption of the individual self into spirit. It therefore often entails a renunciation, a letting go of personal life aims and the controlling independence of the ego. It pertains to the mystical sacrifice of one's self and devotion of one's life to God, as one serves as a vessel for spirit or aligns one's life with the Tao, the underlying flow of meaning and way of all things.

* * * * *

The Enchanted World of Childhood: Moon-Neptune

In considering next Moon-Neptune alignments, we will observe a shift to the felt, emotional, and soulful forms of expression associated with the Moon. Neptune, in these cases, often manifests in the idealistic longing for home or a return to the enchanted world of childhood. The ideal is projected onto, or found within, forms of experience associated with the Moon: childhood, the home, the past, the mother, the feminine, the earth, and nature.

The emotional quality of Moon-Neptune is typically that of a soulful longing for a more enchanted existence or for a place of retreat, tranquility, and belonging—a spiritual home or sanctuary. Neptune acts on the Moon to sensitize the feeling reactions to life, making us emotionally porous, as if our filters were open, all barriers down, and we empathically feel into the joys and sorrows of others and of the world. This particular archetypal complex is also connected to the capacity of the anima to enchant and captivate the soul, stirring emotional longings and fantasies that lure us towards a condition of womblike bliss and eternal security, free from the crude assaults of sense experience and from life's troubles and pressures, back to the magical world of childhood, that place of timeless play and dreamy reverie—back to the time when one was safe and cared for, held close to the bosom of one's family, and secure within the fluctuating ebb and flow of feeling and fantasy that characterizes the childhood experience. Even as the mature worldly ego develops and displaces the childhood nature as the dominant function or complex of psychological life, the archetypal child, in touch with the magical wonder of life, remains active deep within us. In those people with major Moon-Neptune alignments, this dimension of experience often remains, in one form or another, a central component of the personality.

The Moon-Neptune archetypal complex finds a particularly fitting form of expression in poetry, supporting a subtle and sensitive feeling for life and for humanity, and an imagination and emotional nature that draws one close to the divine, as in the case of William Wordsworth, born with the Moon conjunct Neptune.

Wordsworth's great ode "Intimations of Immortality" articulates, with moving profundity and simplicity, the fall from our home in God at birth, the poignant loss of the natural spirituality of childhood, and the struggle to recapture it.

> There was a time when meadow, grove, and stream,
> The earth, and every common sight,
> To me did seem
> Apparelled in celestial light,
> The glory and the freshness of a dream.[30]

The world of childhood is bathed in the transcendent glow of spirit, transfiguring every scene into a glorious divine revelation—fresh, pure, natural, and innocent. The Moon-Neptune complex represents that part of us that remains in touch with this experience or expresses the longing to recover it; it pertains to the untainted innocence and purity of the child at play in a dreamlike world. From within this complex, we might proclaim with Wordsworth that "Heaven lies about us in our infancy!" The Moon here is the connection to the past and the child archetype, which, reflecting the interaction with Neptune, give access to an experience of the divine and the heavenly quality.

Chart 22

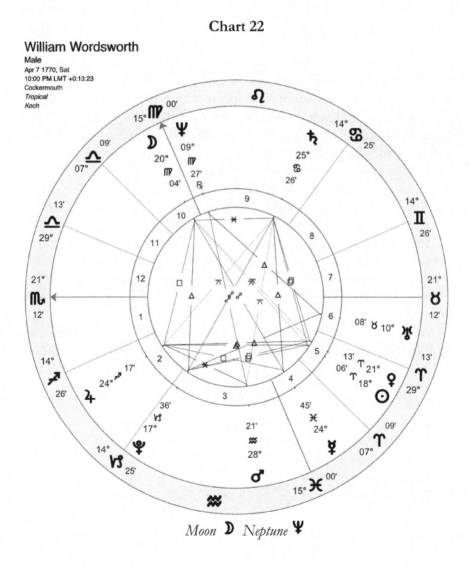

Moon ☽ Neptune ♆

Even as the immediate perception of this condition begins to fade, however much we might resist it, it then passes over, in Wordsworth's recollection, to the idyllic enchanted experience of youth and a kind of nature spirituality—with the Moon manifest as Mother Nature and the Earth, embodying the Neptunian experience of enchantment.

> Ye blessèd creatures, I have heard the call
> Ye to each other make; I see
> The heavens laugh with you in your jubilee;
> My heart is at your festival,
> My head hath its coronal,
> The fulness of your bliss, I feel—I feel it all.[31]

Wordsworth the youth was at one with nature, delighting in nature's forms—the springtime, the landscape, the sky, animals, and children, which reveal to him the wonders of heaven. Note that Wordsworth also had natal Jupiter in a square aspect to his Moon, and Jupiter in a trine to a Sun-Venus conjunction—indicating contributory archetypal factors manifest in the sense of fullness, aesthetic wonder, and joyous experience of his youthful recollection.

Yet the direction of the fall away from spirit is set, and, with the coming of maturity, it precipitates a kind of divine homesickness for the lost transcendent God, the heavenly oneness forsaken at birth—an experience immortalized in these famous lines:

> Our birth is but a sleep and a forgetting:
> The Soul that rises with us, our life's Star,
> Hath had elsewhere its setting,
> And cometh from afar:
> Not in entire forgetfulness,
> And not in utter nakedness,
> But trailing clouds of glory do we come
> From God, who is our home.[32]

The sense of God as our home is a manifestation of the archetypal dimensions of experience associated with Moon-Neptune. This experience remains in the memory of childhood, in the dim intuition of our spiritual origin, and in the emotional longing for a return. This is not to reduce Wordsworth's spiritual revelation to "nothing but" an expression of archetypes and astrological configurations, but rather to note the presence of archetypal themes in his revelation and poem. For even the most profound of experiences appear to manifest in accordance the a priori framework of meanings symbolized in the astrological mapping of the cosmological order.

We might draw comparison here, in a different genre, with A. A. Milne, author of *Winnie the Pooh*. Although there is no precise birth time available for Milne, only the date of birth, it is highly probable that he was born with a Moon-Uranus-Neptune grand trine, with Neptune also conjunct Jupiter, and both Saturn and the Moon conjunct Venus.[33] The magical tales of Christopher Robin's adventures in the Hundred Acre Wood, written in part as a response to the loss of innocence wrought by the First World War, conveys well the wonder of the child's imagination and the magical playfulness of childhood, associated with Moon-Neptune, and serves as a portal for us all to reconnect to that experience. The joys of childhood, its happy experiences and memories, are especially associated with the Moon-Venus combination; the archetypal Neptune gives the capacity to sensitively employ one's imagination to bring such memories to life in art and image. The Moon-Neptune complex is the signature of the childhood imagination, which through Milne gave shape to those characters that were to magically enrich the lives of generation after generation of children: Winnie-the-Pooh, Tigger, Eeyore, Piglet, and their companions. For each artist draws on his or her own archetypal inheritance, symbolized through the birth chart, in service of the gods, as it were, articulating particular insights, sensibilities, and experiences for us all. As Joseph Campbell observed, this function is at the heart of "creative mythology."[34]

We might draw comparison as well to J. M. Barrie, author of *Peter Pan*, the classic portrayal in children's literature of the boy who never grew up—the *puer aeturnus* in the language of archetypal psychology. Barrie had a broad T-square with Venus opposite the Moon, Neptune square to Venus, and Neptune square to the Moon. Here too, with this combination, the archetypal child, associated with the Moon, comes into relationship with the timeless, eternal, fairytale quality of Neptune. We can draw comparison also with Walt Disney who had a Moon-Jupiter-Neptune T-square, which we see in the plethora of larger-than-life comical cartoon characters inspiring the childhood imagination, in young and old alike. And likewise, C. S. Lewis, author of the religiously themed children's adventure classics *The Chronicles of Narnia*, had a

Moon-Neptune conjunction in a triple conjunction with Pluto, with Pluto opposite Saturn, and Jupiter trine Neptune.

In Wordsworth's case, his experience of the Moon-Neptune pairing seems to have supported his revelatory poetic genius, associated with the grand trine of the three "transpersonal planets," Uranus, Neptune, and Pluto, which I will consider in Volume IV. The same is true of German poet Friedrich Hölderlin whose work had a formative influence on Hegel, Heidegger, and Jung, among others. Like Wordsworth, Hölderlin had a major Moon-Neptune alignment—a trine—and he too was exquisitely attuned to the spiritual and mythic quality of childhood, a quality lost to the individual and to modern Western civilization at large.[35] Hölderlin took it upon himself to try to resurrect the lost mythic reality, recalling his own close proximity to the gods in his youth, which offered him a form of refuge from the piercing noise of the human world:

When I was a boy
A god often rescued me
From the shouts and the rods of men
And I played among the trees and flowers
Secure in their kindness
And the breezes of heaven
Were playing there too.[36]

In the concluding line of "When I Was a Boy," the poet recalls: "I grew up in the arms of the gods."[37]

But the gods, although eternal, have long since departed from view. They have become, in the minds of men, but a fair memory of the mythic Golden Age. In its association with the past, particularly the emotional trace and soulful essence of the past, the Moon in combination with Neptune can promote a sentimental nostalgia as much as a yearning to recover the lost innocence and wonder of youth, for then it is one's own past, or a past era or civilization, that carries the projection of the Neptunian ideal. Yesteryear always tends to seem more magical, more innocent, than the current day—an innate nostalgia for the cherished memories of the past sees to that. But the way of individuation demands, once more, a differentiation of the Neptunian urge—typically, in this case, a rejection of merely sentimental bonds to the past, while making possible a recovery of the enchantment of the inner child and a cultivation of the compassionate feeling for the unity of all life, outside the often narrow, hard-hearted concerns of the ego.

The Mythic Past and Empathetic Feeling

In another inflection of the Moon-Neptune combination, Hölderlin conceives of the gods themselves as sleeping children, eternal and ever-renewing:

> Fateless, like the sleeping
> Infant, breathe the heavenly ones,
> Chastely guarded
> In modest bud;
> Their spirits
> Blossom eternally . . .[38]

Through much of Hölderlin's poetry there runs a yearning for the recovery of ancient Greece in a mythologization of his homeland (Swabia) in Germany, bringing a spiritual renewal to the civilization. Again, the Moon archetype is present here in the connection to the past as the source of the spiritual-mythic vision, and in the homeland, the place where spirit is to be restored and revealed anew.

> Greece, blessed land, the house of all the immortals!
> See, what we heard in our younger days is true
> Hall for a feast
> Whose floor is the ocean and tables the mountains
> Truly for unique use built aeons ago![39]

You will remember, too, that the Moon is closely associated with the Jungian mother archetype and the mythic figure of the Great Mother. Neptune in combination with the Moon has the effect of sensitizing and universalizing the maternal impulse to care, nurture, and protect. This impulse can be readily directed towards caring for all things, even to the planet as a whole in attuning emotionally to the Earth as Gaia, as well as to the earth beneath our feet. In Hölderlin's case, he expresses a compassionate feeling for the earth, shares in the grief of the earth, a sadness which in good Neptunian manner soon dissolves into the lunar realm of childhood sleep and dream:

I love you, earth, for you are grieving with me
And our grief like the troubles of children turns
Into sleep.[40]

Chart 23

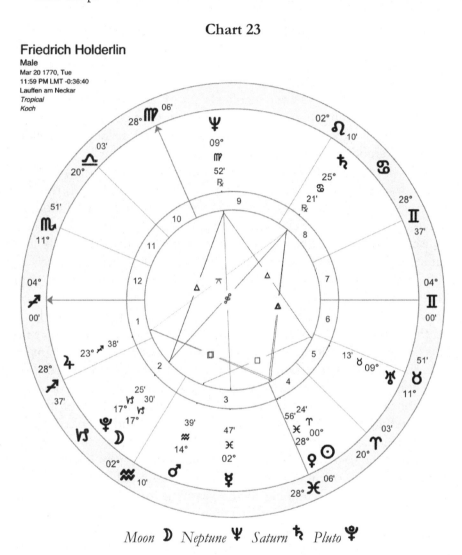

Moon ☽ Neptune ♆ Saturn ♄ Pluto ♇

More problematically, with hard aspects between these two planets, sensitivity can easily become saccharine sentimentality, touchy oversensitivity, or a lack of emotional discernment—all negative anima traits. Neptune dissolves the boundaries of the lunar feeling realm and can make one awash with feelings, tears, yearnings, and sensitivities as one is pulled into a sea of emotion.

In Hölderlin's birth chart, the Moon is in an exact conjunction with Pluto and opposite Saturn—hence the wonder of the childhood world, and the great era of mythic Greece (associated with his Moon-trine-Neptune), becomes lost to him, as if fallen into the underworld of collective experience, which is the basis then for the Neptunian quest to recover this mythic reality and re-imagine it. In many of Hölderlin's poems, a scene of secure tranquility is shattered by the intervention of dark forces—often the gods, or the troubled times. Archetypally, the elemental power of Pluto manifests as a brooding, foreboding, ominous, consuming presence. The denied powers of heaven impinge on the lunar experience of simple comfort and belonging, pulling Hölderlin emotionally into the underworld.

The Moon-Neptune complex can also be understood in terms of the alchemical operation of *solutio*, which dissolves established forms—of the base matter in the alchemical vessel as it is reduced to a solution; of locked-up libido in psychological complexes, which then flood into conscious awareness; and of the emotional core of the personality in a return to the "maternal ground" of the unconscious. However strong and independent the conscious ego might become, emotionally one can remained pulled by the Moon-Neptune complex back to the childhood state of vulnerable sensitivity and dependency—this fragility is the basis of the felt sensitivity towards life and empathetic care associated with this archetypal combination. Yet in the midst of this complex, we might lose the capacity for responsible directed action, will, and self-control. The complex formed by the Moon-Neptune principles can become the emotionally exposed child, needing to be cared for and protected, taking refuge from a world that is felt as too crude and too painful. For individuation, in meeting the challenges of this complex, as one seeks to recover the soul and its enchanted mode of being from the depths of the unconscious, one must take care not to lose oneself in the womb of unconsciousness, succumbing to the yearning for dissolution into the infantile state of absolute emotional unity with the mother.

Hölderlin himself was susceptible to these tendencies, for better and for worse; indeed, for the second half of his life, after falling into an insanity from which he did not recover, he was cared for by kindly guardians, as if he had returned to childhood. Before his mental dissolution, his sensitivity and poetic apprehension of the world also manifested in his nostalgic romantic feeling, conveyed in many of his poems, for the simple life of the people, the community of folk quietly living their lives in towns and villages, which Hölderlin experiences in mythic terms, with the people, gods, and the land in intimate communion, even as this comforting existence was disturbed, even destroyed, by the darker demonic powers of the gods. Hölderlin was moved always to reconcile the themes and energies of the Uranus-Pluto complex into his Neptunian spiritual vision—in accordance with the meaning of the grand trine between these planets.

Reverie, Sleep, and Childhood
Moving from poetry to literature, another fine example of an artist giving expression to Moon-Neptune themes is French novelist Marcel Proust, with natal Moon conjunct Neptune. In Proust's case, his Neptunian sensitivities were predominantly directed towards memories of the past, a nostalgic draw back towards a womb-like existence of childhood, and his experience of his mother.

In the opening pages of *Swann's Way*, the first volume of *À La Recherché du Temps Perdu* ("In Search of Lost Time"), Proust, in the character of an unnamed narrator, exquisitely describes the act of falling asleep and drifting in and out of sleep, with the play of memories, sensations, and feelings washing over him in the twilight between states of consciousness and unconsciousness. Proust's words capture the lunar experience of being in bed, as if back in the womb or in the nourishing memories of childhood, magically and poignantly expressed by the Neptunian facility for acute sensitivity and imagination. The following short extracts are enough to give a flavor of the experience:

> I would lay my cheeks gently against the comfortable cheeks of my pillow, as plump and fresh as the cheeks of childhood....
> I would fall asleep again, and thereafter would reawaken for short snatches only, just long enough to hear the regular creaking of the wainscot, or to open my eyes to stare at the shifting kaleidoscope of the darkness, to savour, in a momentary glimmer of consciousness, the sleep which lay heavy upon the furniture, the room, that whole of which I formed no more than a small part and whose sensibility I should very soon return to share. Or else while sleeping I had drifted back to an earlier stage in my life, now for ever outgrown, and had come under the thrall of one of my childish terrors, such as that old terror of my great-uncle's pulling my curls which was effectually dispelled on the day—the dawn of a new era to me—when they were finally cropped from my head. I had forgotten that event during my sleep, but I remembered it again immediately I had

succeeded in waking myself up to escape my great-uncle's fingers, and as a measure of precaution I would bury the whole of my head in the pillow before returning to the world of dreams.[41]

The capacity for such inspired observances of the thoughts, sensations, memories, and feelings of drifting in and out of sleep relies upon the archetypal function associated with Mercury. For Proust, Mercury was in a square alignment to the Moon-Neptune conjunction. With Mercury also in a conjunction with Uranus (a combination we will consider in Volume III), each observation—which most of us might not consciously attend to let alone record—jumps out as a minor revelation. Uranus, as Tarnas has described, is the archetypal principle of the awakener, which makes things acute and breaks through the habitual and the ordinary. But the area of focus, the topic under Proust's perceptive eye, is his exquisite sensitivity to the Moon-Neptune experience of the emotional state of being in bed, slipping into unconsciousness, with ego concerns and defenses relaxed, open to reverie and the drifting sensations and memories that surround sleep.

The Idealization of the Maternal, the Feminine, and the Family

A few pages later in *Swann's Way*, Proust offers a "remembrance" of the narrator's idealization of his mother, with its clear religious overtones—a theme reflected in Proust's own life:

> My sole consolation when I went upstairs for the night was that Mamma would come in and kiss me after I was in bed. But this good night lasted for so short a time, she went down again so soon, that the moment in which I heard her climb the stairs, and then caught the sound of her garden dress of blue muslin, from which hung little tassels of plaited straw, rustling along the double-doored corridor, was for me a moment of utmost pain; for it heralded the moment which was to follow it, when she would have left me and gone downstairs again. So much so that I reached the point of hoping that this good night which I loved so much would come as late as possible, so as to prolong the time of respite during which Mamma would not yet have appeared. Sometimes when, after kissing me, she opened the door to go, I longed to call her back, to say to her "Kiss me just once more," but I knew that then she would look displeased, for the concession which she made to my wretchedness and agitation in coming up to give me this kiss of peace always annoyed my father, who thought such rituals absurd,

and she would have liked to try to induce me to outgrow the need, the habit, of having her there at all, let alone getting into the habit of asking her for an additional kiss when she was already crossing the threshold. And to see her look displeased destroyed all the calm and serenity she had brought the moment before, when she had bent her loving face down over my bed, and held it out to me like a host for an act of peace-giving communion in which my lips might imbibe her real presence and with it the power to sleep.[42]

The conception of his mother's presence and her goodnight kiss as a holy act of "peace-giving communion," almost as the visitation of a goddess, emerges from the Neptunian capacity to mythologize, idealize, and romanticize experiences—in this case those associated with the Moon: motherhood, tender care, falling asleep, emotional needs and habits. The Moon-Neptune archetypal combination can be personified in the form of female deities, which become the object of one's devotion. Proust's Moon-Neptune conjunction is placed in the first house in a conjunction with the Ascendant, which, astrologers agree, gives it special prominence in life, shaping the basic mode of meeting and filtering experience. The Moon-Neptune conjunction is also in a trine to Venus and to Saturn, with the planets together forming a grand trine. Venus lends the experience of the goodnight kiss its romantic quality and is apparent in the profound love and affection which Proust holds for his mother. Saturn is evident in the disapproving judgment of the father, the self-judgment, the anticipated loss of the moment of blissful union through the kiss, and the desire therefore to delay the kiss so as to put back the painful loss and separation from the mother. We saw earlier the Venus-Saturn theme of losses in love and a protectiveness around the pain of romantic loss; Neptune brings heightened sensitivity and imagination to this experience—its preciousness, subtlety, and (in relation to Saturn) the lament for the brief duration of the encounter and the separation from the mother.

Alongside the idealization of the mother, Moon-Neptune energies can support the idealization of and projection of a kind of innocent, pure femininity—a quality that can shape the lives and personalities of people born with Moon-Neptune aspects. Audrey Hepburn is a fine example, portraying in film roles the innocent, enchanting, sensitive, childlike woman, who is at the same time mysterious, baffling, and perhaps gullible. The Moon-Neptune complex can sometimes manifest as an almost ethereal or translucent quality. A similar childlike innocence and vulnerability was evident in Marilyn Monroe, who had a

Moon-square-Neptune natal aspect. In her case too, there arose an idealistic longing for a family situation of which she was deprived as a child—something that she could not in fact attain.

Chart 24

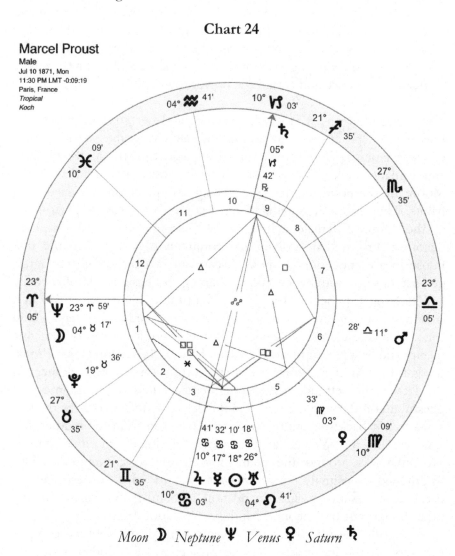

Moon ☽ Neptune ♆ Venus ♀ Saturn ♄

The emotional sensitivity associated with Moon-Neptune alignments is a personality characteristic and biographical theme evident even in otherwise strong, forceful "masculine" personalities. For example, Al Pacino (Moon square Neptune), Marlon Brando (Moon trine Neptune), Robert De Niro (Moon-Saturn-Neptune T-square), the three actors best known for their portrayal of ruthless mafia figures in film, each exhibit in these roles a touching sentimentality around family, holding up family as the guiding ideal of life, as that to be revered and honored, above all else. We have already noted De Niro's comical portrayal of sentimentality towards his deceased mother in *Meet the Parents*, and Brando and Pacino, as the older Don Corleone and Michael Corleone respectively in *The Godfather* films, make devotion to the family almost akin to a religious creed. The Moon-Neptune complex can promote an idealization of family, and, in a different manifestation of its archetypal themes, lead one to a universal sense of family, perhaps in the form of a spiritual community of some sort, or a developed feeling for our common humanity transcending bloodline and the personal sphere of life, in the recognition that we are a single human family in which everyone is a part of everyone else. A sense of universal care naturally arises from such a realization. Yet equally, we might note here Moon-Neptune's association with undifferentiated feeling, and the tendency to seek refuge in and become dependent upon group spirituality rather than developing one's own.

Sleep and Prophecy, Spirituality and the Unconscious

In another inflection of the Moon-Neptune complex, we find the prophetic gifts of American psychic Edgar Cayce, known as the "Sleeping Prophet" because of his ability to enter into a trance-like sleep to give psychic "life readings" about matters of health, vocation, soul destiny, past lives, lost civilizations, astrology, and more. Cayce, with a Moon-Neptune conjunction, also reportedly had the startling ability to photographically memorize books by sleeping on them under his pillow. The Neptunian prophetic and visionary capacities, and the association of this archetype with non-ordinary states of consciousness, were for Cayce manifest through unconscious channeling (reflecting the Moon's association with sleep) as well as the homespun style of the readings themselves with the channeled material, although often profound, having a homey familiarity in tone, and sometimes lacking precision, discernment, and accuracy. The Moon-Neptune combination can take form in the psychic or medium in which the lunar realm of feeling is pervaded by influences and intuitions from the "spirits" of subtle realms of reality. Moon-Neptune can furnish one with the ability to pick up on others' emotions, perhaps unconsciously, and to assume the role of a kind of spiritual mother figure. As always with Neptune, the capacity to differentiate one's conscious personality from the archetypal role is key for individuation.

The connection between spirituality and the unconscious is also present in Sigmund Freud, born with the Moon and Neptune in a square alignment. Although known for his materialistic atheism (primarily associated with the Saturn-square-Neptune aspect in his birth

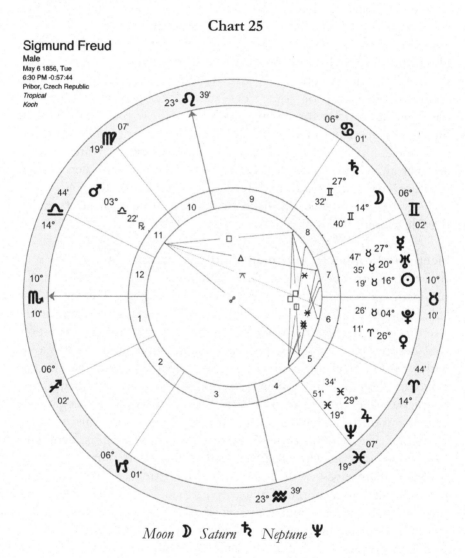

Chart 25

Moon ☽ Saturn ♄ Neptune ♆

chart), Freud gave expression to the Moon-Neptune complex in his characterization of religion as arising from an "oceanic feeling," with spirituality explained as a return to the childhood experience of the unbounded id. Recall here Neptune's association with the ocean, non-differentiation, and the dissolution of boundaries, conjoined with the realm of feeling and childhood associated with the Moon. Touching on several of the Moon-Neptune themes discussed above, in *Civilization and Its Discontents*, Freud observes: "Oceanic experience . . . induces feelings of an indissoluble bond, of being one with the external world as a whole, that represents a regressive escape from the demands of reality and a return to the selfless state of maternal unity."[43] Becoming one with the whole world also reflects the presence of Jupiter, which is conjunct Neptune and square to the Moon in Freud's birth chart—recalling Jupiter's association with wholeness, expansion, and moving out into the wider world.[44]

As the quote from Freud indicates, the Moon-Neptune complex is associated with a regressive return to the experience of oneness with the mother, to a womblike condition of absorption in a kind of unconscious paradise. In Stanislav Grof's model of the psyche, you will recall, Neptune (and particularly Moon-Neptune) is associated with the first perinatal matrix, the stage of the birth process prior to the onset of contractions when the fetus exists in "oceanic" oneness in the aquatic fluid of the mother's womb.[45] In combination with Jupiter, this complex is particularly associated with the experience of the "good womb" and later the "good breast"—the blissful condition of preconscious unity of the baby and the mother. In mythic terms, this relates to the paradisiacal preconscious existence of the primal humans (symbolized by Adam and Eve in the Old Testament) before the emergence of self-consciousness and the moral differentiation of the opposites of good and evil, pleasure and pain, male and female.

Sanctuary for the Soul
Many of the aforementioned themes can manifest during transits of Neptune to the Moon, usually lasting for a period of three-to-four years. For instance, when Jung passed through a transit of Neptune square to his Moon during the early 1920s, he describes in his autobiography and letters his preoccupation with the search for a place of spiritual retreat from the world where he would be free just to be, to live his "true life," more fully recovering a sense of enchantment and communion with nature. This quest was realized when Jung bought land by Lake Zurich, in 1922, where he was later to build stone towers, as a monument to the gods and inner figures prominent in his experience. It was a place where he could step out of time and into his "Number 2" personality—the Self.

Chart 26

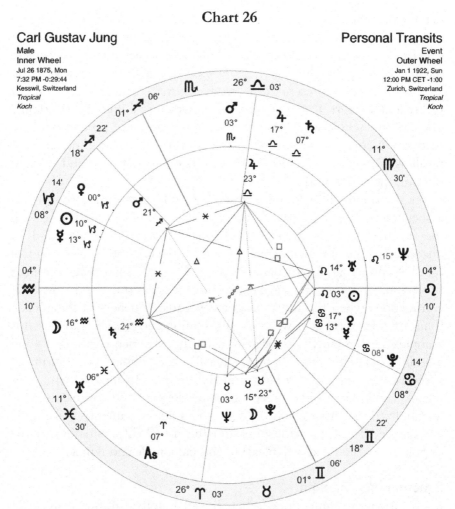

The above personal transit chart for January 1, 1922 shows transiting Neptune ♆ (outer wheel) at 15 degrees Leo, square to Jung's natal Moon ☽ (inner wheel) at 15 degrees Taurus.

"It was settled from the start," Jung recollects, "that I would build near the water. I had always been curiously drawn by the scenic charm of the upper lake near Zürich, and so in 1922 I bought some land in Bollingen. It is situated in the area of St. Meinrad and is old church land, having formerly belonged to the monastery of St. Gall."[46] Both the setting by water and the religious purpose of land are Neptunian themes, manifest here in relation to the lunar impulse to find a place of home, comfort, and belonging. Jung found deep spiritual sustenance in his new home, and saw its significance in mythic terms: "At Bollingen I am in the midst of my true life . . . Here I am, as it were, the 'age-old son of the mother' . . . . He exists outside time and is the son of the maternal unconscious."[47] This development in Jung's life, reflecting the Moon-Neptune quality of that moment, supported a felt connection to nature and the environment, in a further expression of this archetypal complex. "At times I feel as if I am spread out over the landscape and inside things, and am myself living in every tree, in the splashing of the waves, in the clouds and the animals that come and go."[48]

Jung had transiting Neptune square to his Moon between 1920 and 1924—a period that also saw the passing of his mother (in 1923), prompting him to idealistically revisit his memories of her. It was at this time, too, that Jung was engaged in the articulation of the anima concept, so central to his psychology, and in the keeping of dream journals. Each of these activities and experiences reflects the archetypal themes associated with the Moon-Neptune combination.

As in Jung's own case, experiences that may arise during this transit include an idealization of the past, as one becomes more nostalgic and sentimental; the craving for a peaceful place of retreat, such as an idyllic home or sanctuary; dreaming of a blissful family life; and feeling a universal sense of belonging and community, or a unity with nature and the world. In psychological experience, during these transits one's consciousness can be pervaded by yearnings and fantasies that lead one away from the world or draw one into emotional confusion, sensitizing the feelings and opening the heart to the suffering of all life in a stirring of the universal mother archetype.

*   *   *   *   *

Revelation and Confusion: The Receptive and Deceptive Mind

All the Neptunian themes we have already encountered—such as projection, the dissolution of boundaries, a connection to the imaginal and mythic, the urge towards transcendence and escapism, spirituality and religion, enchantment and mystery—are also evident in correspondence with Mercury-Neptune alignments, both in birth charts and in transits. In these cases, as we would expect, Neptunian phenomena find expression in association with the dimensions of life pertaining to the archetypal Mercury, including thinking, the acquisition of knowledge, reading, writing, speaking, and perception.

As we have seen, the archetypal Neptune lies behind the tendency to project the ideal, to see things in idealized or romantic terms. In connection with Mercury, there can be, rather superficially, an attraction to roles or activities associated with Mercury, which provide a source of inspiration but also of escape. Among its many forms of expression, Mercury-Neptune is associated with the mystique of books, the wonders of learning and knowledge—perhaps providing an escape from the painful struggle of life through reading, daydreaming, or analysis, such as endless planning, thinking, and talking things through. For it is far easier to read and think about life, discussing others' viewpoints and ideas or simply acquiring books and knowledge, than it is to live one's own life and dare one's own adventure. Likewise, under the influence of the Mercury-Neptune complex one can find oneself allured by the role of writer or scholar, poet or seer, losing oneself in the image of these lives and pursuits, which can pull one away from one's authentic life direction—although often the projection and mystique give a clue as to one's true vocation, and then it becomes a matter of subjecting the enchanted vision to rational scrutiny and realizing it in one's own way rather than putting on the role like a cloak.

Despite the danger of a flight from reality, on the other hand, under the combined influence of the Mercury-Neptune principles, books can be a source of transcendence and enchantment, as in the sentence that opens the mind to spiritual insight or the poetic turn of phrase that enables one to enter a state of mystery and wonder, if only for a brief time. The function of Mercury becomes the portal through which one might access the numinosity associated with Neptune.

In the early stages of individuation, the Mercury-Neptune complex can open the mind to spiritual truths and aesthetic perceptions that lie out of common sight, and thus open one's consciousness to the mystery of existence, precipitating the spiritual adventure. Equally, however, this archetypal complex can give rise to states of pervasive intellectual confusion, with the mind forming endless associations between ideas and open to flights of fantasy that cloud the capacity for clear intellectual discernment and understanding. One's thinking can be blurred by fantasies and projections, perhaps illusions and delusions, and this can give rise in turn to muddled communications, perceptual difficulties, the obscuring of truth, with the mind lost in the world of fantasy, overlooking important practical details and the plain facts of the matter. The result can be lying, both to others and to oneself, as one becomes persuaded of one's own truth irrespective of obvious facts, with the ability to rationalize and explain away any such deceptions. Yet the Mercury-Neptune complex can also furnish one with the innate gift of persuasion as one's words are used to conjure and sell an image, dream, or ideal. Donald Trump, born with Mercury opposite Neptune, exemplifies a number of these forms of expression, in his case often magnified and dramatized by the Jupiter impulse towards broad strokes and generalizations, self-confidence and aggrandizement.

The susceptibility to fuzzy thinking, an impressionable mind failing to subject ideas and opinions to critical examination, and failing to think critically for oneself, are traits associated, in Jungian psychology, with a poorly developed animus *logos* function. Mercury-Neptune themes can be seen in the mind that is easily moved by inspirations and suggestions, soaking up thoughts as if from the ether, perhaps taking others' ideas as one's own (recalling the Neptunian talent for impersonation and imitation). The complex can be seen in intellectual passivity, the indiscriminate assimilation of ideas, and the reflecting of others' views and opinions like a mirror—of "being thought" or simply "having thoughts" rather than intentionally thinking. The Mercury-Neptune combination is associated with holistic thinking, symbolic thinking, or the free flow of ideas rather than the discrete directed thinking characteristic of the rational ego. It can be as if the rational mind has not been fully differentiated from the state of *participation mystique*. This lends itself to a ready appreciation of unity, wholeness, and threads of meaning connecting us all, but less so initially to differentiated thought.

The complex formed by these archetypes can also sometimes manifest in a gentle and sensitive style of communication—perhaps quite literally as a gentle, indistinct, or irenic voice, and in a highly sensitive nervous system, often ill-suited to the sensory bombardment of the modern world; and also sensitive in the perception and comprehension of life, with the mind attuned to the mosaic of patterns and meanings usually hidden from the more literal-minded. This complex finds a more natural and fitting mode of expression engaging with a world of subtle impressions, intangible truths, and in the attempt to render the ineffable into words and images. In combination, these archetypes can open one to the perception of spiritual and artistic truths, seeking the underlying unity and forms behind surface appearances, as the rational mind and fallible powers of communication grapple to convey the inexpressible mystery and wonder of things through word or image or other artistic media.

Metaphor and the Mythic Imagination

One specific form of expression of Mercury-Neptune is the study of religion. For instance, Elaine Pagels, a leading scholar of Gnostic scriptures, has a grand trine involving Mercury, Neptune, and Saturn-Uranus (in a conjunction)—a vocation perfectly symbolized in this astrological configuration. We see in this example not only the Mercury-Neptune theme of deciphering and interpreting religious texts in order to convey their meaning, but also both the Saturn-Neptune theme of ancient religion (recalling Saturn's association with the old) and the Uranus-Neptune theme of the religious epiphany, the sudden spiritual revelation, as well as, in this case, the controversial challenge presented by Gnosticism to Christian orthodoxy. Thus, taken together the various archetypal factors take concrete form in the study of the meaning and consequences of the unexpected discovery of heterodoxical ancient spiritual texts (in Egypt in the 1940s), offering revelatory insight into early Christianity and heretical religious sects, particularly as a vehicle of gnosis. We will return to consider combinations of Saturn, Uranus, and Neptune at a later point.

The use of the power of the mind to penetrate to spiritual truths is also well exemplified by Joseph Campbell, whose life we discussed earlier in the context of the Saturn return. With a natal Mercury-Neptune square aspect, Campbell lent his formidable powers of comprehension and the articulation of perennial truths to the study of mythology the world over (his Mercury-Neptune square, as we will shortly consider, was also aligned with Jupiter—hence the breadth and the grandeur of his intellectual vision).

Asked by his friend Alan Watts, "what is your yoga?," his response, much to Watts' bewilderment, was "underlining sentences."[49] For Campbell, reading and study constituted his spiritual path. Aspects to Neptune in the natal chart tell us something significant about how we might access the spiritual dimension of life, about which archetypal functions are in direct relationship with the Neptunian spiritual instinct. In Campbell's case, the opening to spirit came through words, reading, writing, study—each associated with Mercury. Indeed, he remarked elsewhere that his studies of the world's myths and religions stirred within him a "mild, slow-burning rapture."[50]

Also apparent in Campbell's life experience was the recognition of the limits of rational understanding in the face of the ultimate mystery. The study of myth could lead one to the edge of this mystery, but no further. Myth, he often remarked, is the penultimate truth. The course of spiritual realization leads beyond all concepts of God, beyond all concepts in general. Yet myth and poetry—Neptunian-inspired expressions of Mercury—could put one in a state of mind that is receptive to religious truth. Thus Campbell's emphasis on developing the capacity to read myths and religions poetically, metaphorically, rather than getting stuck in the reading of them as factual, historical, and literal truths. And having devoted his life to unearthing the symbolic meaning of myth and thus recovering the value of myth for modern culture, he was also to proclaim that, in the final analysis, we are not really seeking meaning, but rather "the experience of being alive."[51] Again, he was giving expression to the Neptunian transcendence of the intellectual meaning and understanding associated with Mercury. In these alignments, Neptune acts to dissolve the need for knowledge and understanding, as one progressively surrenders to the flow and experience of life. In the face of the immediate experience of life's mystery one no longer needs to know. "Deliver me from reasons why," Jim Morrison petitioned in The Doors song "The Crystal Ship," conveying a sentiment emerging from the archetypal complex associated with his own Mercury-Neptune natal square.[52]

In another expression of Mercury-Neptune themes, Morrison was also inspired to create a new myth through putting his lyrics and poems to music with The Doors. Indeed, we find major Mercury-Neptune aspects in songwriters known for their poetic turn of phrase or for their capacity to mythologize through their music and lyrics. Bob Dylan and Bruce Springsteen, remarkable examples in both respects, have major Mercury-Neptune hard aspects. Mercury-Neptune aspects naturally correlate with the storyteller, the mythmaker through words. The complex often furnishes one with the capacity to empathically reach out to others with one's words, to meet them where they are, and to say what they need to hear—skills well suited to teaching and preaching and inspirational speaking. Not least, Mercury-Neptune aspects are associated with the visionary mind, manifest as the prescient power to discern and give form to hidden and emerging truths, and to synthesize different areas of intellectual understanding into a unifying vision.

Intellectual Synthesis and Universal Theorizing

In the case of Georg Friedrich Hegel (born August 27, 1770), with the Sun and Mercury conjunct to Neptune, we see an example *par excellence* of the capacity of the Mercury-Neptune complex to bring forth a seamless intellectual vision that includes everything in its scope, and to approach universal truths through the power of thought.

In Hegel's work, there is also a projection of the ideal onto "Reason" (which Hegel capitalizes), the domain of Mercury, such that Reason is conceived as the portal to the universal and is associated with perfection. As we read in the Introduction to *The Philosophy of History*:

> The only Thought which Philosophy brings with it to the contemplation of History, is the simple conception of Reason; that Reason is the Sovereign of the World; that the history of the world, therefore, presents us with a rational process. . . . It is there [in philosophy] proved by speculative cognition, that Reason . . . is Substance, as well as Infinite Power; its own Infinite Material underlying all the natural and spiritual life from which it originates, as also the Infinite Form—that which sets this Material in motion. On the one hand, Reason is the *substance* of the Universe; viz., that by which and in which all reality has its being and substance. On the other hand, it is the Infinite Energy of the Universe . . . . It is the infinite complex of things, their entire Essence and Truth. . . . While it is exclusively its own basis of existence, and absolute final aim, it is also the encouraging power realizing this aim; developing it not only in the phenomena of the Natural, but also of the Spiritual Universe—the History of the World. That this "Idea" or "Reason" is the True, the Eternal, the absolutely powerful essence; that it reveals itself in the World, and in that World nothing else is revealed but this and its honor and glory—is the thesis which . . . has been proved in Philosophy, and is here regarded as demonstrated.[53]

Universal, infinite, eternal, spiritual—these are all Neptunian characteristics and descriptions, applied to the realm of reason, thought, and ideas associated with Mercury. Reason effectively takes on the status of God. In Hegel's world conception, reflecting the presence of the Sun in this archetypal complex, "Reason" becomes the "Sovereign of the World" and finds fulfillment in the "honor and glory" of the divine, shining like the Sun itself.

Another example of a grand intellectual synthesis and unitary perspective, again applied to the understanding of the entire sweep of human history, is provided by Will Durant, born with Mercury opposite Neptune (and Pluto), who co-authored the magisterial fourteen-volume *The Story of Civilization* series, with his wife, Ariel Durant. In a note to the reader in *Rousseau and Revolution*, which the Durants thought would be the last volume of *The Story of Civilization*, they reflect on the underlying motivation behind the endeavor: "Our aim has been to write *integral history*: to discover and record the economic, political, spiritual, moral, and cultural activities of each civilization, in each age, as interrelated elements in one whole called life."[54]

Chart 27

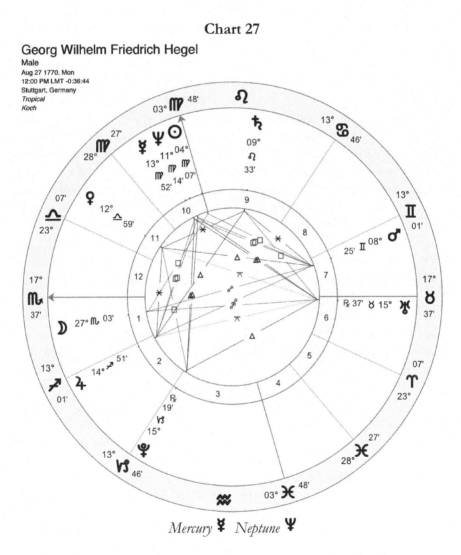

Mercury ☿ Neptune ♆

We find a similar urge towards theoretical synthesis and an approach to spirituality through reason in the work of "integral philosopher" Ken Wilber, who has a close-to-exact trine between Mercury and Neptune in his birth chart (born January 31, 1949). Dubbed the "Hegel of

Eastern philosophy," Wilber synthesizes vast areas of human thought, from East and West, and also introduces a developmental scheme that posits the transcendence of reason through the cultivation of various levels of spiritual consciousness—a formulation entirely in keeping with one theme of the Mercury-Neptune complex, as we have seen. One of his early books was *No Boundary*, a title that captures well the capacity of the Mercury-Neptune-inspired intellect to perceive underlying and encompassing unities behind the apparent separateness and division of life revealed by analytical thought.

In considering this wide range of expressions of the Mercury-Neptune archetypal combination, then, we can discern a characteristic pattern that moves one in the direction of individuation. To characterize it in broad strokes, the process leads from intellectual passivity, impressionability, and sometimes fantasy thinking and delusion to a pristine clarity of understanding and spiritually inspired mind; from endless associations, ruminating, and intellectual confusion to a striving for intellectual synthesis in a seamless universal vision; from the romanticism and mystique of particular ideas and ideologies and intellectual roles towards the intellectually empowered imagination, poetic-metaphorical insights, visionary understanding, and the mythically informed intellect—and perhaps even the transcendence of knowing completely, as the intellect is given over to the service of the Self, as one relinquishes one's own need to know or understand. A similar pattern applies to communication, as one comes to recognize that the power of the spoken and written word is to be used not for one's own gratification or betterment, but in accord with the Tao-like flow of life, with one's words, one's voice, serving as a channel for the power of spirit to be expressed through the flow of ideas, perhaps revealing a prophetic intellectual vision or articulating a near-inexpressible truth about reality. Mercury-Neptune is especially associated with the experience of the flow of consciousness, thoughts, and ideas. Under the influence of this complex, a person does not always know what he or she is going to say, but the act of communication opens up a channel from which ideas and words start to emanate.

* * * * *

Idealization of Beauty and the Spell of the Siren: Venus-Neptune

Personified in the mythic deities Aphrodite, Cupid, Eros, and Kama, the archetypal-astrological principle Venus pertains to love, romance, and beauty—domains of experience that are ripe for the enchanted projection, idealization, and wishful yearning associated with Neptune. In our exploration of the pantheon of Jungian archetypes in Part III, we noted that *maya*-like projection, enchantment, romantic allurement, the desire of Eros, and joyous life feeling come together in the Jungian archetype of the anima. The astrological combination of Venus and Neptune is especially closely linked with that archetype and with individuals who act as carriers of romantic projections for the entire culture.

Thus we find major aspects between Venus and Neptune in the birth charts of a wide range of actresses who became compelling anima figures, embodiments of the cultural form of the ideal of female beauty in recent history. The list includes Sophia Loren, Bridgette Bardot, Bo Derek, Britt Ekland, Scarlett Johansson (all Venus conjunct Neptune), Marilyn Monroe and Audrey Hepburn (Venus trine Neptune), Joan Collins, Jane Fonda, Madonna, Nicole Kidman, Charlize Theron, Sharon Stone, Catherine Zeta-Jones, Kate Beckinsale, and Pamela Anderson (all Venus square Neptune). This dimension of the Venus-Neptune complex is conveyed especially well in beauty expressed as image through film which then captivates the popular imagination. The actresses in this list, as with others born with Venus-Neptune aspects, expressed and embodied a particular form of beauty that helped shape and inform cultural ideals in recent decades, with Hollywood film stars fulfilling the need for many people for some form of connection to a more ideal, enchanted, and inspirational existence to that offered by mundane life. Of course, for both the beholder and perhaps especially the carrier of the cultural ideal, there is the danger of being trapped by the projected image of beauty, especially if one feels that one must always live up to the impossible image of perfection and therefore cannot accept one's mortal failings, blemishes, and imperfections.

This combination is associated too with subtle pleasures and enjoyments or touches of the sensual—soft fabrics, champagne and subtle aromas, the scent of perfume, or "clean white linen and . . . fancy French cologne," to borrow from Joni Mitchell's "Carey," with the lyrics an expression of the archetypal complex associated with Mitchell's own natal Venus-Neptune alignment.[55] This archetypal complex often manifests as a fine sensitivity that permits the nuanced appreciation of the aesthetic and the sensual. At its best, it is the antithesis of the crude and the gaudy, yet under the influence of these archetypes one can easily be seduced by a beautiful image or an alluring product that reinforces the ideal representation one has of oneself. The fashion victim, devoted to the cultivation of the perfect look, can also emerge from this particular complex of archetypal principles.

As we have seen, the imaginative yearnings and Eros-feelings associated with the anima can be bound up with an illusory image of a more ideal life, of a perfect love, of the bliss that one feels one deserves as reward and compensation for life's hardships and struggles. The image offers a source of escape into a mode of being in which one's yearnings are fulfilled, through which one can touch again the magical feeling of truly being alive. The longer one goes without such fulfillment, the more the heart yearns for it—thus we can understand the association of Venus-Neptune with the motif of the Sirens' call. Unless one has been able to differentiate the emotional sphere of desires and feelings associated with the anima, one remains particularly susceptible to falling under the Sirens' spell—a potential acutely present when the Venus-Neptune complex is activated, indicated by a major natal alignment or a transit of Neptune to Venus.

Here we see the characteristic dual-edged Neptunian propensity to lead one back towards the recovery of an enchanted mode of being in the world and pull one unwittingly into the delusory spell of *maya*, in a flight from reality. Again we might recognize the need for careful differentiation to meet with adequacy and competence the challenge presented by Neptune during individuation. For if one has clarified for oneself one's spiritual values and ideals, one has a point of reference from which to relate to the hypnotic allure of fantasies and desires as they arise—to tie oneself to the mast of one's spiritual direction, just as, in Greek myth, Odysseus instructed his crew that he be bound to the mast of his ship in order to resist the hypnotic melodies of the Sirens. If one cannot hear the voice of the anima, one's life is impoverished, for it offers heartfelt rejuvenation and connection to soul that often fall outside of the primary singular direction of individuation and the dictates of the Self. But if one gives oneself away to the anima, the possibility of individuation might well be lost, as the rewards of the anima prove to be fleeting gratifications and passing states of bliss rather than an enduring path to meaning, realization, and the fulfillment of one's potential.

A similar tendency to serve as carriers of romantic projection is also evident in men with major Venus-Neptune natal aspects. This archetypal combination is present in the birth charts of a number of celebrated romantic leads, often those noted for their dreamy, romantic qualities, and for starring in romantic films, including Robert Redford,

IDEALISM AND IMAGINATION: THE SPIRITUAL REALM OF NEPTUNE

Richard Gere, Jude Law, Matt Damon, Andrew McCarthy, Tom Hanks, Terrence Stamp, and Christopher Reeve. One especially noteworthy example, given the mythic associations with Venus-Neptune, is the British actor Orlando Bloom, who was cast in the role of Paris in Wolfgang Peterson's 2004 film *Troy*, portraying, in his affair with Helen of Troy, the most famous instance of romantic love in Greek myth—a role entirely befitting his natal Venus-Neptune square. (Helen was played by Diane Kruger, who has natal Sun conjunct Venus and Moon square Neptune.)

Chart 28

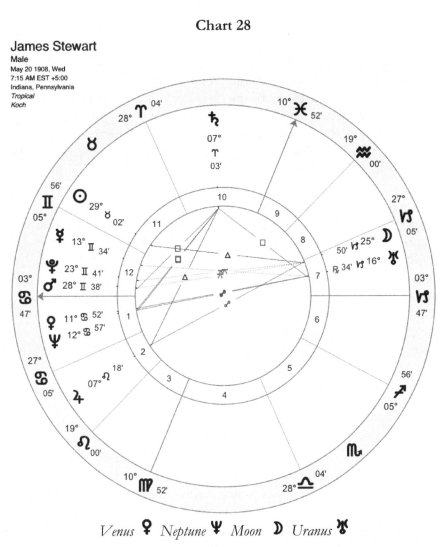

Venus ♀ Neptune ♆ Moon ☽ Uranus ♅

The Fairytale Romance and Aesthetic Sensitivity

Similarly, James Stewart, born with Venus and Neptune in major aspect (see Chart 28), is associated with what is perhaps *the* most romantic gesture in film—offering to lasso the Moon for his beloved, Mary, in *It's a Wonderful Life*: "What is it you want, Mary? You want the Moon? Just say the word and I'll throw a lasso around it, and pull it down . . . I'll give you the Moon, Mary . . . and then you can swallow it, and it will all dissolve, see, and the moonbeams will shoot out of your fingers and your toes and the ends of your hair . . ."[56] Fittingly, in Stewart's birth chart Venus and Neptune, in a conjunction, are in an opposition alignment with the Moon and Uranus—captured by the strikingly unusual (Uranus) romantic gesture involving the Moon, and even the Neptunian dissolution of the Moon itself.

The combination of Venus and Neptune can stir the imagination for fairytale romance in even the most sober-minded individual. In this way, the experience of Venus provides a medium and portal to the enchanted world of Neptune. Beauty is the vehicle of the ideal, romantic love the means to experience wonder and magic. Yet falling under the spell of the anima, and yearning for the promise of fulfillment of the anima, can also weaken one's capacity for clear judgment, and lead to an absence of morality in romantic and sexual matters. Neptune can blur ethical boundaries and in combination with Venus seduce us through our desires. In film, the morally ambiguous dimension of Venus-Neptune is well portrayed, for example, by Robert Redford in *Indecent Proposal* and Richard Gere in *Pretty Woman*. Both actors have major Venus-Neptune natal conjunctions. In politics, one thinks of former US President Bill Clinton's affair with Monica Lewinsky and the infamous denial ("I did not have sexual relations with that woman"). Clinton has natal Neptune in a conjunction with Venus and Mars.

The Venus-Neptune combination is the signature of the romantic, with valentines and red roses, wedding bells and dreams of a happy-ever-after in love. When these archetypes act in concert, both through the archetypal birth pattern and particular periods of one's life, as indicated by transits, they can inspire the fairytale romantic imagination and underlie a susceptibility to projection in love, as one falls under the spell of the anima. Venus-Neptune tends to evoke feelings of eternal love, in the fairytale style of forever and ever, as the romantic sentiments of Venus come into contact with the Neptunian sense of the ideal, the everlasting, and the perfect. Listen, for instance, to the words of Jon Bon Jovi, with a Sun-Venus conjunction, trine to Neptune, in the Bon Jovi track "Always":

> I will love you, baby—always.
> I'll be there for ever and a day—always
> I'll be there till the stars don't shine
> 'Till the record's stuck
> and the words don't rhyme. . .
> And I'll love you for always.[57]

Elsewhere, in Bon Jovi's best-known hit, "Livin' on a Prayer," the song's struggling young lovers are supported only by their own faith in each other, clinging to their dreams even in the realization they might not work out—with the harmonious trine between Venus and Neptune in Jon Bon Jovi's chart indicating the ready capacity to draw on faith in love. In another variation on this theme, portrayed in "I'll Be There for You," Bon Jovi sings of a man hoping to save his relationship, in spite of his failings thus far, in "praying to God you'll give me one more chance, girl."[58] Again, the Neptunian capacity for religious faith is called upon in support of love and romance.

Venus aspects to Neptune also indicate the combination of the spiritual and the aesthetic, the poetic and the mythic, as in the case of John Keats (born October 31, 1795), who had a Sun-Neptune-Venus triple conjunction. In a number of his poems, Keats expresses his idealization of and mythic view of the feminine ("Mermaid") and of pleasure ("Fancy"). For example, consider the lines in "I Cry Your Mercy-Pity-Love—Aye, Love!"

> I cry your mercy—pity—love!—aye, love!
> Merciful love that tantalizes not,
> One-thoughted, never-wandering, guileless love,
> Unmasked, and being seen—without a blot!
> O! let me have thee whole,—all—all—be mine!
> That shape, that fairness, that sweet minor zest
> Of love, your kiss,—those hands, those eyes divine,
> That warm, white, lucent, million-pleasured breast,
> Yourself—your soul—in pity give me all,
> Withhold no atom's atom or I die
> Or living on perhaps, your wretched thrall,
> Forget, in the mist of idle misery,

> Life's purposes,—the palate of my mind
> Losing its gust, and my ambition blind!⁵⁹

Note here the combination of the Neptunian sentiments of pity, mercy, perfection, and purity ("without a blot") manifest in the Venusian realm of romantic love. The romantic projection is such that the love is conceived as divine, an escape from, and means of transcendence of, the miseries of life. A summary of the central thrust of Keat's poetry, on the Poetry Foundation website, captures well the intersection of the Venus and Neptune principles in his work:

> The struggle of the poet to create beauty had become itself paradigmatic of [the] spiritual and imaginative quest to perceive the transcendent or the enduring in a world of suffering and death. For Keats, characteristically, this quest for a transcendent truth can be expressed (or even conceived of) only in the terms of an intense, imaginative engagement with sensuous beauty: "I am certain of nothing but of the holiness of the Heart's affections and the truth of Imagination—What the imagination seizes as Beauty must be truth—whether it existed before or not—for I have the same Idea of all our Passions as of Love: they are all in their sublime, creative of essential Beauty."⁶⁰

As Hegel idealized Reason, reflecting the Mercury-Neptune combination in his chart, so Keats idealized Beauty, Passions, and Love—each associated with Venus, reflecting themes associated with his Venus-Neptune natal alignment.

In art, the symbolist painter Gustave Moreau had a Sun-Venus conjunction square to Neptune, an archetypal combination that took form in his many paintings on mythical and biblical themes. So too the Venus-Neptune combination is well expressed in the decorative styles of Édouard Vuillard and Pierre Bonnard, and in the abstract symbolism of Paul Klee. And the same archetypal combination is also present in sports stars widely recognized for their artistry, including soccer players Johann Cruyff, of the great 1970s Netherlands team, and the Brazilian legend Pele; and Roger Federer in tennis, whose style of play was characterized by sublime "balletic grace" and finesse.⁶¹

This archetypal pairing tends to give rise to a poetic or artistic sensibility even in figures whose dominant traits and life experiences are of a different character entirely, as in the case of Adolf Hitler, whose early artistic interest and thwarted career as a painter seem utterly incongruent with his warped ideology, monstrous inhumanity, and maniacal political and military ambitions.

From Eros to Agape: Love for the Divine

The poetic and artistic forms of Venus-Neptune suggest something of the inherent movement of this complex towards sublimation and increasing subtlety. In terms of individuation, the telos of Neptune, as we observed in the earlier examples, is in the direction of the recovery of purity and the movement towards the spiritual and the unitary from the fallen and the fragmented. The Venus-Neptune complex is connected with a spiritualized expression of the anima, or the blurring of spirituality and romantic love, taking the form of anything from romantic flights of fancy and unconscious romantic projection to a mystic's love of the divine and a transcendence of personal romantic inclinations.

One significant form of expression of the Venus-Neptune complex, then, is the sublimation of Eros, when the romantic urges associated with Venus are both spiritualized and universalized. We might think, for instance, of the mystic's love for God, which is often marked by its quality of personal affection and devotion, as personal feelings of love for a particular individual are directed instead to a divinely infused love for all of humanity and all of nature. Sublimated and universalized romantic urges can transform Eros to Agape, a divine unconditional form of love. Personal desire can be dissolved, as love is expressed in platonic form.

The life of Pierre Teilhard de Chardin (born May 1, 1881) provides one example of these expressions of the Venus-Neptune complex. He had natal Venus and Neptune in an almost exact conjunction, with the two planets also in a close conjunction with the Sun. In his own life, Teilhard embodied this theme in the move towards a universalization of personal love and the sublimation of romantic affection. He refrained from romantic relationship, even when this seemed like it might be attractive and available to him. Biographers have noted his platonic relationship with his cousin, Marguerite Teilhard-Chambon, despite their strong romantic feelings for each other. Yet the Venus dimension of experience was not simply to be ignored. As Teilhard himself notes in his essay "Human Energy":

> When a man loves a woman with a strong and noble passion that exalts his being above its common level, that man's life, his powers

of feeling and creation, his whole universe, are definitely held and at the same time sublimated by his love of that woman.[62]

And again:

> It is no longer a matter of retreating (by abstinence) from the unfathomable spiritual powers that still lie dormant under the mutual attraction of the sexes, but of conquering them by sublimation.[63]

Note, in addition to the Venus-Neptune propensity to combine the romantic and the spiritual, and its movement towards sublimation, the presence of Pluto in these words—in the focus on power, particularly latent or dormant powers in the depths, and on conquering them. We will explore the connection of the Pluto archetype to power drives, will, depths, and overcoming in Volume III. Teilhard himself was born during the Neptune-Pluto conjunction of the late nineteenth century.

His mysticism was profoundly shaped by his scientific research and philosophical reflections on evolution, but also it was fundamentally rooted in his love for humanity, for the world itself, for matter, and for God and the person of Jesus Christ. "A universal love is not only psychologically possible," Teilhard remarked, "it is the only complete and final way in which we are able to love."[64] And, making a similar point: "Love alone can unite living beings so as to complete and fulfill them for it alone joins them by what is deepest in themselves. All we need is to imagine our ability to love developing until it embraces the totality of the people of the Earth."[65] Both quotes capture strikingly well he universalization of love associated with the Venus-Neptune combination.[66]

*   *   *   *   *

The Idealized Masculine: Mars-Neptune

Whereas the Venus-Neptune complex is associated with the idealization of the feminine, often in the form of the idealization of women and beauty, the Mars-Neptune complex is associated with the idealization of the masculine and with the capacity to see in specific men an embodiment of the archetypal masculine, associated with the animus. Joni Mitchell (Chart 39) and Kate Bush (Chart 29) provide two examples of prominent singer-songwriters who convey this dimension of the Mars-Neptune pairing in a number of tracks, reflecting their natal hard aspects between the corresponding planets. In Joni Mitchell's "Willy," on the album *Ladies of the Canyon*, for example, one gets the sense that she is relating to the archetypal masculine—in multiple forms—as much as to an individual man: "Willy is my child, he is my father. And I would be his lady all my life."[67] Again, the archetypal Neptune acts to mythologize and universalize those dimensions of experience associated with the planets with which Neptune is in aspect, enabling one to connect the personal and the specific to the transpersonal and the universal.

Likewise, Kate Bush, with a Mars-Neptune opposition (part of a grand cross with the Sun and Uranus), also provides a striking example of the Neptunian capacity to conceive of and project onto an image of the archetypal masculine. In "The Man with the Child in His Eyes," written when she was only thirteen, she presents an image of something like an idealized animus, bathed in the mythic imagination and inspiring her devotion. The man of her fantasy is an imaginary mysterious presence, understanding and compassionate, unknown to others, and giving eternal love.

> I hear him
> Before I go to sleep
> And focus on the day that's been.
> I realize he's there
> When I turn the light off
> And turn over.
> Nobody knows about my man
> They think he's lost on some horizon.
> And suddenly I find myself listening
> To a man I've never known before
> Telling me about the sea
> Oh his love is to eternity.[68]

The tendency to see the man as a child, evident in both of these songs, is indicative of the presence of the Moon, the archetypal child, in relationship with Mars, the archetypal masculine. Joni Mitchell was born with the Moon, Mars, and Neptune in major alignment. Likewise, in Kate Bush's chart it is highly probable that the Moon and Mars are in major alignment, although the precise time of her birth is not known. Note, too, in Kate Bush's lyrics, the symbolic juxtaposition of the man

(Mars) and water (Neptune)—in this case the sea—together with the characteristic Neptune theme of "eternity."

Chart 29

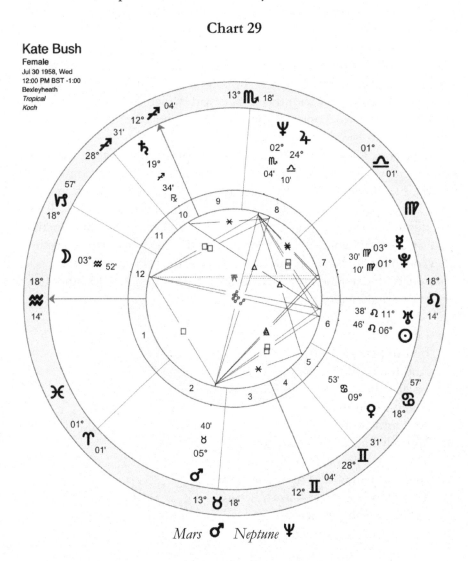

Mars ♂ *Neptune* ♆

In "Wuthering Heights," inspired by the Emily Brontë novel of the same name, Bush, as "Cathy," addresses herself to Heathcliff, the romanticized animus figure portrayed in the novel:

Ooh, it gets dark, it gets lonely
On the other side from you.
I pine a lot, I find the lot

Falls through without you.
I'm coming back, love
Cruel Heathcliff, my one dream
My only master.
Too long I roam in the night
I'm coming back to his side, to put it right.[69]

One further comment might be added on Kate Bush's and Joni Mitchell's respective expressions of Mars-Neptune. In Mitchell's work, among many other ways Mars-Neptune manifests, we see the combination of movement and water, as in "River"—"I wish I had a river, I could skate away on."[70] It is often in the manner of the Mars-Neptune archetypal complex to move away from difficulties, or to flow around them, to avoid conflict and difficulty rather than confront them. Mars-Neptune is associated with the avoidant or escapist action.

Likewise, Kate Bush brings together the Mars theme of running but linked with a Neptunian sacrifice to God, in her single from the late 1980s "Running Up That Hill":

And if I only could
I'd make a deal with God
And I'd get Him to swap our places.
Be running up that road
Be running up that hill
Be running up that building.[71]

In Jungian terms, then, the Mars-Neptune complex is associated with the idealization of the animus or with men who come to embody the animus, perhaps inspiring something like a religious sacrifice to the men in one's life, even when, in some cases, this does not serve one's greater good. Neptune, as we have seen, tends in its unconscious form of expression towards a lack of discernment, inspiring belief and faith but not always good judgment. This complex, perhaps especially in women, is associated with the act of idealizing men, and with projecting onto others the capacity for strength, independence, decisiveness, and courage, associated with Mars and the animus. The withdrawal of projections in individuation enables one to realize these qualities within oneself, as a psychological function to be integrated with the conscious ego.

The Man with No Name

Clint Eastwood gave iconic cinematic expression to the Mars-Neptune archetypal combination in his own life through his portrayal of multiple forms of a mysterious and morally ambiguous hero in Westerns and thrillers. Recalling the association of Mars with the archetypal warrior, when these two principles are in significant relationship Neptune acts on Mars, as it were, to shroud the warrior in mystery, to lend it mystique, and, as in Eastwood's case, to blur the moral boundaries of action and violence as to what is good and what evil. Born on May 31, 1930, Eastwood has Mars trine Neptune and square to the Moon, alongside a T-square featuring Saturn, Uranus, and Pluto.

The quintessential expression of the mysterious warrior is Eastwood's character "The Man with No Name," the protagonist in the series of Sergio Leone's so-called Spaghetti Westerns, filmed in Italy in the 1960s: *A Fistful of Dollars*, *For a Few Dollars More*, and *The Good, the Bad and the Ugly*. In each, Eastwood is the nameless poncho-wearing, cigarillo-smoking, quick-drawing gunslinger, whose charisma and mystique gave us one of the most instantly recognizable images of cinema. Eastwood's reflections on playing the role draw out key elements of the Mars-Neptune complex:

> I wanted to play it with an economy of words and create this whole feeling through attitude and movement. It was just the kind of character I had envisioned for a long time, keep to the mystery and allude to what happened in the past. . . . I felt the less he said, the stronger he became and the more he grew in the imagination of the audience.[72]

Note here the Neptunian emphasis on the imagination, vision, mystery, and allusion explicitly coupled with the Mars themes of action, movement, and strength.

The theme of the mysterious warrior is also prominent in a number of Eastwood's other Westerns. For instance, in *High Plains Drifter* he plays another mysterious stranger who is unknown to the other characters in the film, the ghost of murdered Marshal Jim Duncan. Likewise, the "Preacher" in *Pale Rider* is an "out and out ghost," who goes around quoting from the Bible as he responds to help those in need and metes out violent justice—the combination of Martial aggression, violence, and attack with Neptunian religion and compassion.[73]

Chart 30

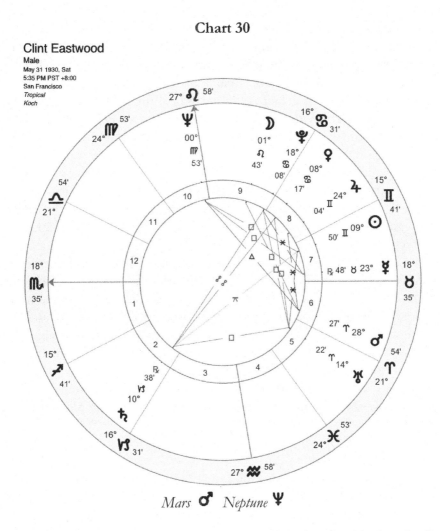

Mars ♂ Neptune ♆

In the 1970s, Eastwood took on another iconic role, this time in the cop thriller genre, portraying "Dirty Harry" (Harry Callahan), the morally ambiguous cop who repeatedly crosses and challenges ethical boundaries. He battles crime as a force for good, but breaks the law in doing so—reflecting not only the moral ambiguity of the Mars-Neptune complex, but also the Saturn-Uranus theme of the lawbreaker, to be discussed in Volume III (Eastwood has the two planets in a square aspect). As Dirty Harry, he is a police officer, upholding the law, but also a kind of vigilante, a law unto himself, while also fighting against ruthless vigilantes (in *Magnum Force*).[74] Again, he is a man of mystery; little is known of his background, and various explanations are offered as to the origin of his nickname. He is known only to his neighbors in his apartment in Nob Hill, San Francisco, as the "cop who lives upstairs."[75] Callahan's anger and impatience towards liberal politics and tolerant policing, which often seemed impotent in dealing with the problems of violent crime and unable to bring perpetrators to justice, inflamed ideological wars across American culture—Mars the anger and battles, Neptune the ideology, tolerance, and weakness, with elements here again of the Saturn-Uranus complex, associated with cultural tensions and divisions. The Mars-Neptune complex can underlie behavior that is weak, avoidant, and slippery in the expression of anger and assertion, with Neptune having an innervating influence on the strength and courage associated with Mars, or aggression can come through in indirect ways, in disguise, as it were—as in passive aggression.

Ultimately, having portrayed violent roles throughout his career, Eastwood was led to meditations on death and violence in his later films *The Unforgiven* and *Mystic River*, which he directed. The haunting and poignant quality of these films, the contemplation of death, and the maturation of his attitudes towards violence, reflect Eastwood's Saturn-Neptune natal alignment (a trine), an archetypal combination that we will consider more fully below. We might recall here a similar transition in the life of Alfred Nobel, also with Mars and Neptune in major alignment—the sublimation and spiritualization of the Mars warrior instinct.

The Spiritual Warrior

In another form of expression, a Mars-Neptune aspect brings together spirituality and movement through such practices as yoga, movement therapy, dance, and swimming—activities in which one can lose oneself in the flow and physically attune to the spiritual dimension of life. This archetypal complex stands behind the capacity to attune to subtle rhythms based on intuitive energetic feel and thus is especially associated with forms of the martial arts, such as Tai Chi Chuan and Aikido, based on combat through the cultivation of *chi* or *ki*—the subtle energy of the universe.

The founder of Aikido, Morihei Ueshiba, born December 14, 1883, had Mars square to Neptune, and he was also born during a Saturn-Neptune-Pluto triple conjunction (see Chart 31). His life journey through the martial arts was characterized by a gradual shift towards softer, gentler combat techniques and a focus on *ki*, as he became increasingly spiritual in his way of being later in life. This profound transition in his approach to the martial arts was marked by three major spiritual experiences. In 1925, Ueshiba emerged unharmed and victorious after being attacked by a naval officer wielding a *bokken* (a wooden stick or katana). A biography written by his son, Kisshomaru Ueshiba, contains vivid accounts of the episode:

> The man's eyes burned with a fierce desire to hit and kill. He began to attack relentlessly, one attack following hard on from the last one. Each time O Sensei easily avoided being hit, and seemed to flow away from the blows of the wooden sword. Eventually, exhausted from his all-out effort, the officer simply fell over, and that was the end of it.[76]

Shortly afterwards, in his garden, Morihei Ueshiba describes the spiritual experience precipitated by the combat:

> I felt the universe suddenly quake, and that a golden spirit sprang up from the ground, veiled my body, and changed my body into a golden one. At the same time my body became light. I was able to understand the whispering of the birds, and was clearly aware of the mind of God, the creator of the universe. At that moment I was enlightened: the source of *budō* [the martial way] is God's love—the spirit of loving protection for all beings.[77]

Budō, he realized, "is not the felling of an opponent by force; nor is it a tool to lead the world to destruction with arms. True *Budō* is to accept the spirit of the universe, keep the peace of the world, correctly produce, protect and cultivate all beings in nature."[78] We see here the transpersonal influence of Neptune on Mars. By itself, Mars inclines us to self-assertion, to fight for ourselves, to exert energy to get what we want. The Neptune archetype universalizes, spiritualizes, and sensitizes the expression of this Mars energy, resulting, as in this case, in fighting for the universal good, exerting oneself on behalf of the world, acting out of oneness and compassion, rather than self-serving ends.

Kisshomaru Ueshiba's biography, quoting his father, gives further detail on his Morihei's attunement to universal energy and the experience of the characteristic flow associated with the Mars-Neptune pattern of being, with the Neptunian dissolution of the individualistic aggression of Mars:

Immediately afterwards, I felt as if I was enlightened. Anyone who contracted himself and became smaller by thinking about the achievement of victory would see nothing. But the person who embraced all things with love and affection, who let *ki* govern the flow of events, could open a space of becoming one with the opponent, in *ki*, in mind, and in the movements of the body. The one who was enlightened would be, as we call it, the winner. But this would be victory without "winning"—real victory, winning over one's self. This would be the victory of merging with one's opponent, of humans becoming one with God, of the universe becoming part of love's creative energy. It would surpass the mere victory or defeat of individuals. It would be absolute victory of the God of Takemusu, and this is the supreme objective of the path of Bu, the martial way. These things are what I understood.[79]

Commentaries on Ueshiba's life describe a transition to ever more subtle techniques and mastery of his art, as Aikido became a form of spiritual practice more than a method of combat. For instance, it is reported that Ueshiba gave greater emphasis to a mastery of the flow of *ki* rather than the details of techniques, and he practiced *kokyū-nage*, or "breath throws," which utilize attackers' own force rather than exerting one's own strength against them. In a variation of something like the Neptunian alchemical practice of *ablutio* or washing, Ueshiba is reported to have practiced "cold-water *misogi*" as a religious rite of cleansing.[80] His cultivated sensitivity to the flow and rhythms of the universe reportedly gave him the capacity to evade bullets, to perceive the intention before an attack, such was his degree of attunement to the subtle dimensions of reality associated with Neptune.

Further major spiritual experiences followed in 1940 and 1942, in which Ueshiba seemingly transcended all martial arts techniques and saw his past martial arts teachings and trainings in an entirely new light. His spiritual journey through the martial arts culminated in 1942, in the midst of the bloody battle of World War Two, in Ueshiba's vision of the "Great Spirit of Peace."

Ueshiba's legacy is preserved in the philosophy underpinning the art of Aikido, revealing the spiritual dimension of the "The Way of the Warrior." As one book on Aikido concludes:

It is not a means to kill and destroy others. Those who seek to compete and better one another are making a terrible mistake. To smash, injure, or destroy is the worst thing a human being can do.

The real Way of a Warrior is to prevent such slaughter—it is the Art of Peace, the power of love.[81]

Chart 31

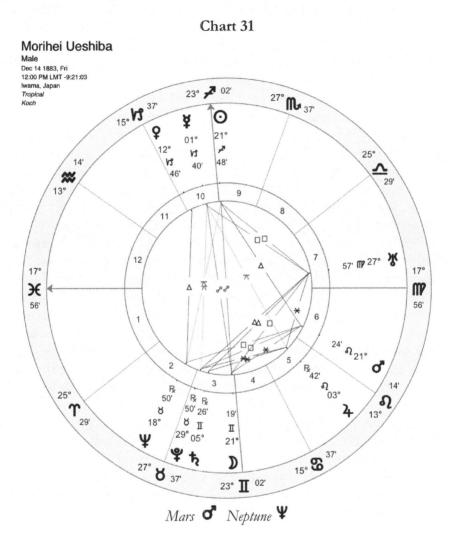

Mars ♂ Neptune ♆

Sensitivity and Spiritual Seeking

The combination of Mars and Neptune sometimes gives rise to physical sensitivity and weakness, perhaps arising from mysterious causes, but it symbolizes too the capacity to achieve transcendence of these conditions through developing subtle awareness of the body and meditative practice. In sports, the leading multiple grand-slam tennis champion Novak Djokovic is a fine example of the range of expression of the Mars-Neptune complex. In the early part of his career, he was forced on several occasions to retire from games with physical ailments, including allergies, and often appeared prematurely fatigued—Neptunian sensitivity impacting his ability to compete. In response, he switched to a gluten-free diet and in time developed a Zen-like capacity for sustained concentration, focusing his imagination on winning, and almost flawless play, as he put together one tournament victory after another. Having achieved so much success, however, Djokovic then became increasingly concerned with the spiritual dimension of experience, struggling to find a way to combine the competitiveness and winning attitude required in top-level tennis with a spiritual philosophy of love.[82] During the Covid-19 pandemic, such is his dedication to being spiritually attuned with his body, that he refused to get Covid vaccinations, disqualifying him from participation in several major tournaments and making him a much-derided figure in the mainstream media, although applauded by many for his stance.

Neptune sensitizes those parts of human nature ruled by Mars—as in the sublimation of aggression into more subtle forms of action, the promotion of "subtle activism" to effect change through psychic or spiritual influences on consciousness, or the redirection of Mars energies to the imaginal world. And just as Neptune can act on Mars to sensitize our actions, opening us to spiritual experience or the sense of flow through movement or shrouding the Mars warrior in mystery, so Mars energy can prompt us to initiate and actively seek out spiritual experience through our own intentions and efforts, as in the "psychonaut" using psychedelic substances to initiate non-ordinary states of consciousness, pursuing adventures in the imaginal realm of the psyche. The Mars capacity for courage and battle then comes through most powerfully in the Neptunian world of non-ordinary states, in the confrontation with the sometimes terrifying imagery or fearful emotions of the inner world. The Mars-Neptune pairing thus stands behind the image of the psychic or spiritual warrior.

Aligning with the Tao: The Dissolution and Sublimation of Will

During transits between Mars and Neptune, one can encounter any number of the above themes for those specific periods of one's life. Often lacking clarity and the ability to direct one's energies in a focused manner at these times, the combined influence of these planetary archetypes tends to leave one susceptible to escapist, deceptive, and avoidant actions, or to a kind of paralysis of the will or physical weakening or experiences of feeling demoralized. These symptoms can be exasperating and difficult to comprehend, seemingly without reason, but, as one moves through the transit, it can give one an intuitive attunement to the natural flow of things, as if, amidst the confusion, debilitation, and procrastination sometimes associated with this complex, there lies a subtle order, guiding actions and timings of events.

Ordinarily, the Mars-Neptune complex is not conducive to forceful acts of will and directed striving. Indeed, attempts to assert one's will can often be undermined and sabotaged. Yet during these transits one finds oneself having to act; one cannot do nothing and cease all activity and avoid all conflict. In taking action, however, one's will is effectively undermined and undone, fulfilling a psychological purpose of the transit, which moves us in the direct of defeat and surrender.

On certain occasions during Mars-Neptune transits, one can have the experience of being attacked or harshly criticized while being unable to defend oneself because of the circumstance; all one can do is submit and yield in the face of the hostility. When all straining and egoic assertion are defeated and dissipated, what remains is something like *wu-wei*—action through non-action—and one can move forward with a sense of yielding and harmonious flow in better alignment with the Tao or the will of God.

* * * * *

Each archetypal complex presents different challenges and requires its own form of response, approach, and attitude. Each furnishes us with different insights and elicits transformation in its own way, distinct from other archetypal complexes. As we can see in the above examples, the type of transformation elicited by Neptune is that of sublimation and transcendence of the personal, moving from the crude and crass towards the subtle, from personal will to divine will, and from egoic oversensitivity to universal compassion. The archetypal Neptune enthralls and enchants, luring us into the world-illusion of *maya*, but leads ultimately from the mystique of projection to genuine spiritual realization, from delusion and confusion to pristine clarity, and from a state of dreaming and wishing to serving as a vessel for spirit. It leads us through experiences of disintegration and dissolution to unity and synthesis.

Neptune works in accordance with the alchemical operation of *ablutio*, washing away confusions, impurities, and blemishes until a state of spiritual perfection is approached, as if one were to become an unblemished mirror or crystal-clear lake. And it works too in accordance with the operation *solutio*, dissolving boundaries and distinctions, in a return to an undifferentiated unity and promoting the attainment of a higher unity or synthesis of individual consciousness with the underlying ground of all being. The Neptunian impulse moves the separated individual consciousness towards a mystical union with all that is—the *mysterium coniunctionis* of alchemy.

Notes

[1] Tarnas, "The Ideal and the Real: Saturn-Neptune," 186–187, in *The Birth of a New Discipline*, 175–199.
[2] From a letter sent to Gandhi in 1939, quoted in Albert Einstein, *Out of My Later Years*, 254.
[3] Encyclopedia Britannica, "Alfred Nobel," accessed December 28, 2021, https://www.britannica.com/biography/Alfred-Nobel.
[4] Jung, *Two Essays on Analytical Psychology*, 170–171.
[5] Daniel Arcucci, in *Diego Maradona*, directed by Asif Kapadia (2019).
[6] Asif Kapadia, *Diego Maradona*. See also "The Cult of Diego Maradona—in pictures," *The Guardian*, October 30, 2020, https://www.theguardian.com/football/gallery/2020/oct/30/the-cult-of-diego-maradona-in-pictures)
[7] *Football Italia* website, accessed November 26, 2019, https://football-italia.net.
[8] Arcucci, in Asif Kapadia, *Diego Maradona*.
[9] These descriptions feature in Asif Kapadia, *Diego Maradona*.
[10] Arcucci, in Asif Kapadia, *Diego Maradona*.
[11] "In the Hands of God," *The Guardian,* November 26, 2020, https://www.theguardian.com/football/2020/nov/26/in-the-hands-of-god-what-the-papers-say-about-the-death-of-diego-maradona.
[12] Tim Vickery, "Diego Maradona: How Tormenting England Made Him an Argentine Deity," BBC Sport, accessed November 26, 2020, https://www.bbc.com/sport/football/55074235.
[13] Guillem Balague, "Diego Maradona Dies: Guillem Balague on 'the Magician, the Cheat, the God, the Flawed Genius'," BBC Sport, accessed November 26, 2020, https://www.bbc.co.uk/sport/football/55084504.
[14] Balague, "Diego Maradona Dies."
[15] The phenomenon of the 27 Club is the subject of an archetypal astrological analysis entitled "The Rebirth of Tragedy" by Zachary Kampf, submitted as a doctoral dissertation at Pacifica Graduate Institute in 2022. Kampf focuses on four figures: Janis Joplin, Jim Morrison, Kurt Cobain, and Amy Winehouse. Joplin had the Sun trine to Neptune.
[16] David Bowie, "Bowie Talks to Paxman about Music, Drugs and the Internet," BBC Newsnight, posted January 11, 2016, http://www.bbc.

com/news/entertainment-arts-35286749?post_id=10153271816925848_10153271816905848.

[17] Bowie, "Bowie Talks to Paxman."

[18] Bowie, "Bowie Talks to Paxman."

[19] Bowie, "Space Oddity" on *David Bowie* (London: Trident, 1969).

[20] Bowie, "Ashes to Ashes" on *Scary Monsters (and Super Creeps)* (New York: RCA, 1980).

[21] A number of the same forms of manifestation of the Sun-Neptune complex are also exemplified by the British comic, social commentator, podcaster, and spiritual activist Russell Brand, who has a natal Sun-Neptune opposition. Suffering through his own drug addiction, Brand has done much to bring the topic into the light, using his celebrity status to share first-person insights into the experience of addiction, and arguing that addicts should be treated with compassion as victims of illness rather than incarcerated as criminals. An outspoken critic of the political establishment, mainstream media, corruption, and the capitalist economic system, Brand is one of the most prominent public figures to propound values and ideas outside of the dominant Western materialistic worldview, championing spirituality, the sanctity of the individual, and new-consciousness perspectives, giving expression to the mystic-spiritual-idealistic dimensions of the Sun-Neptune complex.

[22] Bowie, "Star Man," on *The Rise and Fall of Ziggy Stardust and the Spiders from Mars* (London: Trident/RCA, 1972).

[23] A comparison can be made between Bowie and Lady Gaga, born on March 28, 1986, who has the Sun square to Neptune, Mars, and Uranus.

[24] Jung, *Memories, Dreams, Reflections*, 355.

[25] *Meet the Parents*, directed by Jay Roach (Universal Pictures, 2000).

[26] Jung, *Undiscovered Self*, 60.

[27] Campbell, *Hero with a Thousand Faces*, 16.

[28] For Jung's discussion of the "dissolution of the persona," see *Two Essays on Analytical Psychology*, 160/282, 169/287, 297. The "night-sea journey" is a term featured in the work of Leo Frobenius, and later used by Jung and Campbell.

[29] For Jung's discussion of the regressive restoration of the persona, see again *Two Essays on Analytical Psychology*, 163, 166, & 168.

[30] Wordsworth, "Ode: Intimations of Immortality from Recollections of Early Childhood," Poetry Foundation, accessed November 3, 2021, https://www.poetryfoundation.org/poems/45536/ode-intimations-of-immortality-from-recollections-of-early-childhood.

[31] Wordsworth, "Ode: Intimations of Immortality."

[32] Wordsworth, "Ode: Intimations of Immortality."

[33] Without an exact birth time, the position of the Moon can only be estimated, using a so-called "noon chart"—that is, a chart cast for 12 pm on the date of birth. The rapid speed of the Moon's orbit, moving about 12 degrees each day, means that its position can only be known within that 12-

degree range. For the other planets, we can be confident of their position within 1–2 degrees or even minutes of degrees for the outer planets.

34 Christopher Robin Milne also had a broad Moon-square-Neptune natal aspect.

35 The noon chart for Hölderlin (no birth time is available), shows the Moon trine to Neptune (in an outer-planet grand trine with Uranus and Pluto. The Moon is conjunct Pluto and opposite Saturn. See https://www.astro.com/astro-databank/H%C3%B6lderlin,_Friedrich.

36 Hölderlin, "When I Was a Boy," in *Selected Poems*, 13.

37 Hölderlin, "When I Was a Boy."

38 Hölderlin "Hyperion's Song of Fate," quoted in Jung, *Symbols of Transformation* (trans. R. F. C. Hull), 399.

39 Hölderlin "Bread and Wine," in *Selected Poems*, 37

40 Hölderlin "To the Sun God," in *Selected Poems*, 21.

41 Proust, *Swann's Way*, 2–3.

42 Proust, *Swann's Way*, 15.

43 Freud, *Civilization and Its Discontents*, 39.

44 Salvador Dali, the painter best known for his portrayal of symbolic imagery of dreamscapes in surrealist paintings, had a major Moon-Neptune natal configuration, bringing together Neptunian imagery with the lunar realm of dream.

45 Stanislav Grof, *Psychology of the Future: Lessons from Modern Consciousness Research* (New York: State University of New York Press, 2000), 37–45.

46 Jung, *Memories, Dreams, Reflections*, 223.

47 Jung, *Memories, Dreams, Reflections*, 225.

48 Jung, *Memories, Dreams, Reflections*, 225.

49 The exchange between Campbell and Alan Watts is recounted in Campbell and Frazer Boar, *The Way of Myth*, and Campbell. *The Hero's Journey* (edited by Phil Cousineau), 81.

50 Campbell with Bill Moyers, *The Power of Myth*, 122.

51 Campbell and Moyers, *Power of Myth*, 1.

52 Jim Morrison wrote the lyrics for The Doors song, "The Crystal Ship" on *The Doors* (Elektra Records, 1967).

53 Hegel, *Philosophy of History*, 9.

54 Will Durant and Ariel Durant, *Rousseau and Revolution: The Story of Civilization*, vol. XIV, vii.

55 Joni Mitchell, "Carey" on *Blue* (Reprise, 1971).

56 *It's a Wonderful Life*, directed by Frank Capra (Liberty Films, 1946).

57 Bon Jovi, "Always," on *Cross Road* (Mercury-Polygram, 1994).

58 Bon Jovi, "I'll Be There for You," on *New Jersey* (Mercury-Vertigo, 1988).

59 Keats, "I Cry Your Mercy-Pity-Love!–Aye, Love," Poetry Foundation, accessed December 29, 2021, https://www.poetryfoundation.org/poems/50326/i-cry-your-mercy-pity-love-aye-love.

60 "John Keats," Poetry Foundation, accessed November 3, 2021, https://www.poetryfoundation.org/poets/john-keats#tab-poems. Text slightly modified for grammar.

61 See Russell Fuller, writing for the BBC after Federer's announcement of his retirement in 2022: "Roger Federer Retires: Swiss Great Played Tennis with a Balletic Grace beyond Modern Compare," https://www.bbc.com/sport/tennis/62985363.

62 Quoted in Ursula King, *Spirit of Fire: The Life and Vision of Teilhard de Chardin* (Maryknoll NY: Orbis Books 1996), 75. See the chapter "Faces of the Feminine" in that book for an illuminating discussion of the role of women and the feminine in Teilhard's life and work.

63 Teilhard de Chardin, *Heart of Matter*, 59f.

64 Teilhard de Chardin and Blanche Gallagher, *Meditations with Teilhard de Chardin*, 101.

65 Teilhard de Chardin and Blanche Gallagher, *Meditations with Teilhard de Chardin*, 100.

66 The placement of Teilhard's Sun and Venus in Taurus is reflected in the characteristic earthy cast of his mysticism, which focused on the spirit in the heart of matter, and re-conceived Christianity in terms of the evolution of the material universe. In Volume IV, I will consider the Plutonic evolutionary dimension of Teilhard's work.

67 Joni Mitchell, "Willy," on *Ladies of the Canyon* (Reprise Records, 1970).

68 Kate Bush, "The Man with the Child in His Eyes" on *The Kick Inside* (EMI Records, 1978).

69 Kate Bush, "Wuthering Heights" on *The Kick Inside* (EMI Records, 1978).

70 Joni Mitchell, "River," on *Blue* (Reprise Records, 1971).

71 Kate Bush, "Running Up That Hill (A Deal with God)" on *Hounds of Love* (EMI Records, 1985).

72 Clint Eastwood, on playing the "Man with No Name," in Patrick McGilligan*, Clint: The Life and Legend* (New York: OR Books, 2015), 133.

73 "Pale Rider," accessed April 22, 2024, https://www.clinteastwood.net/filmography/palerider/#audio.

74 *Magnum Force*, directed by Ted Post (Warner Bros., 1973).

75 "Clint Eastwood: Harry Callahan," on Internet Movie Database (IMDB), accessed November 29, 2021, https://www.imdb.com/title/tt0070355/characters/nm0000142.

76 Kisshomaru Ueshiba, *A Life in Aikido: The Biography of Founder Morihei Ueshiba*, 177.

77 Quote cited in Kisshomaru Ueshiba, *Aikido* (Tokyo: Hozansha Publications, 1985). As the Ueshiba biography reports: "Immediately after his encounter with the naval officer, O Sensei had an amazing experience. He walked out of the dojo, and quietly washed off his sweat at the well nearby. Then as he walked back across the garden, just by an old persimmon tree,

suddenly his whole body seemed to freeze in place—he couldn't move a step, but just stood there like a statue without any thoughts or sensations at all. The ground started to tremble and he saw thousands of dazzling golden rays falling from the sky. A glorious and unearthly light welled up to fill the air. Then he felt soft, golden *ki* rising up out of the earth to embrace him" (Ueshiba, *A Life in Aikido*, 178).

[78] Morihei Ueshiba, quoted in Morihiro Saito, *Traditional Aikido*, 38.
[79] Ueshiba, *A Life in Aikido*, 179.
[80] Phong Thong Dang, *Advanced Aikido*.
[81] Winfried Wagner, *Aikido: The Trinity of Conflict Transformation* (Innsbruck, Austria: Springer, 2015), 223.
[82] In another inflection of Mars-Neptune, Djokovic, nicknamed the Joker, became known for his impersonations of his fellow tennis players—the Neptunian capacity for impersonation applied to the martial arena of sport

Chapter 20

The Tenor of Faith and Vision: Jupiter-Neptune and Saturn-Neptune

In further exploring the array of themes and experiences associated with the Neptune archetype, we might again turn to pairings with Jupiter and Saturn for comparison and contrast. For the archetypal influence of Jupiter and Saturn on Neptune does much to determine the quality and tenor of one's vision of the world, the sense of life's possibilities, and an orientation and attitudinal stance towards ideals, dreams, and religious experience.

The Fool's Journey and the Impossible Dream
We have seen a number of examples thus far in which comedy, in permitting a larger-than-life expression of typical human experiences, offers a particularly vivid, because exaggerated, portrayal of archetypes. When considering the expression of the Jupiter-Neptune complex in the arts, therefore, we might turn first to comedy to gain insight into the nature of this complex and thus begin to understand its significance for individuation, both as an aid and an obstacle.

We touched on the birth chart of Jim Carrey in our earlier discussion of Sun-Saturn alignments, noting then that many of his films and the roles he plays, while conveying essential elements of the Sun-Saturn complex (such as a downtrodden character or restrictive and belittling life circumstance) more prominently showcase qualities and themes associated with the Jupiter-Neptune combination. Chief among these is the capacity for eternal optimism, to believe that what one hopes for and dreams about can come true, however small the odds, however remote the possibility of its realization might seem. The Jupiter-Neptune complex can incline towards a form of naïve idealism, devoid of realism and blind to problems and pitfalls, but buoyed by faith and optimism. Such traits are conspicuously evident in the character of Lloyd Christmas, played by Carrey in the enduringly popular Peter

Farrelly movie *Dumb and Dumber*, which follows the adventures of two dim-witted friends from Rhode Island (Lloyd and Harry, played by Jeff Daniels) on a journey to Aspen to return a lost briefcase to its owner, Mary Swanson (played by Lauren Holly), for whom Lloyd has developed a romantic crush after serving briefly as her limo driver on a trip to the airport in Rhode Island. Throughout, the film is concerned with the motif of the journeying fool, in which the hapless blunders and idiotic extravagances of Lloyd and Harry prove no obstacle to the pursuit or ultimately the success of their mission—indeed the foolishness often works in their favor, with the naïve lack of strategy and unconsciousness enabling them to prosper, as often applies in life too. In this form of expression it is as if consciousness remains in a naïve and innocent *participation mystique*—the travelling companions in *Dumb and Dumber* have little in the way of worldly wisdom and discriminating consciousness, with nothing more than a rudimentary grasp of the workings of the world. Yet the very naivety and ridiculous foolishness are what enable them to prevail, with folly and wisdom the opposites that touch at their farther reaches. The Jupiter-Neptune complex underlies the naïve trust and faith that guides their journey. Both Carrey and Daniels have major hard-aspect alignments between Jupiter and Neptune in their birth charts: Carrey has Jupiter opposite Neptune; Daniels has Jupiter conjunct Uranus, square to Neptune. Both men also have major alignments between the Sun and Saturn: Carrey the conjunction, Daniels the square.

Lloyd's capacity to believe in the impossible is nowhere better exemplified than in a humorous scene in which he declares his romantic feelings to Mary Swanson. Having returned the briefcase to Mary in Aspen, and basking in her bemused appreciation, Lloyd takes the opportunity to ask her about their prospects:

Lloyd: What are the chances of a guy [*sic*] like you and a girl [*sic*] like me . . . ?
Mary: Not good.
Lloyd: Not good like one out of hundred?
Mary: I would say more like one out of a million.

Lloyd pauses to take in what Mary has said—coming as a crushing blow, one would expect. But, rather than feeling disconsolate and downhearted, he rebounds with optimism bordering on the incredible:

Lloyd: ... So you're telling me there's a chance! Yeah!¹

The ability to focus on the one-in-a-million chance in one's favor rather than the overwhelming odds against is an admirable and endearing quality, even if it flies in the face of reality. At times, following the way of individuation, or pursuing what Joseph Campbell has called one's "bliss," one has to maintain faith in the possibility of the successful outcome of one's transformative journey, in spite of all evidence that things are unlikely ever to work out. The Jupiter-Neptune complex opens the imagination to the vision and faith that may carry one along towards greatness and the fulfillment of one's dreams. And, of course, without the vision and aspiration, without reaching for the dream, there is no prospect of ever attaining it. In its pure form, then, Jupiter-Neptune dreams big dreams and believes in the likelihood of their realization.

In his own life, Jim Carrey put this Jupiter-Neptune gift to work in the service of his own dreams. As an aspiring actor, hoping to make it big one day, he visualized his future success and wrote himself a $10-million check payable for "acting services rendered," which he kept in his pocket. Remarkably, some years later he received $10 million for *Dumb and Dumber*,² with Jupiter granting successful fruition to the Neptunian dream and vision for the Jupiterian experience of success, wealth, and bounty.

Wish Fulfillment and the Dissolution of Inflation

In *Bruce Almighty*, Carrey's portrayal of television news reporter Bruce Nolan offers another example of the Jupiter-Neptune theme of wish fulfillment. Having been overlooked for promotion to news anchor and then having lost his job and been mugged in the street, the hard-done-by Bruce has an encounter with God (played by Morgan Freeman) and is then bestowed with God's powers. To his amazement Nolan is able to manifest his every wish simply by imagining it—another instance of dreams coming true associated with Jupiter-Neptune. For a time Nolan is able to satisfy his every whim and fancy, but in his role as God he soon finds himself besieged by other people's prayers, with the seemingly endless petitions for one thing or another manifesting as persistent voices in his head. Whatever method he tries to manage the incoming flow of prayers proves inadequate, until he eventually transfers prayers to email requests and answers "yes to all."³ In Jupiterian fashion, this is wish fulfillment on a grand scale, with everyone getting just what they have asked for, which brings with it the inevitable catastrophic consequences. Recall that in its more problematic mode of expression Jupiter is associated with excess and extravagance just as Neptune can incline to an inarticulate unconsciousness and lack of discrimination. In Bruce's experience of assuming God's powers, the film essentially explores the Jupiterian theme of inflation. Bruce is, one might say, in the role of the ego swollen by the influx of transpersonal fantasies and powers, using his God-given powers for show and for self-serving ends. He becomes adrift in the world he creates and in his falsely generated success, caught up in the image of that life once his wishes have been fulfilled. Inevitably, he beings to lose touch with reality. The archetypal influence of Neptune portrayed in the film, however, also effects the dissolution of the Jupiterian inflation. Neptune dissolves the Jupiterian excess and the spurious popularity Bruce achieves; it shows the emptiness of success that comes unearned, and exposes Bruce to the wider world of human suffering through his Godlike abilities. Ultimately, the dissolving power of Neptune leads to surrender, compassion, and the realization of the fallibility of the all-too-human will.

From the excess of prayers in *Bruce Almighty* we turn to the excess of lies in another of Carrey's films, *Liar, Liar,* and then in *Cable Guy* to an excessive exposure to film and television shows—other instances of the Jupiterian magnification of Neptunian phenomena: dreams, religion, deception, and image. (Note here too that Carrey has an exact Mercury-Jupiter conjunction, opposite to Neptune. The Mercury-Neptune combination is sometimes associated with deception through words, and, with Jupiter, the telling of tall tales.) In *Cable Guy*, having spent his childhood alone in front of the television, neglected by his parents, Carrey's character's entire worldview and life experience as an adult are utterly saturated with references to television shows and films, such that they displace virtually any connection to reality.

In *The Truman Show*, in which Carrey plays Truman Burbank, his character's entire life experience takes place within a television show—in this case, one big deception rather than, or as well as, many lies. The only real thing in the show is Truman himself. The cast, comprising all of the people in Truman's life, is privy to the deception and perpetuate it, with the help of 5000 cameras and the intrusive monitoring of Truman's every move. Truman's entire existence is false, make-believe, an illusion, from which he struggles to emancipate himself, ultimately sailing across the "ocean" to the edge of his known reality. The television-set world conjures an image of deception that is Jupiterian not only in its scale but in its quality, manifest in the false happiness and wholesome veneer of a 1950s American Dream ("Hi honey, I'm home," "Have a nice day," and so forth), in which everyone is always nauseously pleasant.

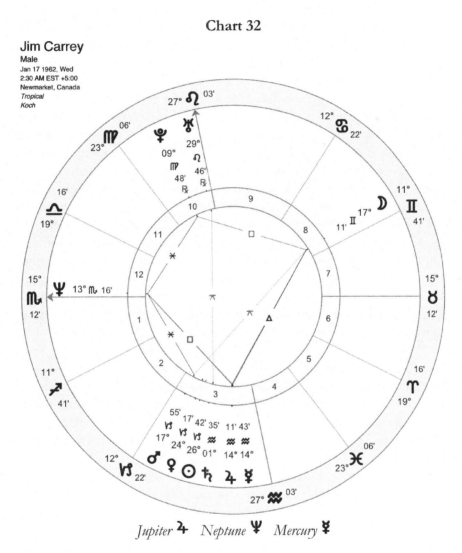

Chart 32

Jupiter ♃   Neptune ♆   Mercury ☿

High Ideals, High Expectations

If grand deception represents one pole and possibility of the Jupiter-Neptune complex, another is the inclination towards the pursuit of high ideals—or in some cases living with high, perhaps overly high, expectations for what life might bring. The Jupiter-Neptune personality has the ability—potentially at least—to imagine a picture-perfect life, in whatever form that might take. Of course, the problem then might well be perpetual disappointment and dissatisfaction when life fails to live up to one's hopes and expectations.

The archetypes of Jupiter and Neptune, acting together, can also underlie the fantasy and ideology of growth and self-betterment, which can, consciously or unconsciously, pervade one's worldview. This complex can manifest too as the pursuit of a plethora of different spiritual paths, often drawn from far and wide, given the easy access to worldwide religions we enjoy today. The rich combination of spiritual perspectives can inspire a sense of the universality of spiritual teaching but it can also be spirituality overdone, with too many religious teachings and practices, health remedies, natural medicines, plant rituals, retreats and workshops, and the like. One can also easily be lost in the image of a positive-thinking spirituality and growth, of affluence and well being, centered on one's happiness and the actualization of one's potentials, and perhaps therefore obscuring reality rather than leading towards enlightenment. While promoting an aspiration towards the summit, the Jupiter-Neptune fantasy can pull one away in escapist detachment from the pains and sufferings of the valley of the soul—a point made by James Hillman, who had natal Jupiter and Neptune in alignment with Saturn (evident in the critique).

The Promised Land
In traditional astrology, Jupiter has long been associated with foreign lands and long journeys; accordingly, when Jupiter acts in combination with Neptune there can be the projection of the ideal onto foreign countries and cultures, which shimmer in the Neptunian mystique,. The "promised land" is to be found on the faraway shore or in some dreamed-of unknown place, one veiled in the allure of the projection. In music, one artist who captures something essential of this dimension of the Jupiter-Neptune archetypal complex is Bruce Springsteen—he has a Jupiter-square-Neptune alignment in his birth chart.[4] The characters in Springsteen's songs "believe in a promised land," as we hear on a track on *Darkness on the Edge of Town*.[5] They yearn to leave the restriction of humdrum reality in their hometowns and head off to some "alien distant shore" in the belief that there, one day, they might come to the realization of their dreams and find a life of blissful happiness.[6] What comes through in many of Springsteen's songs is the

optimistic yearning for a better life and the sustaining belief that it might indeed be attained in a glorious moment of redemption.

A fundamental Neptunian motivation is the yearning for heaven, for paradise; Springsteen's characters pursue a big dream or a big vision with the hope that, if fulfilled, this might restore the blissful state, present for many of us in childhood—Springsteen also has the Moon in a major relationship to Neptune. In "Born to Run," his most famous song, the romantic hero and his girl are caught up in "a runaway American Dream"—a dream without limit, the dream of success, of finding happiness, of making it big, all reflecting Jupiter-Neptune's association with expansion and boundlessness. "The big top is for dreamers," Springsteen writes in "Mary Queen of Arkansas," again connecting Jupiterian amplification and magnitude with Neptunian dreams.[7] Inspired by romantic idealism his characters dream big dreams, and they live in expectancy that one day their dreams will be fulfilled:

Someday girl, I don't know when,
We're gonna get to that place
we really wanna go.[8]

Yet the big dream can often turn out to be the big illusion in which the heroes of his imagination are "driving all night chasing some mirage," finding only "a great grease paint ghost on the wind," only "a great false dawn."[9]

Often, for Springsteen's characters, it is the lure of the open roads and the untold promise of unknown distant lands that hold the possibility of redemption, happiness, and fulfillment. Jupiterian experiences, that is to say, take on a magical allure, carrying the Neptunian projection of the ideal, drawing Springsteen's characters out into the world in pursuit of their dream, in search of a place "where paradise ain't so crowded," a place where they can finally, "walk in the sun."[10] The final destination of Springsteen's wandering characters is often unknown ("You don't know where you're going, but you know you won't be back").[11] The wandering is prompted by a feeling or an intuition rather than a clear vision of where it is heading. In "Frankie," on *Tracks*, combining themes of the unknown future destination and the sense of magical wonder, the narrator explains:

Well Frankie I don't know what I'm gonna find
Maybe nothing at all, maybe a world I can call mine,
Shining like these street lights down here on the strand
Bright as the rain in the palm of your hand.[12]

Chart 33

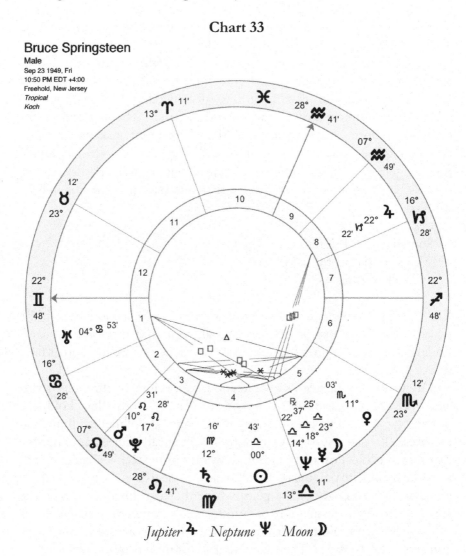

Jupiter ♃ *Neptune* ♆ *Moon* ☽

Unsurprisingly, the same Jupiter-Neptune combination (especially indicated by hard aspects) can, on occasion, manifest as aimless wandering that leads nowhere, as futile drifting and dreaming, relying too much on faith that life will provide. There is something naïvely trusting and uncritically idealistic in the Jupiter-Neptune complex, which can give rise to the tendency to see the world through rose-tinted glasses and to avoid all contact with the often unpleasant reality of one's life situation. Nevertheless, one of the most appealing qualities of Springsteen's music is the pervasive sense of faith and optimism, the feeling that, however improbable, everything will indeed work out, in spite of all difficulties and no matter how bad the current situation, and that "one day we'll look back and it will all seem funny."[13]

In "The River," from the album of the same name, Springsteen introduces the motif of returning to water for renewal. Relating to the archetypal Neptune, water symbolically represents the unconscious, the source of life, and it is by travelling to the river or ocean that the characters, worn down by the frustrations and limitations of life, seek to reconnect to the life-vivifying flow of inspiration and dream in order to redeem the desolate "badlands" in which they live. Of all the religious themes associated with Jupiter-Neptune, redemption is perhaps the one that best expresses the meaning of this complex, as this combines both spirituality (Neptune) and uplift (Jupiter), and the successful resolution (Jupiter) of spiritual idealism and yearning (Neptune) that enables one to return to life with renewed optimism, faith, and a sense of meaning (expressing both Jupiter and Neptune).

Universal Spirituality and the Myths of the World

With this combination, experiences of travel, spending time abroad, and immersing oneself within foreign cultures can be the source of numinous feeling and spiritual sustenance—such as travelling overseas to pursue spiritual retreats and pilgrimages. Jupiter gives an international, multicultural, and even global vista to the Neptunian pursuit of religious experience.

Given these themes, it is not surprising, then, that a number of leading figures who popularized the study of world mythology and religion have major Jupiter-Neptune alignments in their birth charts, including Carl Jung (see Chart 20), Joseph Campbell (Chart 14), and Mircea Eliade (Chart 34). As we have seen, Jung referenced myths and religions from far and wide in the formulation of his model of a universal archetypal psychology. Campbell authored multiple volumes and multiple series of volumes (*The Masks of God, The Atlas of World Mythology*) exploring the myths of the world across history, bringing a Jupiterian expansive and holistic perspective to his studies of the mythic and mystical dimensions of life, just as he celebrated the universal core truths—the perennial mythology, as he called it—within the diverse mythic cultures of the world.

Likewise, Eliade wrote the three-volume *A History of Religious Ideas*, surveying world religion, and also published substantive works on yoga, shamanism, alchemy, and initiation rites together with a number of books on symbolism, images, and religious paths. And, to give one more example, James Hillman also had a major hard-aspect Jupiter-Neptune, similarly reflected in his rich cultural imagination and breadth of vision, inspired especially by the Italian Renaissance, and the polytheism of his mythic sensibility.

Chart 34

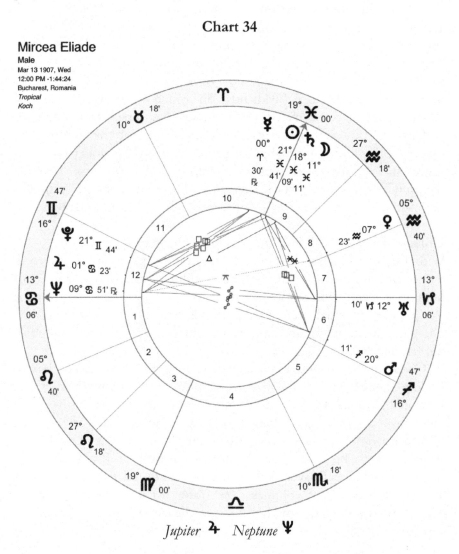

Jupiter ♃ Neptune ♆

In elevating the status of myth in modern culture, all four figures were expressing another dimension of the Jupiter-Neptune complex. Campbell especially saw myth in exalted, even grandiose terms—construing myths and understanding their import through a Jupiterian lens, which inclines one to amplify, raise up, celebrate, and perhaps exaggerate. The following passage, from the opening paragraphs of *The Hero with a Thousand Faces*, illustrates the point:

> Throughout the inhabited world, in all times and under every circumstance, the myths of man have flourished; and they have been the living inspiration of whatever else may have appeared out of the activities of the human body and mind. It would not be too much to say that myth is the secret opening through which the inexhaustible energies of the cosmos pour into human cultural manifestation. Religions, philosophies, arts, the social forms of primitive and historic man, prime discoveries in science and technology, the very dreams that blister sleep, boil up from the basic, magic ring of myth.
>
> The wonder is that the characteristic efficacy to touch and inspire deep creative centers dwells in the smallest nursery fairy tale—as the flavor of the ocean is contained in a droplet or the whole mystery of life in the egg of a flea. For the symbols of mythology are not manufactured; they cannot be ordered, invented, or permanently suppressed. They are spontaneous productions of the psyche, and each bears within it, undamaged, the germ power of its source.[14]

Campbell was responsible in no small degree for spreading a greater awareness of myth, and disseminating its spiritual message throughout contemporary Western culture, giving myth a broad appeal and widespread popularity even in an age of empirical science, secularism, and austere rationality. His primary intuition of a unitary and universal view of the mythic-religious history of the human race, emerging from its common biology and psychology, well reflects the holism and universalism associated with Jupiter and Neptune. Yet this viewpoint left him open to criticism that he overlooked important cultural differences between myths.

Campbell is perhaps best known, even by those not familiar with his writing, for the axiom "follow your bliss."[15] He exhorted people to try to find and follow their passion in life, for that would be the pathway to a flow of positive experiences of bliss that could subsume all struggle and suffering, allowing them to access their own spiritual support in the midst of the life they are living, rather than waiting for the hereafter. In so doing, he was giving his own form of expression to the Jupiter-Neptune wish-fulfillment theme, supported by the spiritual powers at work in the universe. In *The Power of Myth* interviews with Bill Moyers, Campbell spoke of "invisible hands" coming to our aid when we follow our bliss—an affirmation of the benevolence of a life lived in accord with the Tao-like flow of spirit.[16]

We see a further expression of the Jupiter-Neptune complex in Campbell's belief in the ultimate goodness and beauty of existence, in which the horrors and sufferings we encounter are but the "foreground to a wonder."[17] Also reflecting Campbell's Jupiter-Neptune sensibility is the very act of mythologizing the journey of life—for the journey, as we have seen, is essentially a Jupiterian theme, just as myth, spirituality, and the inclination to focus on the archetypal and universal are Neptunian. Thus, in sum, we see in Campbell's life and work several essential elements of the archetypal pairing of Jupiter and Neptune: from his overarching faith in the possibility of spiritual realization and bliss in this life to his promulgation and dissemination of the universal spiritual truths of world mythology; and from his elevation of myth to the status of a spiritual revelation to his wonder at the magic power of myth and the ubiquitous manifestation of mythic motifs in human experience, not least that of the mythic-mystical journey of the hero.

Campbell's elevation of the mythic reflects the association of Jupiter with experiences of ascent, manifest in the realm of Neptune, but this, of course, is only one form of expression of this particular theme. Reflecting Tarnas's insight into the multidimensional nature of astrology, we find the same themes manifest in consistent ways across all dimensions of reality. We turn now to consider further examples in film that provide illustrations of this multidimensionality, conveyed both in imagistic content and in style.

Disillusionment with Hedonism and the Sublimation of Eros

The work of Federico Fellini provides fine examples of a number of themes associated with the three-archetype combination of Venus, Jupiter, and Neptune. In Fellini's birth chart, you will recall, there is a Jupiter-Neptune conjunction with a trine to Venus, which we will include in the analysis here too. In his celebrated film *La Dolce Vita*, released in 1960, the opening scene features the bizarre spectacle of a statue of Jesus, with arms spread, hoisted by helicopter, and transported high in the sky above Rome. The quite literal elevation of the religious in the images in this scene parallels Campbell's elevation of the mythic in his grandiose vision of myth's importance in human experience. Jupiter represents the impulse towards height, ascent, and amplification. Characteristically, reflecting the presence of Venus in the configuration of archetypes, Fellini blends in the aesthetic and erotic, with the helicopter crew involved in flirtatious banter with bikini-clad sunbathers on a rooftop below.

Chart 35

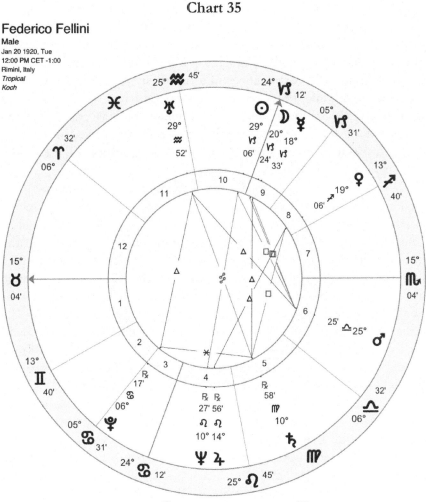

Venus ♀ *Jupiter* ♃ *Neptune* ♆
(12 pm birth time used as no accurate birth time available)

In *8½*, similarly, Fellini gives us one of the cinema's most memorable *sublimatio* scenes—the alchemical operation associated with the experience of rising up in airy detachment. The film opens with footage of film director Guido Anselmi, played by Marcello Mastrioanni, suffering some kind of nervous breakdown or existential crisis while stuck in his car in traffic, hemmed in on all sides, and surrounded by the banal disinterest and distracted pleasures of the drivers and passengers in the vehicles around him. In an anxiety-stricken state, he escapes through the roof of his car, and then, in a surreal sequence, finds himself floating up into sky, as if flying in a dream, which marks, we are led to assume, his temporary transcendence of or flight from his particular life circumstance. The film then follows his experiences in a health spa or clinic, in which he works to overcome the creative block underlying his psychological problems. The cinematic depiction of height and ascent is itself an expression of Jupiter-Neptune, with the opening scenes of *La Dolce Vita* and *8½* in different ways suggesting the elevation of the mythic and religious, and psychological ascent as escape and retreat.

La Dolce Vita is concerned with the cultural manifestation of the religious and the mythic in the context of an increasingly secular modern Rome, with the population ever hungry for a miraculous manifestation of the divine. While the search for the miraculous in that film ends in farce and tragedy, as a crowd, gathered in response to a reported sighting of the Madonna, turns into the stampede of an angry mob, Fellini introduces us to experiences of religious and mythic themes in another way, manifest through the aesthetic and the pleasurable—that is, through dimensions of experience associated with Venus. Earlier, we considered examples of the forms of expression of the Venus-Jupiter combination in Fellini's films: the high life of parties, romantic and sexual adventures, hedonism, beautiful cultural settings, and so forth. Fellini's Jupiter-Neptune becomes apparent too, however, in his ability to reveal the mythic manifest within the seemingly secular and hedonistic lives depicted in his film. For example, in one memorable scene Marcello makes his exit from a party with the voluptuous American actress, Sylvia, played by Anita Ekberg. After parking his car in the deserted streets of Rome in the early hours, Sylvia beseeches Marcello to find some milk for a stray kitten. When an exasperated but entranced Marcello duly returns with a saucer of milk, he watches Sylvia frolicking in the Trevvi Fountain, playfully toying with the kitten on her head, as if she were toying with Marcello's anima. Mesmerized by the siren-like Sylvia, Marcello agrees to join her in the fountain where, against the mythic backdrop of sculptures of the Roman gods, she pours water on his head as if to baptize him. At that moment, dawn breaks, the water of the fountain stops flowing, and momentary silence descends on the Eternal City.

We can recognize in this scene the Venus-Neptune theme of the idealization of the feminine, especially in the juxtaposition of the Christian revelation of the Virgin Mary with Marcello's idealization of Sylvia. Indeed, multiple dimensions of the anima interpenetrate here: the erotic attraction and allurement, the sirens motif, the soul or inner child (symbolized by the kitten) held captive by the anima (Sylvia), the mythic dimension of the anima as that which connects to the eternal images of the collective unconscious (suggested by the sculpted mythic figures in the fountain), and the mystical-religious dimension of the anima as an expression of the spiritual feminine, like the Virgin Mary, delivering us to the world of spirit and the eternal silence. The entire episode is thus a masterful portrayal of multiple anima themes, with Fellini, drawing on the archetypal talents associated with his Jupiter-Neptune conjunction trine to Venus, infusing the mythic and the spiritual into the erotic, illustrating how awareness of a mythic reality can pervade human experience even when we have lost our living connection to myth or orthodox religion. The mythic themes remain, manifesting within the dramas of the soul and cultural life of the city, even if the gods have ostensibly departed.

Marcello's romantic and sexual escapades, associated with the Venus-Jupiter combination, are in some sense being spiritualized, leading from crass hedonism to mythic revelation and spiritual experience—the audience witnesses this even if he himself remains tragically unable to realize his creative calling and higher values. It is here that we might recognize the archetypal influence of Neptune, sensitizing and sublimating, veiling things in divine mystery and wonder, pulling us into its spell as we are introduced to the spiritual dimension of life, not as an appendage to normal life, but as its essence and fulfillment. Spiritual life, as Joseph Campbell once remarked, is the "bouquet of nature"; it is not something superimposed on it.[18]

It is indicative of the nature of the trine between Venus and the Jupiter-Neptune conjunction that the experience of pleasure, romance, and beauty intrinsically supports the exploration of and experience of the mythic and spiritual. In this relationship, the mythic and the sensual, the mystical and the romantic are mutually accessible and congruent dimensions of life experience rather than inherently incongruent, as we can imagine they might be in other contexts and from different archetypal viewpoints.

While the aesthetic and romantic adventures of Marcello in *La Dolce Vita* reveal their mythic background, Fellini also explores Marcello's saturation in, and disillusionment with, hedonism and the socialite lifestyle. Jupiter elevates, sometimes raising us to a higher moral vantage point and moving us towards growth. Neptune sublimates, manifesting in this case as the disillusionment with Jupiterian high life and the Venusian pursuit of the momentary enjoyment of pleasure, which ultimately prove to be superficial and empty, even as they also offer a means of escape from life. We see this kind of sublimation in Marcello's longing to be a writer and his attraction to a purer, innocent form of the anima, symbolized in the film by the young waitress Paola. Shocked by his friend's infanticide and suicide, however, Marcello falls into despair and disintegrates into crass hedonism, ultimately ignoring the calls of his soul, symbolized by Paola, to leave behind the common crowd and the Dionysian nihilism that characterizes his life at that point.

Neptune dissolves and disintegrates, leading us back to the oceanic source. The question to be settled in life is whether this merger is regressive, a falling back into the non-differentiation of the mass and instinctual life, or progressive, preserving and enhancing individual consciousness in spiritual union with the unitary source of life.

*   *   *   *   *

The Saturn-Neptune Complex

The following analysis of the Saturn-Neptune complex in this section is indebted to examples presented by Richard Tarnas in graduate seminars and journal articles on archetypal astrology and the arts, including discussion of Ingmar Bergman and Joni Mitchell. Much of what I came to understand of the Saturn-Neptune complex emerged from my immersion in the work of these artists. Below, informed by Tarnas's research, I include select examples of particularly salient illustrations of Saturn-Neptune themes in their work, alongside a range of other examples from birth charts and transits.

When the Saturn and Neptune archetypes combine, indicated by prominent natal or transiting aspects between the planets, one finds a sensitive and imaginative capacity to enter into the core experiences associated with Saturn, including death and suffering, endings and loss, time and aging, just as the Saturnian capacities for judgment, negation, maturation, and discipline are brought to bear on Neptunian areas of life, including religion and spirituality, dreams and ideals, fantasies and visions. The resulting archetypal complex comprises an especially rich array of qualities and types of experience. There is no better artistic expression of this complex than in the work of Ingmar Bergman.

Chart 36

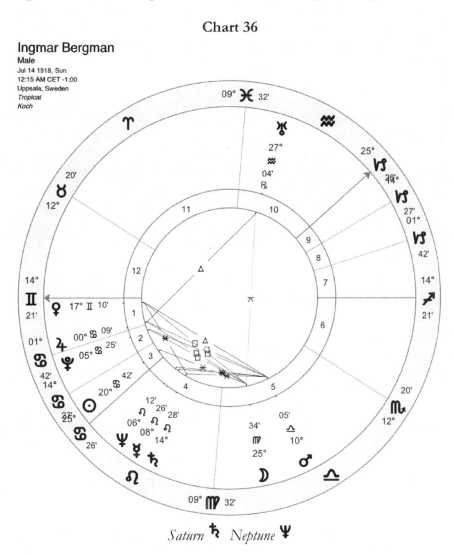

Saturn ♄ *Neptune* ♆

"The Artistic Haunting" and Transcendence through Death

Much could be said about the presence of Saturn-Neptune themes throughout Ingmar Bergman's films, but one scene in particular, in *Through a Glass Darkly*, offers vivid insights, in concentrated form, into central elements of the psychological reality of the Saturn-Neptune complex. Near the beginning of the film, set on a Swedish island, we witness a family performance of a play called "The Artistic Haunting," put on by Karin, a young married woman, and her seventeen-year-old brother, Minus, for the entertainment of their father, David, on his return from a period overseas. In the play, Karin (played by Harriet Andersson) is in the role of the spirit of a deceased Castilian princess seeking to persuade her brother Minus (Lars Passgard), playing the role of a king, artist, and suitor, to sacrifice his life to be with her for eternity in death and thus to prove his love in an ultimate act of faith.

The title of the play, "The Artistic Haunting, or The Tomb of Illusions" captures the essence of its thoroughly Saturn-Neptune flavor. The tomb evokes the *senex*-Saturnian reality of cold stone and death, enclosing the Neptunian experience of illusion. The haunting quality is typical of this complex, as are ghostly apparitions and dark visions.[19] As the performance begins, we are told that Minus, as the king and suitor, is a "poet without words" and "painter without paints" (an instance of Saturnian negation applied to the Neptunian artistic sensibility), who is promised eternal life and oblivion if he sacrifices himself in death before the clock strikes two, and joins the princess in the hereafter. "Oblivion shall own me, and death alone shall love me," he declares.[20]

Karin, as the princess, comes to the idealistic king Minus as an alluring proposition, which, at first, he yearns to accept, to prove himself to her in faith and deed, and to prove that he is worthy as a "true artist."[21] As the fateful hour approaches, however, with the prospect of death growing ever closer, he has to decide whether his romantically inspired suicide pact with the princess will really deliver him to blissful oblivion or whether, rather, the vision is mere illusion and therefore not to be trusted. Tarnas has highlighted the tension between fact and illusion, reality and deception, as central to the Saturn-Neptune complex. Saturn attunes us to the hard facts of concrete reality, tangible data, and empirical experience; Neptune opens our consciousness to the spiritual world and subtle unseen realities, and promotes the yearning to believe, to have faith, or to directly experience transcendence of the mundane world. But are these spiritual and imaginal experiences true? Do these realities really exist? Can our religious epiphanies and idealistic yearnings be trusted, or are they deceptions and illusions that we must outgrow as we seek to face and accept the reality of life as it is? Is the Neptunian longing for transcendence nothing more than a flight or escape from facing up to life in the material world, with all its sufferings and limitations? Such questions emerge from the dialectic between Saturnian consciousness and Neptunian consciousness, often demanding ongoing renegotiation and integration, especially if one has these two planets in natal hard aspect. Often, the Saturnian-senex consciousness might negate and judge as delusory or escapist the Neptunian proclivity towards belief, faith, and spirituality. In this case the complex promotes, Tarnas has observed, skeptical doubt or materialistic atheism, as exemplified by figures such as Marx and Freud, both with natal Saturn-Neptune hard aspects. The latter's view of the belief in God as an illusion, based on the infantile need for a protective father, well exemplifies this position, as does his sense that religion, even if it is a metaphysical illusion, serves a valuable sociological function. In other forms of expression, however, Saturn grounds and actualizes rather than negates Neptune, helping to translate religious belief and spiritual consciousness into practical action in the form of a pragmatic spirituality or ideology, helping in tangible ways to relieve human suffering, carrying spirit in the world, with works proving faith, as it were. For instance, in addition to the Saturn-Neptune aspect in Karl Marx's chart, studies have highlighted the correspondence between Saturn-Neptune world transits and developments in socialism.[22]

In "The Artistic Haunting," Minus, overcome by doubt ("have I gone mad?," he asks himself), cannot carry through his promised suicide.[23] His faith fails him at the decisive moment, and he retreats into a kind of aloof detachment, realism, and ironic distancing, in the face of what might have been ("Oh well, such is life!").[24] Death, the fundamental Saturnian reality, was offered as a means of transcendence or escape into a blissful oblivion, if the test of faith could have been met and if, indeed, the artistic haunting and vision of the princess were real.

In this film and others, Bergman's treatment of psychopathology, dark and disturbed states of consciousness, the morbid imagination, the sobering realization of illusory belief, the alienation from God, and the loss of faith powerfully illustrate the psychological depths of the Saturn-Neptune complex. These themes are especially evident in Karin's delusional schizophrenia in *Through a Glass Darkly*, which explores the experience of existential meaninglessness and the absence or unreality of God, but ultimately offers a kind of humanistic secular alternative, based on the idea of God as human love.

Such experiences might present themselves to any of us during personal transits of Neptune to Saturn, but the experience of these transits in non-ordinary states of consciousness can be especially powerful. In an archetypal astrological analysis of a series of "bad trips" on LSD in 1967, during a personal transit of Neptune square to Saturn, Jungian scholar Scott Hill describes his dramatic encounter with many of these themes, in experiences reminiscent of Bergman's play in *Through a Glass Darkly*:[25]

> After an initial series of ecstatic psychedelic episodes during the spring of 1967, my carefree teenage adventures with psychedelic substances carried me into depths of madness and hell that I could previously never have imagined. The four later experiences became pervaded by a terrifying call from beyond to end my life in what I perceived as an absurd world. This vision of redemption through suicide unfolded within a pervasive, sustained, and overpowering sense of another dimension of reality, a terrifyingly immense stillness that was inexplicably but undeniably sacred. The deep, absolute, and transcendent nature of this stillness implicitly and mysteriously called all earthly existence into question and challenged me—despite the absence of any prior religious tendency—to redeem myself by sacrificing my life in this world in order to be with God in Heaven.
>
> Throughout each of these four difficult experiences, I struggled with the dilemma of whether I had gone insane or had instead discovered something deeply, disturbingly true about the profoundly spiritual nature of my existence. These two possibilities were often bewilderingly conflated, and during each experience I struggled to resolve them in what felt like an eternal hell of confusion.

Reflecting on one of his psychedelic experiences, he recalls:

> And with wisps of fog drifting inland from the ocean, I was captivated by the mysteriously rich beauty of the landscape. Although the place had the same general features as the coast with which I was familiar, it now seemed oddly unreal. We seemed to be in a fairytale land, and I was suddenly overcome with the terrifying conviction that in our climb out of the canyon my friend and I had somehow emerged into another world. My sense of this was so

strong that I was convinced we were either in another world or I had gone mad.[26]

In Hill's recollections, just as in Bergman's "The Artistic Haunting," we find a stark portrayal of the Saturnian experience of death or suicide as a means to spiritual transcendence, associated with Neptune, with pervasive doubt and confusion as to what is truly real, feeding into a fear of insanity.

Loss of Faith, Alienation from Spirit

Under the archetypal influence of the Saturn-Neptune complex, whether indicated by a natal alignment or a major transit between the two planets, one can find oneself enveloped in a dark atmosphere, as if lost in a dense fog. Everything can appear confused and uncertain, as one's capacity for clear engagement with reality is compromised by a tendency to suffer from negative projections, such that the world itself appears veiled in darkness, perhaps even inherently false or insubstantial in some sense—as in Hill's experience, above. Even if the world once glowed in divine radiance and once was filled with a sense of spiritual purpose and a proximity to God, when these two archetypes come into relationship such experiences might fade away, appearing now as nothing more than distant memories or even naïve delusions. One might come to a sobering realization of the truth, painfully revealed behind the deception in which one was formerly living—or so it seems. Naturally, in such a state of mind one might readily dismiss prior spiritual experiences, ideals, and dreams as unreal—as nothing more than fanciful wishing and thus to be discarded in the facing of the hard facts of reality. Of course, such negative judgments might well prove, in the fullness of time, to be illusions themselves, arising from a doubting, perhaps morbid and defeated, state of consciousness, unable to retain faith in the face of disappointing experiences that puncture one's ideals and fall short of one's hopes for life. The dialectic between truth and illusion, clear judgment and distorting projection, facts and ideals, can lead to skepticism and even bitter cynicism as one turns against one's own former "mistaken" beliefs and delusions. To save face, and partly redeem oneself, it might seem then that the only course of action is to try to save others from falling under similar deceptions. The deflating, sobering experience of Saturn-Neptune can create an ardent skeptic out of a believer.

Such experiences of loss of faith can naturally have an incapacitating impact on one's will and levels of motivation and belief. The Saturn-Neptune complex is associated with states of pervasive disillusionment and depression, apathy and moral fatigue, futility and regret or lament for what has passed or what might have been. Such adverse manifestations of the complex can obviously pose significant problems for individuation. One must somehow maintain faith in the rightness of one's path and the validity of one's revelation in spite of testing external circumstances that might serve to stir and reinforce one's inner doubts. This archetypal combination, however, also draws out the moral capacity to cleave to one's ideals and spiritual truths regardless of the seemingly contradictory evidence presenting itself through one's current circumstance, regardless even of feelings of loss of faith and pervasive discouragement. The Saturn-Neptune complex can help us build faith, Tarnas has observed. It might help to furnish us, too, with the capacity to cope with disappointments and to discern more deeply what is true, beyond the evidence of the senses and the wishful longings and sentiments of the human mind. With clear Saturnian judgment, one might be able to see through any false images and romanticized projections onto the world and onto oneself. The Saturn-Neptune combination has much to do with the unmasking of deception, the withdrawal of projections, and seeing beyond the distorting power of archetypal images that can blind us to the truth of our existence. For the direction of individuation leads, as Jung stressed, to the attainment of a clear and realistic view of the world.

The Spirit of the Times: Saturn-Neptune World Transits

When the slow-moving outer planets form major geometric alignments with each other, especially the hard aspects (conjunctions, oppositions, and squares), the entire zeitgeist is pervaded by themes and experiences associated with the combination of the corresponding archetypes. As we have seen, these alignments are known as *world transits*, for they pertain to the entire world. Events taking place and creative projects born under these transits tend to carry, in significant ways, the archetypal qualities associated with the current astrological alignments.

World-transit correlations may be illustrated by considering cultural phenomena arising during the Saturn-Neptune opposition alignment of late 2004 to 2008. In the middle of this period, in June 2006, the English alternative pop band Keane, riding the success of their 2004 album, *Hopes and Fears*, released a second album, *Under the Iron Sea*, which went on to achieve critical acclaim, going triple platinum in the

UK and gold in the US, with over three-million record sales globally to date.[27] In essential ways, the album seemed to tap into and articulate the collective zeitgeist, with its distinctly Saturn-Neptune flavor. Commenting on the album in 2006, the band characterized the songs as creating "a kind of sinister fairytale-world-gone-wrong," and expressing "a feeling of confusion and numbness represented by a dark place under an impenetrable iron sea"—with both descriptions strikingly capturing themes and experiences associated with the Saturn-Neptune complex.[28]

The second track on the album, "Is It Any Wonder?," begins with the sobering realization of a kind of self-deception in the belief and expectation that we can live in a world that conforms to our high ideals ("the kingdom of the good and true"), a belief that, in retrospect, appears naïve and foolish, the stuff of fairytales, rather than reality.

> I, I always thought that I knew
> I'd always have the right to
> Be living in the kingdom of the good and true.
> And so on, but now I think I was wrong
> And you were laughing along
> And now I look a fool for thinking you were on, my side.[29]

We are later presented with images of an "old cathedral" and "sad lonely spires," suggesting the loss of the enchanted world of religious belief, which now exists as nothing more than abandoned relics from a time before the alienation from spirit.[30]

As we have seen, Tarnas has characterized the combination of Neptune and Saturn as the "ideal and the real" in which the Neptunian sense of what life might be, what we expect it to be, is painfully contrasted with the reality of what it actually is.[31] Not infrequently, this perception can give rise to a sense of deflation and demoralization but also, once the illusion has been exposed and accepted, to an aspiration to make one's life conform more closely to the ideal through one's own efforts. Yet initially, during periods marked by transits between these planets, the overwhelming sense can be one of world weariness, existential malaise, moral exhaustion, a sense of defeat, and debilitating confusion as to what is true and real and what mere illusion, captured by Keane's lyrics in this track.

Is it any wonder I'm tired?
Is it any wonder that I feel uptight?
Is it any wonder I don't know what's right?

Chart 37

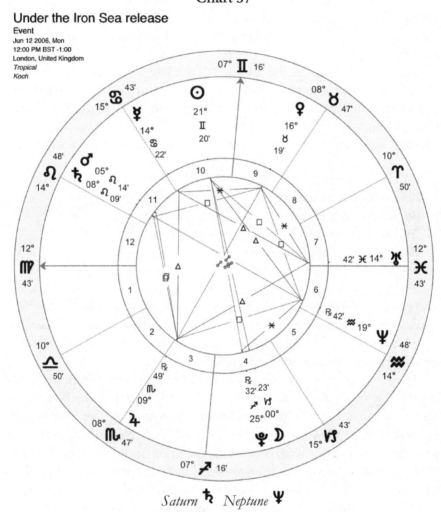

The above is the event chart for the release of Keane's Under the Iron Sea *on June 12, 2006, midway through the Saturn-Neptune world-transit opposition and carrying the archetypal qualities of that historical moment.*

And in "Bad Dream," on the same album:

> I wake up, it's a bad dream
> No one on my side
> I was fighting
> But I just feel too tired.[32]

In the experience of the bad dream we meet again the Saturn-Neptune association with the dark vision, the disturbed state of consciousness, with the Saturnian world of suffering and problems, limitation and death, coming through the Neptunian experience of the dream.

Another Saturn-Neptune theme explored on this album, on the track "Crystal Ball," is that of existential confusion and doubt as to what is real, with the debilitating sense of unreality afflicting the protagonist's basic sense of self.

> Who is the man I see
> Where I'm supposed to be?
> I lost my heart, I buried it too deep
> Under the iron sea.[33]
> . . .
> Lines ever more unclear
> Not sure I'm even here,
> The more I look the more I think that I'm
> Starting to disappear.[34]

The song was written by keyboard player Tim Rice-Oxley who has natal Sun opposite Neptune (evident in the theme of the disappearing self). The lead singer of Keane, Tom Chaplin, has natal Sun square Neptune, as part of a T-square with Saturn, lending itself to the expression of Saturn-Neptune themes in Keane's music.

The song also presents words and images from fairytales to convey a longing for redemption and the restoration of the lost life, now fallen and buried in the depths—under the iron sea.

> Oh, crystal ball, crystal ball
> Save us all, tell me life is beautiful,
> Mirror, mirror on the wall.[35]

Similarly, in "Is It Any Wonder?" the sense of confusion and self-loss give rise to the experience of being trapped in the wrong time:

> But sometimes
> I get the feeling that I'm
> Stranded in the wrong time
> Where love is just a lyric in a children's rhyme.[36]

Remarkably, almost identical themes were portrayed in the acclaimed British television miniseries *Life on Mars* from the same year (broadcast January 2006 to April 2007, during the same Saturn-Neptune world transit), starring John Simm as Detective Inspector Sam Tyler. Set in Manchester, England, the series explores Tyler's attempt to make sense of his reality after waking from a car accident to find himself some thirty years earlier in time, in what appears to be 1973. The premise of the show is that Tyler is "trapped in the wrong time," and must figure out what he needs to do to return to his life in the 2000s.[37] As he struggles to accept the often disturbing, yet nostalgically familiar and poignant, reality in which he finds himself, he comes to doubt the very basis of his existence, wondering if he has gone insane or is trapped in a coma or has died. The grim, often brutal, reality of 1973 in northern England is so different from the modern world he knew before the accident that it is as if he has woken up on Mars—hence the name of the show, which is accompanied by David Bowie's song of the same name (which was released as a single in the UK in 1973). As in the lyrics of the Keane song quoted above, Tyler does not know if he is "even here" in any real sense. In episode two of the first season, he stares in the mirror while shaving, wondering who he is, with the sense that his former life and identity are falling away, lost in time. The given facts of his experience are all subject to considerable doubt and uncertainty—a theme often accompanying Saturn-Neptune transits. Unsurprisingly, to his police colleagues in 1973 Tyler appears confused, in the grip of psychopathology, afflicted by nightmares and dark states of consciousness, with medical treatment in the future 2000s (as we witness in certain episodes) leaving him impaired and heavily medicated, in a stupor—Saturn is manifest here as the problem, Neptune the medication and altered state of consciousness. Indeed, also prevalent during transits between Neptune and Saturn, notably during personal transits between these planets, is the occurrence of mysterious, hard-to-diagnose illnesses that leave one feeling sick, weary, fatigued, confused, and perhaps therefore dispirited, doubting everything that formerly seemed secure and true.[38]

Chart 38

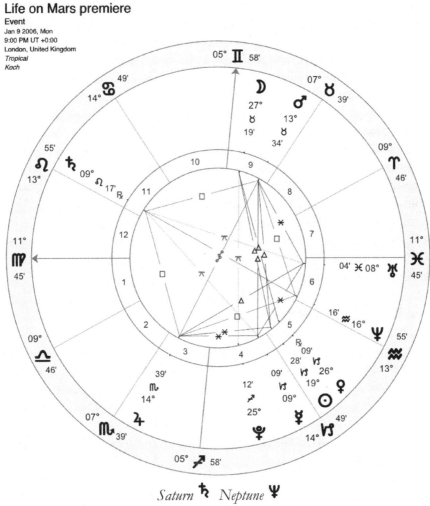

Event chart for the premiere of Life on Mars, *June 9, 2006.*

Throughout the two seasons, the Saturn-Neptune themes are as numerous as they are pervasive: the loss of faith and struggle to maintain faith in spite of the nightmarish or surreal reality in which Tyler finds himself, the fading dream and hope of a return to his life in the future, the doubt as to the reality of his existence, the problematic consequences of drugs and medication, the poignant sense of revisiting his past and meeting his mother and long-estranged father, feeling haunted by old memories, the utter confusion as to what is real and what illusory (with the world of 1973 eventually taking on a greater reality than his previous life in the 2000s), a pervasive paranoia (with some justification) that he is being watched and in communication with unseen powers, and the sense of self-loss and alienation from all he formerly took to be certain and true as he continually has to commit to a reality he does not believe to be real.

In a related theme to Bergman's "The Artistic Haunting," *Life on Mars* ends with Tyler, having returned to the 2000s, now unable to accept that reality, and choosing to take his own life, to die or hospitalize himself again, in order to return to the now more-real world of 1973—death as the means of transcendence of this world and an escape into a more ideal or truer existence. Behind these themes lies the religious-metaphysical drama depicted in the biblical Fall of Man, marking the exile from the idyllic paradise of Eden into the suffering and alienation of ego-consciousness. In one possible expression of Saturn-Neptune, the return to paradise or entrance to heaven is to be realized through death—or is it?

The Poignant Passing of Time

Identifying Saturn-Neptune themes in Keane's lyrics and elsewhere invites comparison again with Bergman's treatment of these kinds of experiences. His *Wild Strawberries* (1957), for instance, begins by taking us into the jarring nightmare of Isak Borg (played by Victor Sjöström), a retired doctor who is soon to be awarded a prestigious honorary degree at Lund Cathedral, in recognition of his long service, commemorating fifty years since he received his first doctorate. Borg's disturbing dream, in the opening sequence of that film, sets the tone for the entire narrative and presages it symbolically. As a horse-drawn funeral carriage crashes into a roadside lamppost, dislodging the lid of a coffin as it falls onto the street, the dream introduces Borg to his own dead self, stirring within the coffin, with the corpse reaching out to grab Borg by the hand, as if to force him to face himself—those parts that were seemingly dead or disowned, in his shadow. Thus we see Saturn as the shadow and death manifest in the Neptunian realm of the dream. Here, in another expression of a Saturn-Neptune theme, the clock time of Chronos is dissolved, suggested by the appearance in the dream of a clock and a watch without hands.

Saturn-Neptune themes are notably manifest in the experience of the poignant, and the act of looking back, in nostalgia for the past, or in lament for the life one might have lived and the precious dreams that are lost, forever gone into the mists of time, or unattainable ideals that were forsaken in meeting the practical realities of life. Neptune gives the imagination for and sensitivity to the Saturnian experience of ending, loss, and passing. The revisiting of times past, imagined as a very real experience, was the core idea behind *Wild Strawberries*. "So it struck me," Bergman reflected, "—what if you could . . . just walk up in a realistic way and open a door, and then you walk into your childhood, and then you open another door and come back to reality, and then you make a turn around a street corner and arrive in some other period of your existence, and everything goes on, lives."[39] The return to the past and the witnessing of the events of childhood and young adulthood in *Wild Strawberries* are at once movingly poignant, as Isak laments what might have been, and painful, for they compel him to face the bittersweet memories of his life and to come to terms with the flaws in his character, especially his selfish hard-heartedness, which stand in stark contrast to the image of him as an esteemed doctor, revered in the community. Here again we meet the Saturn-Neptune theme of the contrast between image and reality, with the benevolent persona (of the "world's best doctor") cloaking the painful reality of the unacknowledged and integrated shadow. The film essentially explores Isak standing in judgment of himself as he moves, by the end of the film, towards compassionate acceptance of his life.

Love's Dreams and Reality
Similar themes present themselves in the music of Joni Mitchell, who has a Venus-Neptune conjunction in a square alignment with Saturn. Especially prominent is the contrast between the fairytale romantic ideal and the reality of love relationships, as in "Willy" from *Ladies of the Canyon*:

> Willy is my joy, he is my sorrow
> Now he wants to run away and hide
> He says our love cannot be real
> He cannot hear the chapel's pealing silver bells
> But you know it's hard to tell
> When you're in the spell if it's wrong or if it's real
> But you're bound to lose
> If you let the blues get you scared to feel.[40]

Chart 39

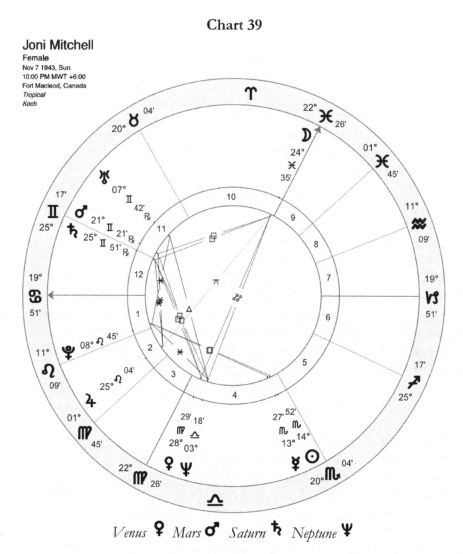

Venus ♀ *Mars* ♂ *Saturn* ♄ *Neptune* ♆

As we have seen, by itself Venus-Neptune, in one form of expression, is associated with the fairytale romantic imagination, inspiring dreams of true love, and the experience of the magic and wonder of love. But here, with Saturn in relationship to Joni Mitchell's Venus-Neptune complex, we find instead the questioning of the reality of love, with her beloved in the song unable to believe in or experience the fairytale romantic quality of Venus-Neptune. The song addresses too the experience of being caught in the spell of romance—with Saturn, as judge and reality principle, doubting whether the enchantment of the love experience, associated with Venus-Neptune, is to be trusted. Is this experience to be believed in, or is one to fall back into a more pragmatic and realistic Venus-Saturn reality? We might call to mind here Billy Joel's treatment of Venus-Saturn themes, including self-protectiveness in love based on past disappointments and wounding that prevent the opening of the heart to new romantic possibilities. Joni Mitchell brings these themes into relationship with the Venus-Neptune fairytale romance and the Moon-Saturn theme of being "scared to feel."

She reveals different inflections of the Venus-Saturn-Neptune archetypal configuration in other songs. "Tin Angel," the first track on the album *Clouds*, gives an interesting twist, for it describes the loss of the fairytale valentine's romantic dream with the entrance into the imperfect reality of a relationship with a man who falls far short of her dreamed-of prince. The dream, the idealized fantasy or memory of love, is traded for the concrete attainment of a real relationship. Ironically, then, in finding love, Mitchell mourns the loss of her romantic fantasy—with the experience of mourning also expressing the Saturn-Neptune complex:

> Letters from across the seas
> Roses dipped in sealing wax
> Valentines and maple leaves
> Tucked into a paperback.
> Guess I'll throw them all away
> I found someone to love today.
>
> Dark with darker moods is he
> Not a golden Prince who's come
> Through columbines and wizardry
> To talk of castles in the sun.[41]

Obviously, what cannot be conveyed in any textual analysis of this kind, but what is absolutely essential to grasping the archetypal quality of astrological configurations, is the experience of listening to the music or watching the film, which makes possible a far fuller, more vivid entrance into an archetypal reality than can be evoked by words alone. The music of "Tin Angel," for example, can stir the mood and feel of Saturn-Neptune—of dark mystery, perhaps disturbing, or melancholic and mournful, or bitter-sweet, tinged with poignancy.

The River of Death

A retrospective glance at other world-transit alignments of Saturn and Neptune reveals the prominent expression of many of these themes across the culture at those times. For example, it was during the Saturn-Neptune opposition of the early 1970s that Richard Adams published *Watership Down*, telling the adventures of a colony of rabbits. During the next hard-aspect alignment between these two planets, the square of 1978–1980, a film version of the book was released (October 19, 1978), together with Art Garfunkel's "Bright Eyes," a single from the soundtrack (released 1979), which remained at the top of the UK singles chart for six weeks.[42] The book, film, and song all convey the heartbreaking poignancy of the fate of the rabbits, dealing with themes of death, loss, and pain, as in the following lyrics:

> Is it a kind of a dream
> Floating out on the tide
> Following the river of death downstream
> Oh, is it a dream?
>
> There's a fog along the horizon
> A strange glow in the sky
> And nobody seems to know where it goes
> And what does it mean?[43]

These lines from "Bright Eyes" convey well the Saturn-Neptune feelings and motifs in the song and film: the questioning of the reality and meaning of a dark vision (is it real or a dream?), the image of the "river of death," and the mourning for the tragic fading of life and light from the once vital but now wounded hero-rabbit Hazel, with the suggestion that what seems like the final reality of death might prove itself to be part of the great dream of life.

The Saturn-Neptune world transit of the early 1970s also coincided with the release of Don McLean's "American Pie" (in October 1971), mourning the tragically young deaths of Buddy Holly, Ritchie Valens, and the Big Bopper (Jiles Perry Richardson, Jr.) in a plane crash in February 1959, and lamenting the passing of the idealism of the early rock-and-roll era in American culture. Tarnas has noted the connection between Saturn-Neptune world transits and the experience of collective mourning, as accompanied the deaths of President John F. Kennedy and Princess Diana of Wales, both occurring during Saturn-Neptune hard-aspect alignments.[44]

Chart 40

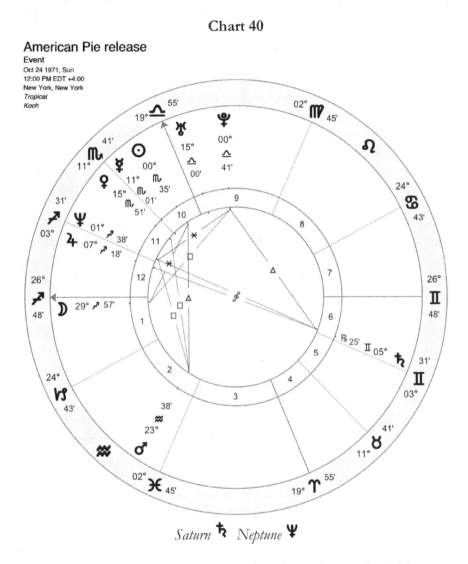

The above is the event chart for the release of "American Pie" by Don McLean on October 24, 1971 during a Saturn-Neptune opposition.

The assassinations of two of the Kennedy brothers in the 1960s—John F. Kennedy in 1963 and Robert F. Kennedy in 1968, while campaigning for the Democratic Party presidential nomination—marked the end of an idealistic era in US politics, with the curtailed

John F. Kennedy presidency later mythologized as a modern-day Camelot. Both Kennedy brothers had major natal aspects between Saturn and Neptune: John the conjunction, Robert the square. And both assassinations took place under world transits between Saturn and Neptune: John's in November 1963 during a Saturn-square-Neptune alignment; Robert's in June 1968 when Saturn was quincunx to Neptune, two degrees from exact.

Over fifty years later, one of Robert's sons, Robert F. Kennedy, Jr, ran his own campaign as an independent candidate for the 2024 US presidential election, based in part on an attempt to reconnect to the lost idealism of the Sixties, to recover the American Dream for the working and middle classes, and restore the spiritual and moral vitality and the physical wellbeing of the nation—all themes connected to the Saturn-Neptune complex.

Kennedy, Jr., has a natal Saturn-Neptune conjunction, with both planets square to his Sun, providing us, therefore, with an excellent example of a range of expression of the corresponding planetary archetypes, in relation to other prominent archetypal factors symbolized in his chart. Surveying major themes of his life experiences and his presidential campaign will allow us to draw together our analyses of the Saturn and Neptune principles and to examine further their modes of interaction.

Spiritual Heroism, Recovery, and Restoration of Lost Ideals

In addition to the Saturn-Neptune aspect, Kennedy's birth chart (Chart 41) is distinguished by a Sun-Uranus-Neptune T-square—comprising a Sun-Uranus opposition, with Neptune square to both of these planets. The course of his biography and the fundamental orientation of his personality exhibit characteristic themes and traits of the Sun-Neptune complex. Belonging to the most famous, most idealized, family in American politics, and with a life therefore lived in the public eye, in the wake of the assassinations of his uncle and father Kennedy fell into heroin addiction, which lasted for fourteen years. "I became a drug addict when I was fifteen years old," he confessed, "about a year after my dad died." His life therefore mirrored the Sun-Neptune archetypal pattern of idealization, escapism, and dissolution or disintegration, discussed earlier, with drugs offering an escape from his suffering, anxiety, and feelings of discomfort, which he was unable or unwilling to be with. The addiction pulled him away from the religious practices and principles of his youth. He had been raised in a pious religious environment of Irish Catholicism, with prayers after meals, recitations of the rosary each day, bible readings, and church visits for Mass, but his sense of God faded during his addiction and became a "distant concept," he noted.[45] "When you're an addict you're living against conscience ... you push God to the peripheries of your life."[46]

Kennedy was striving to get off drugs, but he could not break his drug habit through an act of will, even though he reports having "iron willpower as a kid." He had "tried everything [to stop] for a decade," but he was confounded and defeated by the addiction. Neptune, as we have seen, can lead to the experience of surrender—a "defeat for the ego," as Jung put it, as a prelude to the emergence of the Self as something like God within. In certain cases addiction can serve to effect this kind of surrender.

Kennedy recognized that the path to sobriety would entail a fundamental reorientation. He was to be inspired by the religious conversion of a friend, a fellow drug addict, who was totally cured, left with no desire whatsoever to take drugs. "I wanted to completely realign my self, so [that] I was somebody who got up every day and just didn't want to take drugs," Kennedy explains. He was seeking a "spiritual realignment, a transformation." He referenced St Augustine, St Paul, and St Francis as examples of figures who had undergone just this kind of conversion experience. At that time, when he was consumed by the yearning to be cured of his addiction, wondering how it could happen, he experienced a synchronicity, fittingly involving Jung's book *Synchronicity: An Acausal Connecting Principle*. "I picked it up off a table; I don't know who left it there." Reading the book, he came to understand synchronicity as "a way that God intervened in our lives that broke all the rules of nature." It was his "first real exposure" to Jung. "The reason I read that book," he adds, "is because The Police had an album out by the same name."[47] Experiencing the synchronicity led him to Jung's autobiography *Memories, Dreams, Reflections*.[48] This episode precipitated Kennedy's spiritual reorientation around this time, and his yearning to be free of addiction was then effortlessly realized: "I had a spiritual awakening and my desire for drugs and alcohol was lifted miraculously, and to me it was as much a miracle as if I'd been able to walk on water."[49]

In Volume III, we will explore in some detail both the Sun-Uranus themes of sudden awakening and liberation and the Uranus-Neptune themes of the religious epiphany and startling experiences of synchronicity (the "miracle" in Kennedy's remark)—which together came to manifestation in his spiritual awakening. He was led, through the addiction and the miraculous emancipation from it, to the discovery of a spiritual orientation to life, reflecting a central dimension of a Sun-Neptune pattern.

His experience of the Sun-Neptune complex, however, was significantly colored by the Saturn archetype, as we would expect given his natal Saturn-Neptune conjunction. In the tragic loss of his uncle and father as a child, and the pervasive confusion and suspicion as to what is really true about the causes and circumstances of their deaths, the young Kennedy was exposed to major themes of the Saturn-Neptune complex. As an adult, he was led to doubt, question, and ultimately reject the accepted narratives about both assassinations.

Chart 41

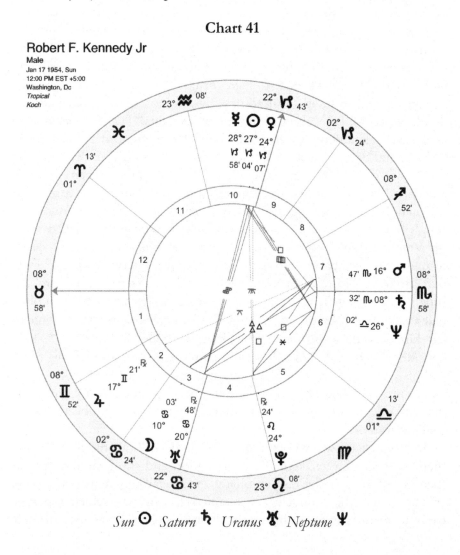

Sun ☉ *Saturn* ♄ *Uranus* ♅ *Neptune* ♆

His encounter with the problematic side of drugs, which led to his arrest and prosecution for possession, and his long struggle for sobriety were further expressions of the Saturn-Neptune combination. So too was his spirituality, which at first had a pragmatic caste. He was struck by the fact that people who believe in God have a better chance of a faster and more successful, more enduring recovery than people who do not—he thus had a practical reason to believe. "If believing in God was gonna help me . . . then I was going to do that," he explained, irrespective of whether God really exists.[50]

During an interview in 2024, in response to the questions "what is your understanding of God?" and "who is God?," Kennedy elaborated:

> How do you start believing in something that you can't see or smell or hear or touch or taste or acquire with your senses? . . . Jung provides the formula for that, and he says "act as if"—you fake it 'til you make it, and so that's, you know, what I started doing: I just started pretending there was a God watching me all the time and . . . life was a series of tests and there was a bunch of moral decisions that I had to make every day. And if I make a whole bunch of those choices right, I maintain myself in a posture of surrender, which keeps me open to my higher power like to my God. . . . So much about addiction is about abuse of power. All of us have some power, whether it's, you know, good looks or whether it's connections or education or family or whatever, and there's always a temptation to use those to fulfill self-will. And the challenge is how do you use those always to serve instead God's will and you know the good of our community and that to me is kind of the struggle. And when I do that I feel God's power coming through me and that I can do things, I'm much more effective as a human being. That gnawing anxiety that I lived with for so many years in my gut, it's gone, and that I can kind of like put down the oars and hoist the sail, and the wind takes me, and I can see the evidence of it every day of my life.[51]

In another interview, Kennedy commented that he was able to relate to the tentative "act as if" approach, whereas at that time he would have been unable to accept a stronger assertion of the validity of the existence of God.[52] The metaphysical agnosticism he found in Jung's approach to religious phenomena—bracketing the question of whether God really exists and focusing on the psychological reality and empirical value of belief or transcendent spiritual experience—resonated with his own position at that time, and was therefore just what he needed to read at that moment.

In Kennedy's remarks, above, we may recognize the Sun-Neptune gift for acting and "pretending there was a God watching me" as a variation, one might say, of the *imitatio Christi*, with the Saturnian element manifest in the pragmaticism of the belief and the sense of his every move being watched and judged—an expression of the super-ego theme we saw in our earlier discussion of the Sun-Saturn complex. This complex is plainly evident too in the conceptualization of life in terms of "tests" and "moral decisions," like the wise old man testing the fortitude and character of the hero. On another occasion, he remarked, "the trick to life is to not have expectations but just to know what your duty is and to do it," further expressing the Sun-Saturn quality of doing one's duty and meetings one's responsibilities (in this case to God).

The surrender to a higher power, the sacrifice of self-will in favor of God's will, and the experience of being in the Tao-like flow of life express perfectly the kind of spiritual orientation that is befitting of the Sun-Neptune complex, bringing Kennedy relief from his Saturnian struggle and "gnawing anxiety." Kennedy's ongoing spiritual challenge, he remarked, is to "maintain that posture of surrender"[53] even when good things happen, "when the cash and prizes are flowing into your life"[54] and the need for divine guidance and support are therefore diminished—a Saturnian dedication to the Sun-Neptune act of surrender to a higher spiritual power.[55]

Thereafter, Kennedy made his spiritual realignment central to his life. After his arrest in September 1983, he committed to rehab in the 12-step program created by Alcoholics Anonymous—these events taking place in coincidence with his Saturn return in his late twenties and a Saturn personal transit to his Neptune.[56] He has followed the 12-step program now for 40 years. "It is a central organizing principle of my life," he notes. His commitment to this path includes attending daily meetings and "doing my meditations while I hike," which helps him "stay on a spiritual keel" and "walk with one foot in the material world and the other in the spiritual world"—with Saturn and Neptune both appeased, one might say.[57] As we have seen, the Saturn-Neptune complex is associated with sobering up, literally and metaphorically, with Saturn as the reality principle meeting and challenging the Neptunian tendency towards escape, avoidance, and delusion. It is associated, too, with spiritual discipline and the intersection of spirit and matter—themes captured well by Kennedy's words.

In facing the challenge of sobriety, Kennedy drew sustenance from a line in Isaiah (40:31): "Be still and know that I am God." "That had a huge impact on me," he reports. Attuning to this stillness, accepting discomfort, allowing it to pass through him without striving to fix it, was an approach central to his spiritual resolution of his addiction. He goes as far to assert that being still, he believed, "should be ultimately the ambition of a spiritual enlightenment."[58]

Referring again to the relationship of the planetary archetypes to the basic perinatal matrices (BPMs) of Grofian psychology, the Saturn-Neptune complex is connected, Grof and Tarnas have shown, to the experience of a toxic womb—when the Neptunian aquatic intrauterine existence in the womb is adversely effected by drugs or medicines in the mother's bloodstream, such that the fetus's environment is experienced as poisoned. As described in Grof's summary:

> In both its positive and negative forms, the first perinatal matrix (BPM I) is unmistakably reflective of the archetype that astrologers link to Neptune. The positive aspect of BPM I includes the reliving of episodes of undisturbed intrauterine existence, as well as the concomitant experiences of dissolution of boundaries, interpersonal fusion experiences, oceanic ecstasy, cosmic feelings of unity, transcendence of time and space, and awareness of the mystical and numinous dimensions of reality. The negative aspects of BPM I are associated with regressive experiences of prenatal disturbances. Here the dissolution of boundaries is not mystical but psychotic in nature; it leads to confusion, delusion, a sense of chemical poisoning, bizarre metaphysical distortions, and paranoid perceptions of reality. This matrix also has a psychodynamic connection with alcoholic or narcotic intoxication and addiction.[59]

Due to its association with the problematic, restrictive, and fearful side of life, the archetypal influence of Saturn inclines towards the negative aspects of BPM I, described by Grof. This association is borne out in worldly affairs in the correspondence between Saturn-Neptune alignments and toxic poisoning, pollution, and the problematic side of pharmaceutical drugs and vaccines, all of which have been central preoccupations in Kennedy's life.

Following his spiritual reorientation and period in rehab, Kennedy went on to develop a successful career as a lawyer, prosecuting high-profile cases against corporations responsible for polluting the nation's waterways and poisoning its people. Having been sentenced to hundreds of hours community service, he worked as an environmental lawyer for Hudson River Foundation, later becoming its chief prosecuting attorney. He then helped form Waterkeeper Alliance in the early 1990s, protecting the country's waterways from corporate pollution and poisoning. A 2008 article in *Vanity Fair* summarizes Kennedy's role within a subsidiary, the Hudson Riverkeeper:

> Kennedy's early work with Hudson Riverkeeper set lasting standards for environmental law and inspired the creation of hundreds of similar organizations throughout the United States and abroad, helping to fuel the keeper movement. With Hudson Riverkeeper and the National Resources Defense Council, he won historic victories against massive corporate polluters such as Con Edison and General Electric, forcing the former to abandon development plans that would have destroyed critical spawning grounds and the latter to contribute to cleanup efforts for P.C.B.s [polychlorinated biphenyls] and other poisons dumped in the river. He also led negotiations on a crucial watershed agreement providing reservoirs for New York City's drinking water, now regarded as an international model in sustainable development.[60]

Outside of environmental protection, among his most notable legal cases is the Monsanto "Roundup" weed-killer litigation, representing people suffering from cancer and other health issues caused by chemicals in the product. Kennedy initially won a claimant a $289 million payout in compensation, which led to further awards of billions of dollars. For over twenty years, he also led a sustained campaign against pollution by factory farming. An advocate for renewable energy, he fought against the oil, coal, nuclear, and gas industries, and against the building of new pipelines. And as an environmental attorney, he fought for the cause of poor and oppressed communities, in New York City, Chicago and elsewhere. He was then a powerful advocate for indigenous people's rights in Chile, Quebec, Ecuador, and Mexico. At the time, he was lauded for his environmental work by *Time*, *Rolling Stone*, and *People* magazines, and became an idealized figure, especially in the eyes of the liberal establishment. Indeed, *Time* named Kennedy a

"Hero for the Planet" because of his efforts to clean up the Hudson River, in stark contrast to how he would later be depicted.⁶¹

These examples serve to illustrate Kennedy's practical idealism, that is, practical action suffused with a spiritual vision and idealism—the Saturn-Neptune theme of "spirit in the world," we encountered earlier. The impulse to conserve, protect, and hold accountable through law arises from the Saturn archetype in service of the Neptunian capacity to sympathetically identify with the plight and suffering of individuals, groups of people, and nature at large. A motivation arising out of the complex is to protect or restore a state of purity—the innocent womblike condition of BPM I.

Themes associated with the Saturn-Neptune complex also come to the fore in Robert Kennedy, Jr's stance on childhood vaccinations and other pharmaceutical interventions. Kennedy reports being influenced by groups of mothers whose children developed serious injuries and medical conditions, such as severe autism, after vaccinations. The mothers would regularly attend his talks, beseeching him to investigate on their behalf. Eventually taking up their cause, after initial reluctance, Kennedy went on to establish what would become the Children's Health Defense. In challenging the safety of vaccines, highlighting possible links to autism and other conditions, Kennedy was condemned by many in the mainstream media and scientific establishment, and branded a "conspiracy theorist," a peddler of debunked or dangerous claims, even a "crank." From the perspective of many others, however, he was a champion of the truth, exposing ignorance and delusion about vaccine safety and the undue influence of the pharmaceutical industry within medical regulation and government policies. One way or another—whether in connection with the assassinations of his father and uncle, or in connection with vaccines or suspicions about the motives of those in positions of power—the attempt to determine truth from deception has been a central theme of his life experience, corresponding with the Saturn-Neptune conjunction in his birth chart.

Kennedy came to greater prominence and public awareness during the Covid-19 pandemic with his protest against government mandates, particularly vaccine mandates, and government-directed media censorship of free speech in relation to this issue. (He successfully sued the Biden administration for censoring his own social-media posts.) He also took aim at Anthony Fauci, then the Chief Medical Advisor to the US government, who had dubiously positioned himself in the role of scientific savior as the pandemic unfolded, with Kennedy (and others) exposing as questionable, misleading, or even false Fauci's assertions and denials on Covid-19's origins, his role in supporting gain-of-function research at Wuhan, his ever-shifting statements about vaccine safety and effectiveness, his dismissal of alternative medical treatments, and his pronouncements about the effectiveness of masking and distancing policies. Many of these claims are detailed in Kennedy's exposé *The Real Anthony Fauci*. Kennedy's stance on this issue feeds into and reflects a wider skepticism about truth as propounded in mainstream narratives and a pervasive distrust of government agencies.

As a result of his views on Covid, one can scarcely encounter Robert F. Kennedy, Jr's name today without it being attached to the label "anti-vaxxer." Routinely smeared by large sections of the mainstream media and by the political and scientific establishment for, in their eyes, promoting misinformation and conspiracy theories, Kennedy has been forced to stand his ground in the face of fierce, often *ad hominen* attacks.[62] (Other archetypal factors are also at work here, not least those associated with his Mars square to Pluto, to be considered in the next volume, and his Mars-Saturn conjunction.)

Especially prominent in Kennedy's life and personality is the Sun-Uranus outsider theme, associated with his Sun-Uranus opposition. His experience of being an outsider or an unusual individual, at odds with dominant narratives and consensus opinion, and sometimes flouting accepted norms of behavior, is coupled with experiences correlating with his Sun and Venus square to Saturn: becoming publicly isolated from his family and friends, and being smeared and attacked by the mainstream media, and being rejected and ostracized by the ruling powers of the Democratic Party. He had to accept such estrangement, criticism, and hostility as essential elements of his spiritual mission (his "dharma," as he put it in one interview), drawing comparison with the similar fates suffered by inspirational figures that he admired, such as Augustine, Francis of Assisi, Lincoln, and Churchill. As we will consider in Volume III, the Sun-Uranus complex is associated with the experience of going one's own way in life and following one's unique path, breaking with the common crowd and with social expectation.

His experiences during the Covid-19 pandemic, especially getting "de-platformed" and witnessing the covert widescale censorship of free speech, contributed to his decision to run for president in 2024. Ultimately, having been censored and kept off the debate stage by the Democratic Party, he felt compelled to join forces with the Republican Trump campaign, under the slogan "Make America Healthy Again."

We will explore the astrological background to the pandemic, and the commitment to free speech and the espousing of radical ideas, associated with Kennedy's Mercury-Uranus opposition, in Volume III. Here, we will concern ourselves with the ongoing expression of Kennedy's Sun-Neptune idealistic heroism and the Saturn-Neptune flavor of his pitch for the presidency, especially his focus on America's distance from its past ideals and his aspiration to restore them.

His candidacy exemplified multiple dimensions of the Saturn-Neptune complex. Most notable initially was his focus on the need to recover America's lost ideals, drawing contrast between the political idealism of the 1960s, during his uncle's presidency and father's candidacy, and the corruption, decline, forlorn hopelessness, and malaise of contemporary America in the 2020s, particularly afflicting America's youth: "We're in a spiritual dead zone right now where we have a whole generation of kids who are feeling alienated, dispossessed, disconnected from any feeling of community, and the beginning of spiritual renewal is restoring that sense of community." The language—the "spiritual dead zone"—reveals the Saturnian coloring of Neptune, as does the dark vision of the zeitgeist.

Again illustrating the Saturn-Neptune theme of the problematic side of drugs and medication, Kennedy highlighted a tragic consequence of the dispiriting alienation of America's youth: drug addiction and death from overdose. We are "losing 110,000 kids a year from overdose," he disclosed, as he bemoaned the "levels of mental illness" and "dependence on psychiatric drugs." "The drug industry," he adds, "sells 120 million doses of SSRI's [antidepressants] every year and 120 million doses of Benzos [anti-anxiety sedatives] and another 118 million doses of ADHD medication, of Adderall, of Concerta, Ritalin. . . . That's more than a prescription for every single American." To combat this, Kennedy pledged to set up healing centers to deliver free of charge care to those with addiction.[63]

Other major elements of his campaign were a focus on cleaning up air, waters, and food supplies, to address the "chronic health epidemic" arising from toxic and technological poisoning; and tackling corruption in the form of "corporate capture" of government agencies by big business, especially the pharmaceutical industry. In a campaign missive of October 2024, he announced: "And let me tell you one other kind of pollution I'm going to help get rid of. It is the pollution of our government agencies by corporate money. It's called, corruption. When Big Pharma money, Big Ag money, and Big Tech money pollutes

Washington DC, it's not long before their chemicals pollute the entire country."[64] Thus we see a continuation of the Saturn-Neptune themes of toxicity, drug abuse, poisoning, and corruption, which Kennedy sought to clean up in service of the restoration of America's forsaken ideals.

In a campaign video, released after securing ballot access in California for the 2024 election, Kennedy put forward his vision of "a symbol of America's homecoming to an authentic populism of unity, peace, and prosperity. . . . [and] a return to the Kennedy vision where the government serves the people, people serve one another, and our nation serves its idealistic mission as an exemplary nature, an example of democracy around the globe."[65]

> If we want to meet our obligation as a generation, as a civilization, as a nation, which is to create communities for our children that provide them with the same opportunities for dignity and enrichment and prosperity and good health as the communities that our parents gave us, we've got to start by protecting our environmental infrastructure: the air we breathe, the water we drink, the wildlife, the fisheries, the public lands—those things that are not reducible to private property but by their nature are the property of all of us the commons, the commonwealth, the landscapes, the waterways, that connect us to the 10,000 generations of human beings that lived before there were laptops and that ultimately connect us to God. And God talks to human beings through many vectors: through each other, through organized religion, through the great books of those religions, through wise people, through art and music and literature and poetry, but nowhere with such detail and grace and color and joy as through creation; and when we when we destroy a species and we destroy a special place we're diminishing our capacity to sense the divine, to understand who God is and what our own potential is as human beings. Father Martin once told me that the definition of sin is an injury to another human being or to God, to our relationship with God. And my children are going to grow up in a world where they will never see the kind of explosions of color from butterflies that I saw every time I walked into my garden because 80 or 90% of the butterflies are gone. . . [They] will never hear the song birds that I heard; they're not going to see that in their lifetime; they're unaware of it. And it's like God is a tapestry and he's talking to us from all of these different vectors and we're

pulling threads out of that capacity and it is such a crime against our children.⁶⁶

The speech showcases Kennedy as a spiritual and moral leader in the sphere of politics, with the overt Sun-Neptune attunement to the spiritual dimension of life channeled into a practical form of expression, under the influence of the archetypal Saturn. In this speech and many others, Kennedy also occupies the Sun-Saturn role of judge, urging the meeting of responsibilities and obligations, standing in judgment of his country and its failings, decrying the tragic loss of nature's full expression, with its diversity and splendor now in a sad decline.

The Sun-Saturn complex is apparent, too, in the experience of the absent father, with Kennedy, Jr, growing up in the shadow of his father and uncle, whose early deaths effectively froze them and their ideals in time. Their lives, and their absence, shaped his personality, with his political aspirations tapping into the mystique of the Camelot myth and his quest to resurrect the spirit of their generation. The Saturn archetype, one might say, manifest as the missing father and as the connection to tradition and past generations, was eternalized and mythologized by Neptune—a pattern that came to define the expression of Kennedy's life, associated with the Sun. As James Billot observes for *Unherd*:

> The Camelot myth haunts Robert F. Kennedy Jr. He was brought up to believe that he would be the one to pick up the mantle left by Arthur, John F. Kennedy. Even as a precocious 20-year-old—having been hooked on hard drugs since 14, having been expelled from two boarding schools, and having faced a near-fatal heroin overdose—the young Bobby believed it was his "destiny" to be president. Fifty years later, aged 70, Robert F. Kennedy has finally thrown his hat into the ring. He wants to return America to its Camelot era—that brief period of hope and promise during his uncle's presidency—amid widespread disillusionment with the two main contenders for office.⁶⁷

The Camelot myth proved to be central to Kennedy's life orientation, expressing a key dimension of the Sun-Neptune theme of the mythologized heroic individual life, articulated and espoused by Joseph Campbell. "When my uncle was president," Kennedy noted in a campaign video, "everyone was talking about Camelot and I ended up reading a book about Camelot called *The Once and Future King* [by T. H. White]. It gave me the capacity to process pain in a different way"—the Saturnian element.[68] Reading this book seems to have shaped Kennedy's sense of heroic, spiritually informed purpose: "If you're going to do anything important with your life, there's going to be a hero's journey where you go through the valley of death and feel like you're completely alone."

The arc of Kennedy's life, in summary, illustrates in concrete terms the mythic and religious background of the Saturn-Neptune complex: the loss of a naïve or simple idealism, of a mythic golden age, which remains a nostalgic guiding ideal and reference point; confronting and seeking to rectify the fall into a spiritual wasteland of malaise, mistrust, toxicity, and corruption; the aspiration to purify the unclean and poisoned in the environment, society, and politics; and the skeptical questioning of false narratives, assumptions, and images in seeing through deception to truth. In the meeting of these planetary archetypes, the pure religious quality and ideals of Neptune are confronted by the tainted, fallen reality of the material world, associated with Saturn, with its loss, sufferings, and practical limitations, but also the sustained effort to make right our human failings in service of the ideal. The Saturn-Neptune complex thus traces an archetypal trajectory from disenchantment to re-enchantment, from spiritual alienation and loss of faith to renewal of belief and the effort to recover and restore a paradise lost.

Faith in Stone: Saturn-Neptune Personal Transits

Saturn-Neptune personal transits can indicate periods dominated by any number of these themes—such as lost ideals and lost dreams, with an accompanying sense of grief, mourning, deflation, defeat, loss of faith, and world-weariness. Such states of being are obviously detrimental to the more heroic dimension of individuation with its emphasis on self-overcoming, the sacrifice of one's life in the service of the Self, and the capacity to fulfill some world-historic calling. But the same experiences bring soul into our lives, through the imaginative feeling into and sensitivity to the sufferings and losses that impact all of us. The Saturn-Neptune complex affords us the rich experience of another dimension of the wholeness of the Self. A life lived only in terms of "spirit," fueled by a kind of Dionysian-Plutonic heroism, can leave one feeling scorched, hollow, and empty. The Saturn-Neptune complex, for all its association with melancholy states, is a necessary complement to individuation conceived and lived only as heroic transformation.[69] Unsurprisingly, this complex is prominent in the life and work of James Hillman, who critiqued and rejected the heroic dimension of individuation and the realization of the Self, focusing instead, as we have seen, on pathos and pathology as a portal to soul-making.

In general, personal transits of Neptune to any planet can coincide with periods in which the spiritual dimension of life is accentuated in one way or another. The effect of the activation of the Neptune archetype during these transits is to shroud certain aspects of our experience in magic or mystery and make them more alluring. It can also cloud and confuse our judgment and impede clear perception, weaken and dissolve our will and strength, then help us to integrate and synthesize, to form unities from differentiated parts or to come to new spiritual insights, values, and ways of being. When Neptunian energies are constellated during transits, they can stir our imaginative faculties and the flow of fantasy, accompany a yearning for escape and transcendence, and make us more sensitive to life, introducing us to subtle realms of experience, and to the reality of spirit in a transition towards refined and spiritual modes of living and acting.

During a personal transit between Saturn and Neptune, the Saturnian hard facts can confront and expose our idealistic projections, associated with Neptune. That which we had once idealized—people, places, movements, beliefs, and more—may become the source of disillusionment, revealing their shortcomings and failings. This can obviously have a dispiriting impact on us, but it is not without purpose, for it reveals false securities and projections and can contribute to a leave-taking of those images and idols that keep us removed from an experience of life as it truly is.

Under these transits, one might also be motivated to make one's spiritual life more concrete, to give form to the symbolic meaning of one's experience. Thus, it was in 1923, during a long Neptune transit opposite to the natal position of Saturn, that Jung built the first section of his tower on Lake Zürich at Bollingen. It was here, through the structure itself and in engraved sculptures, he created physical monuments that conveyed the symbolism of the meaning of his life.

As Jung reports in *Memories, Dreams, Reflections*:

Gradually, through my scientific work, I was able to put my fantasies and the contents of the unconscious on solid footing. Words and paper, however, did not seem real enough to me; something more was needed. I had to achieve a kind of representation in stone of my innermost thoughts and of the knowledge I had acquired. Or, to put it another way, I had to make a confession of faith in stone. That was the beginning of "The Tower," the house that I built for myself at Bollingen.[70]

Chart 42

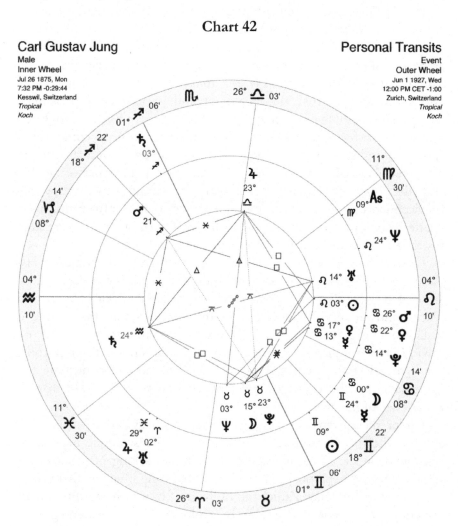

This personal transit chart for June 1, 1927 shows transiting Neptune ♆ (outer wheel) at 24 degrees Leo opposite Jung's natal Saturn ♄ (inner wheel) at 24 degrees Aquarius.

The "confession of faith in stone" captures exceptionally well the intersection of Neptunian and Saturnian themes and motifs.

Other themes were evident during the same transit in Jung's life. Not unlike Joseph Campbell's personal transit of Neptune to his natal Saturn, during his second Saturn return (see Chart 15), when he was so deeply affected by the mythos of the burial rites during the funeral of John F. Kennedy, Jung, in response to an episode of "haunting" in 1927, still during his Neptune transit to Saturn, staged his own burial rites upon the discovery at Bollingen of the skeleton of a fallen French soldier, with a bullet lodged in his elbow: "I arranged a regular burial on my property, and fired a gun three times over the soldier's grave. Then I set up a gravestone with an inscription for him."[71]

I mention these details to give an illustration of the manner in which specific themes become manifest and accentuated in a person's life during transits, even if the particular planets are not in major alignment in that person's birth chart. With an understanding of astrology, one can recognize the themes of Saturn-Neptune in multiple ways during Jung's life at the time and thus draw a connection between the events and their archetypal background: the urge to give concrete expression to the spirit and symbolism of one's life; the haunting presence of spirits (the "lament for the dead"); and the sanctification of death through funeral rites.[72]

During transits of Neptune to Saturn, the perception of the absence of spiritual values and meaning in one's daily life can give rise to the urge to make one's spiritual life an actual reality, to embody it in the way one lives day by day. These transits often initially accompany the realization of one's distance from the divine and a life of spiritual meaning, stirring the aspiration to close the gap between one's visions and ideals as to how one might live, or what life should or could be like, and the reality of how one's life actually is. The response to the perceived distance between spiritual needs and the way one is living can be, for instance, to establish a regular form of spiritual practice.

But equally, as we have seen, these transits can indicate moral disillusionment and defeat. Such experiences are themselves key elements of a spiritual life, of course. The mystical "dark night of the soul" is associated with Neptune transits to Saturn, accompanying the final agonizing death of the ego and all it held dear, when all hope of redemption and all saving thoughts must be forsaken. The things one had formally idealized, one's hopes and dreams, and every attempt to make sense of life and one's experience, and even one's ideas of God, are to be relinquished in this experience—for each may serve as props and devices of the ego and self-will, a final barrier to surrender to the divine. In the midst of these transits, it can seem as if we must exist without spiritual support and that all our former ideals dissolve such that there is nothing secure to cling to.

The intersection between these archetypal principles might also be understood alchemically, in the interrelated alchemical operations of *solutio* and *coagulatio*, captured in the axiom *solve et coagulatio* ("dissolve and coagulate"). Disillusionment, depression, defeat, and weariness are symptoms of the dissolution of the structure of one's life, the dissolution or disappearance of one's former certainty, the weakening of the will, the crumbling of the solid ground beneath one's feet. Yet from within the dissolving structures new psychic contents, insights, and aspects of oneself might then emerge as the psyche coagulates into a new form, only to dissolve again in an archetypal rhythm, like the lapping of the waves against rocks. After the intense struggle of individuation and rebirth, Neptune transits to Saturn can accompany periods less heroic and Dionysian in character, when that which was firmly established and set in one's life disintegrates and one's hold on that particular reality weakens. But a new reality is then formed in its place, perhaps more unified, with a gathering up and reintegration of lost and buried fragments of experience and personality.

In conclusion, the Saturn-Neptune complex is evident within an array of themes and types of experience that, on the one hand, often present obstacles to the ongoing unfolding of individuation but that, on the other, lend a poignant richness to the soul's experience, through pathos and tragedy, through loss and lament, through doubt and disillusionment. This particular combination of archetypes inwardly presses us to make our religious life or spiritual path actual, to develop and commit to a settled form, and thus to embody our highest values and ideals in the concrete acts of life such that the world of practical concerns becomes suffused with spiritual meaning and life gradually recovers its enchanted quality. It marks a progression from naïve ignorance into disenchantment, when the scales of illusion and false belief fall from our eyes, to the building and maintenance of faith in the darkest hours and on, potentially, to re-enchantment, with the recovery of the experience of spiritual meaning and soul in the realization of the symbolic life, and the bridging of the realms of the spiritual and the material, and the religious and the natural.

* * * * *

The Next Destination . . .

As we continue to traverse the archetypal worlds associated with the outer planets, it is to the infernal regions of the Plutonic instincts that we will journey next, in Volume III, there to encounter our devils and demons, compulsions and passions, and a source of primal life power. It is there, in the mythic underworld, that we might hope to recover from our depths the buried treasured of transformed selfhood.

Notes

[1] *Dumb and Dumber*, directed by Peter Farrelly (Burbank, CA: New Line Cinema, 1994).

[2] Wendy Michaels, "Why Jim Carrey Wrote Himself a $10 Million Check Before He Was Famous, Even Though He Was Broke," accessed November 21, 2021, https://www.cheatsheet.com/entertainment/why-jim-carrey-wrote-himself-a-10-million-check-before-he-was-famous.html/.

[3] *Bruce Almighty*, directed by Tom Shadyac (Universal Pictures, 2003).

[4] See my fuller analysis of the significance of the Jupiter-Neptune complex in Springsteen's song lyrics, in "Land of Hope and Dreams: An Archetypal Analysis of Bruce Springsteen's Song Lyrics (Part Two)," in *Cultural Crisis and Transformation, Archai: The Journal of Archetypal Cosmology*, 87–104. The content of this section is adapted from that article.

[5] Springsteen, "The Promised Land" on *Darkness on the Edge of Town*.

[6] Lyrics from "For You," on *Greetings from Asbury Park, New Jersey*.

[7] Springsteen, "Mary Queen on Arkansas" on *Greetings from Asbury Park, New Jersey*.

[8] Springsteen, "Born to Run" on *Born to Run*.

[9] Lyrics from Springsteen, "The Promised Land" on *Darkness on the Edge of Town*, and "Wild Billy's Circus Story" on *The Wild, the Innocent, and the E-Street Shuffle*.

[10] Lyrics from Springsteen, "Incident on 57th Street" on *The Wild, the Innocent, and the E-Street Shuffle* and "Born to Run" on *Born to Run*.

[11] Springsteen, "Land of Hope and Dreams" on *Live From New York City*.

[12] Springsteen, "Frankie" on *Tracks*.

[13] Springsteen, "Rosalita" on *The Wild, the Innocent, and the E-Street Shuffle*.

[14] Campbell, *Hero with a Thousand Faces*, 3–4.

[15] Campbell, with Bill Moyers, *Power of Myth*.

[16] Campbell, with Bill Moyers, *Power of Myth*.

[17] Campbell, with Bill Moyers, *Power of Myth*.

[18] A remark made by Campbell, with Bill Moyers, in *The Power of Myth* interviews.

[19] The haunting quality associated with Saturn-Neptune is well exemplified, in another form, by M. Night Shyamalan's *The Sixth Sense* (Buena Vista Pictures, 1999), in which a young boy, Cole Sear (played by Haley Joel Osment, with natal Saturn conjunct Neptune square to the Sun) is subject to haunting experiences of dead people, who occupy his normal reality. Shyamalan also has a Saturn-Neptune natal opposition.

[20] Bergman, *Through a Glass Darkly*.

[21] Bergman, *Through a Glass Darkly*.

[22] See, André Barbault, "The History of a Prediction," accessed January 6, 2022, http://cura.free.fr/quinq/02barbo.html.

[23] Bergman, *Through a Glass Darkly*.

[24] Bergman, *Through a Glass Darkly*.

[25] See Scott Hill's own archetypal astrological analysis of his series of "bad trips" in "A Vision of Redemption through Death," in *Beyond a Disenchanted Cosmology*, 127–152. See also Hill's *Confrontation with the Unconscious* for a careful examination of psychedelic experiences in relation to Jungian psychology.

[26] Hill, "A Vision of Redemption through Death," 128, 133. Hill also describes these experiences in *Confrontation with the Unconscious*.

[27] See Udiscovermusic, "'Under the Iron Sea': Inside Keane's Introspective Sophomore Set," accessed October 9, 2024, https://www.udiscovermusic.com/stories/keane-under-the-iron-sea-feature/.

[28] Keane, "Under the Iron Sea—A Message from the Band," Keane20 (April 19, 2006), accessed December 6, 2023, https://www.keanemusic.com/under-the-iron-sea-a-message-from-the-band.

[29] Keane, "Is It Any Wonder?" on *Under the Iron Sea* (Island Records, 2006).

[30] Keane, "Is It Any Wonder?" on *Under the Iron Sea* (Island Records, 2006).

[31] See Tarnas's two-part study "The Ideal and the Real: Saturn-Neptune" and "The Ideal and the Real (Part Two) in *Archai: The Journal of Archetypal Cosmology*, issues 1 and 2.

[32] Keane, "Bad Dream," on *Under the Iron Sea* (Island Records, 2006).

[33] These lyrics ("I lost my heart, I buried it too deep, under the iron sea") also reflect Tim Rice-Oxley's triple conjunction of Moon-Mars-Saturn. The Moon is associated with the heart and feeling, which can become inaccessible, blocked, or repressed under the archetypal influence of Saturn. Mars, in traditional astrology, is associated with iron. Additionally, Mars was in major hard aspect with Saturn and Neptune when the album was released.

[34] Keane, "Crystal Ball," on *Under the Iron Sea* (Island Records, 2006).

[35] Keane, "Crystal Ball," on *Under the Iron Sea* (Island Records, 2006).

[36] Keane, "Is It Any Wonder?," on *Under the Iron Sea* (Island Records, 2006).

[37] Graham, Jordan, and Pharoah, *Life on Mars* (Kudos/BBC television, 2006).

[38] Such conditions were explored in the popular television series *House* (NBC Universal Television, 2004), starring Hugh Laurie as medical diagnostician Gregory House. The show debuted in November 2004 as Saturn and Neptune

moved into alignment, and its audience peaked in the US and beyond during the remaining years of the Saturn-Neptune opposition between 2005 and 2008. House is addicted to pain-relief medication—another expression of a Saturn-Neptune theme, with Neptunian medication used to numb and escape Saturnian suffering. As in this example and in *Life on Mars*, experiences taking place during Neptune transits to Saturn can give rise to nebulous fears—some arising from circumstances, but some arising from phantasmagoria and nightmares, which veil the world in a dark distorting projection.

[39] "Wild Strawberries (1957): Trivia." on Internet Movie Database (IMDB), accessed November 29, 2021, https://www.imdb.com/title/tt0050986/trivia/?ref_=tt_trv_trv.

[40] Joni Mitchell, "Willy," on *Ladies of the Canyon*. See the Joni Mitchell website for lyrics to all her songs (https://jonimitchell.com/music/songlist.cfm).

[41] Joni Mitchell, "Tin Angel," on *Clouds*.

[42] Art Garfunkel has a natal Saturn-trine-Neptune alignment.

[43] Mike Batt (lyrics), "Bright Eyes" on Art Garfunkel, *Fate for Breakfast* (Columbia Records, 1979).

[44] See Tarnas, "The Ideal and the Real: Related Saturn-Neptune Patterns in History and Culture" (Part Two), in *Cultural Crisis and Transformation*.

[45] RFK, Jr. World Over interview with Raymond Arroyo, accessed April 27, 2024, https://www. youtube.com/watch?v=tjAFC6grOl4&t=65s.

[46] The Jimmy Dore Show: "How RFK Jr. Beat Addiction with Carl Jung!," accessed May 1,2024, https://www.youtube.com/watch?v=hAjwUtGjHd4&t=1007s.

[47] Jimmy Dore Show: "How RFK Jr. Beat Addiction with Carl Jung!."

[48] Jimmy Dore Show: "How RFK Jr. Beat Addiction with Carl Jung!."

[49] The Lex Friedman Podcast, "RFK Jr: Who Is God? Robert F Kennedy Jr and Lex Fridman," accessed May 1, 2024, https://www.youtube.com/watch?v=3eqcY-oCcqY.

[50] Jimmy Dore Show: "How RFK Jr. Beat Addiction with Carl Jung!."

[51] Robert F. Kennedy, Jr, "Who Is God to RFK?," accessed April 23, 2024, https://www.youtube.com/watch?v=MLx6XVwXCLM.

[52] Jimmy Dore Show: "How RFK Jr. Beat Addiction with Carl Jung!."

[53] Lex Friedman Podcast, "RFK Jr: Who Is God?."

[54] The Jimmy Dore Show, "How RFK Jr. Beat Addiction with Carl Jung!," accessed May 1, 2024, https://www.youtube.com/watch?v=hAjwUtGjHd4&t=1007s.

[55] The Lex Friedman Podcast, "RFK Jr: Who Is God? Robert F Kennedy Jr and Lex Fridman," accessed May 1, 2024, https://www.youtube.com/watch?v=3eqcY-oCcqY.

[56] At the time of Kennedy's arrest, September 1983, a Saturn-Pluto world transit conjunction was aligned with his natal Neptune. Transiting Saturn

moved to within eight degrees of the natal position of Saturn in his chart indicating the onset of his Saturn return.

[57] Jimmy Dore Show: "How RFK Jr. Beat Addiction with Carl Jung!."

[58] Robert F. Kennedy, Jr, "The Ambition of Enlightenment," accessed May 1, 2024, https://www.youtube.com/watch?v=zv88_MeGjPY.

[59] Grof, "Holotropic Research and Archetypal Astrology," in *The Birth of a New Discipline*, 58.

[60] Bruno Navasky, "Robert F. Kennedy Jr. on the Environment, the Election, and a 'Dangerous Donald Trump'," accessed April 30, 2024, https://www.vanityfair.com/news/2016/08/robert-f-kennedy-jr-on-the-environment-election-and-donald-trump.

[61] "Biography: Robert F. Kennedy, Jr," Congress.gov, accessed June 18, 2024, https://www.congress.gov/118/meeting/house/116258/witnesses/HHRG-118-FD00-Bio-KennedyR-20230720.pdf.

[62] Derek Beres, Matthew Remski, and Julian Walker, "The Conspirituality of Robert F. Kennedy, Jr," *Time* magazine, July 5, 2023, https://time.com/6292191/robert-f-kennedy-jr-conspiracy-theory-vaccines-essay/.

[63] Sam Montgomery, "US Presidential Hopeful Robert F Kennedy Jnr Opens Up on Gruelling Heroin Battle—'I Was Born an Addict'," August 13, 2023, https://www.gbnews.com/news/robert-f-kennedy-jnr-addiciton-drugs-presidential-election.

[64] TeamKennedy promotional email, October 3, 2024.

[65] Robert F. Kennedy, Jr, "RFK Jr.: Officially on the Ballot in California," accessed April 30, 2024, https://www.youtube.com/watch?v=iYVp98f48zY.

[66] Robert F. Kennedy, Jr, "RFK Jr: How Nature Connects Us to God," accessed April 23, 2024, https://www.youtube.com/watch?v=QVCwJy5c0Og.

[67] James Billot, "The Growing RFK Jr Coalition: The Insurgent Candidate Is Relishing the Struggle," April 24, 2024, https://unherd.com/2024/04/the-growing-rfk-jr-coalition/.

[68] American Independent Party, "Finish the Story: Nicole Shannahan, Trump, RFK Jr, Make America Healthy Again," accessed September 7, 2024, https://www.youtube.com/ watch?v=UOqOkSHBU9c.

[69] Saturn-Neptune themed experiences are integral to the process of soul-making, as defined by James Hillman, who himself had Saturn and Neptune in square alignment in his birth chart—part of a larger T-square with Jupiter and Mars. He gave expression to Saturn-Neptune themes in myriad ways in his work, of which the following are but a few examples. The act of "seeing through" the literal events of life to reveal their mythic background employs the Neptunian imagination in engaging with Saturnian concrete, literal facts of existence. Recall Hillman's remark, included in Volume I: "Outer historical facts are archetypally colored, so as to disclose essential psychological meanings. Historical facts disclose the eternally recurring mythemes of history

and of our individual souls. History is but the stage on which we enact mythemes of the soul" (Hillman, *Senex & Puer*, edited by Glen Slater (Putnam, CT: Spring, 2013), 29). Reflecting the archetypal influence of Mars in the T-square, for Hillman the literal—that is, the tendency to perceive and construe the world in a literal manner—is the problem, and was subject to his critical attack. As soon as something is literalized it is dead. In a different inflection of the same archetypal dynamics, however, Hillman also brought Saturnian concrete reality to bear on the Neptunian tendency towards abstraction and universal symbolism when it is unrelated to specific circumstances or individual lives. He was critical of the kind of depth psychology that would readily translate specific dream images into archetypes or universal symbols, as one might by looking up universal meanings in a dream dictionary. For Hillman, in working with dreams and images, it is imperative that one "stick to the image." Universal meanings and symbols always manifest concretely and in ways unique to the individual and the circumstance, even as they partake in archetypal patterns. It is this very insight that informs the archetypal approach to astrology too. Thus Hillman holds up the concrete Saturnian reality against Neptunian universal symbolism, even as he draws on Neptunian consciousness to see through Saturnian hard facts.

In further multivalent expressions of Saturn-Neptune, Hillman insists on granting the archetypal dimension of experience its own substantial reality—giving Saturnian form to the Neptunian world of archetypes, and gods and goddesses. The imaginal is not the imaginary in the sense of being made up; rather, it is fundamentally real. Yet, such was his commitment to metaphor and image as a reality of psychological life, he refused to subscribe to a concrete cosmology or worldview, not wishing to fall into the trap of reifying on image. For Hillman, reality is the image, the imaginal, the imagination. This too expresses Saturn and Neptune.

Jupiter is in a conjunction with Neptune in Hillman's chart, as part of the configuration with Saturn. In discussing the Jupiter-Neptune complex, I noted Hillman's breadth of cultural imagination, inspired by his Renaissance sensibility, as a reflection of his Jupiter-Neptune complex. In another expression of this complex, however, Hillman was also critical of an emphasis on spiritual ascent and transcendence in—a Saturnian judgment of the Jupiter-Neptune emphasis on the fantasy of growth that pervades much of psychology and spirituality. He was critical too of meditative paths and psychedelics as means to achieve such transcendence. Again, the Jupiter-Neptune association with height (the *sublimatio* motif we considered earlier) is resisted and judged by Hillman's Saturn-Neptune allegiances and sensibilities. For, Hillman believed, rather than seek ascent away from life's sufferings and pathologies, one must enter into pathology as a form of soulful deepening, to remain within the vales of suffering rather than ascend to the peaks of spiritual highs. Suffering, falling apart in the vales of the pathos of the soul, would then become an opening and opportunity for finding greater soulful meaning in life. Thus Hillman's focus on themes such as suicidal fantasies and the disillusionment of betrayal, associated with Saturn-Neptune. It is characteristic of Jupiter's role in this complex to see such experiences in positive terms.

[70] Jung, *Memories, Dreams, Reflections*, 223.
[71] Jung, *Memories, Dreams, Reflections*, 232.
[72] Tarnas discusses the Saturn-Neptune theme of "the sanctification of death" in "The Ideal and the Real (Part Two)," in *Cultural Crisis and Transformation*, 118–122.

BIBLIOGRAPHY

Abba. "Thank You for the Music." On *The Album*. Polar Music, 1977.
Agassi, Andre. *Open: An Autobiography*. Reprint. New York: Vintage, 2010.
Allen, Woody. *Annie Hall*. United Artists, 1977.
———. *Midnight in Paris*. Sony Pictures Classics, 2011.
———. "Woody Allen on Life." Excerpt from Press Conference for "You Will Meet a Tall Dark Stranger" (Cannes Film Festival). Accessed July 31, 2021. https://www.youtube.com/watch?v=5yVPS8XBoBE.
Arroyo, Stephen. *Astrology, Karma, & Transformation: The Inner Dimensions of the Birth Chart*. Sebastopol, CA: CRCS Publications, 1978.
Balague, Guillem. "Diego Maradona Dies: Guillem Balague on 'the Magician, the Cheat, the God, the Flawed Genius.'" Accessed November 26, 2020. https://www.bbc.co.uk/sport/football/55084504.
Barbault, André. "The History of a Prediction." Accessed January 6, 2022. http://cura.free.fr/quinq/02barbo.html.
Bergman, Ingmar, director. *Through a Glass Darkly*. Janus Films, 1961.
———. *Wild Strawberries*. Stockholm: AB Svensk Filmindustri, 1957.
Bon Jovi. "Always." On *Cross Road*. Mercury-Polygram, 1994.
———. "I'll Be There for You." On *New Jersey*. Mercury/Vertigo, 1988.
Bowie, David. "Ashes to Ashes." On *Scary Monsters (and Super Creeps)*. New York: RCA, 1980.
———."Bowie Talks to Paxman about Music, Drugs and the Internet." BBC Newsnight. Posted January 11, 2016. http://www.bbc.com/news/entertainment-arts-35286749?post_id=10153271816925848_10153271816905848.
———. Interview on the BBC. http://www.bbc.com/news/video_and_audio/headlines/35286547.
———. "Space Oddity." On *David Bowie*. London: Trident, 1969.
———. "Star Man." On *The Rise and Fall of Ziggy Stardust and the Spiders from Mars*. London: Trident/RCA, 1972.
Bush, Kate. "Running up That Hill (A Deal with God." On *Hounds of Love*. EMI Records, 1985.
Campbell, Joseph. *The Hero with a Thousand Faces*. 1949. Reprint. London: Fontana, 1993.

———. *A Joseph Campbell Companion: Reflections on the Art of Living*. Selected and edited by Diane K. Osbon. New York: HarperCollins Publishers, 1991.

———. *The Masks of God, Volume IV: Creative Mythology*. 1968. Reprint, New York: Arkana, 1991.

———. *Myths to Live By: Mythology for Our Time*. London: Souvenir Press, 1973.

Campbell, Joseph, and Bill Moyers. *Joseph Campbell and the Power of Myth with Bill Moyers*. New York: Mystic Fire Video, 1988.

Capell, Richard. *Schubert's Songs*. London: Pan Books, 1973.

Capra, Frank, director. *It's a Wonderful Life*. Liberty Films/RKO Radio Pictures, 1946.

Churchill, Winston. "We Shall Fight on the Beaches." International Churchill Society. Accessed December 22, 2021. https://winstonchurchill.org/resources/speeches/1940-the-finest-hour/we-shall-fight-on-the-beaches.

Clarey, Christopher. "Something Old, Something New at French Open." *New York Times*. June 12, 2017. https://www.nytimes.com/2017/06/12/sports/tennis/something-old-something-new-at-french-open.html.

"The Cult of Diego Maradona—in Pictures." *The Guardian*. October 30, 2020. https://www.theguardian.com/football/gallery/2020/oct/30/the-cult-of-diego-maradona-in-pictures.

The Cure. *Galore: The Singles*. Fiction/Elektra, 1997.

———. "In Between Days." On *The Head on the Door*. Fiction, 1985.

———. "Lullaby." On *Disintegration*. Fiction, 1989.

Dang, Phong Thong. *Advanced Aikido*. North Clarendon, VT: Tuttle Publishing, 2012.

Diamond, Neil. "I Am . . . I Said." On *Stones*. Uni Records, 1971.

Doors, The. "The Crystal Ship." On *The Doors*. Elektra Records, 1967.

Durant, Will, and Ariel Durant. *Rousseau and Revolution: The Story of Civilization*, volume XIV. New York: Simon & Schuster, 1963.

Einstein, Albert. *Out of My Later Years: The Scientist, Philosopher, and Man Portrayed through His Own Words*. Reprint edition. New York: Open Road, 2011.

Encyclopedia Britannica. "Alfred Nobel." Accessed December 28, 2021. https://www.britannica.com/biography/Alfred-Nobel.

Farrelly, Peter, director. *Dumb and Dumber*. Burbank, CA: New Line Cinema, 1994.

Fellini, Federico, director. *8½*. Cineriz, 1963.

———. *La Dolce Vita*. Cineriz, 1960.

Football Italia. Accessed November 26, 2020. https://football-italia.net/.

Freud, Sigmund. *Civilization and Its Discontents*. 1929–1930. The Standard Edition. Translated by James Strachey. New York: W. W. Norton & Company, 1989.

Garfunkel, Art. "Bright Eyes." Lyrics by Mike Batt. On *Fate for Breakfast*. New York: Columbia Records, 1979.

BIBLIOGRAPHY

Goethe, "Erlkönig." Translated by Richard Wigmore. In *Schubert: The Complete Song Texts*. Schirmer Books. Accessed July 31, 2021. https://www.oxfordlieder.co.uk/song/1420.

Graham, Matthew, Tony Jordan, and Ashley Pharoah, directors. *Life on Mars*. Kudos/BBC television, 2006.

Grof, Stanislav. "Holotropic Research and Archetypal Astrology." *The Birth of a New Discipline. Archai: The Journal of Archetypal Cosmology*. Issue I. 2009. Reprint. San Francisco, CA: Archai Press, 2011: 50–66.

———. *Psychology of the Future: Lessons from Modern Consciousness Research*. Albany, NY: State University of New York Press, 2000.

Händel, Georg Friedrich. "Messiah*: A Sacred Oratorio*." 1742. Words by Charles Jennens. Accessed December 6, 2023. http://opera.stanford.edu/ iu/libretti/messiah.htm.

Harding, Michael. *Hymns to the Ancient Gods*. London: Arkana, 1993.

Hegel, Georg Wilhelm Friedrich. *The Philosophy of History. Translated* by J. Sibree. New York: Dover Publications, 1956.

Hill, Scott J. *Confrontation with the Unconscious: Jungian Depth Psychology and Psychedelic Experience*. London: Muswell Hill Press, 2013.

———. "A Vision of Redemption through Death: Saturn-Neptune." *Death, Rebirth, and Revolution. Archai: The Journal of Archetypal Cosmology,* Issue 4. 2012. San Francisco: Archai Press, 2012.

Hillman, James. *Re-Visioning Psychology*. New York: HarperPerennial, 1992.

———. *Senex & Puer*. Edited by Glen Slater. Putnam, CT: Spring Publications, 2013.

Hölderlin, Friedrich. *Selected Poems*. Second edition. Translated by David Constantine. Highgreen, UK: Bloodaxe Books, 1996.

"In the Hands of God." *The Guardian*. November 26, 2020. https://www.theguardian.com/football/2020/nov/26/in-the-hands-of-god-what-the-papers-say-about-the-death-of-diego-maradona.

Joel, Billy. "An Innocent Man." On *An Innocent Man*. Family Productions/Columbia, 1983.

———. "The Longest Time." On *An Innocent Man*. Family Productions/Columbia, 1983.

———. "Piano Man." On *Piano Man*. Family Productions /Columbia, 1973.

———. "Tell Her About It." On *An Innocent Man*. Family Productions/Columbia, 1983.

———. "Uptown Girl." On *An Innocent Man*. Family Productions/Columbia, 1983.

Jung, Carl Gustav. *The Archetypes and the Collective Unconscious*. Second edition. Volume 9, part I of *The Collected Works of C. G. Jung*. Translated by R. F. C. Hull. Princeton, NJ: Princeton University Press, 1968.

———. *Jung on Astrology*. Edited by Safron Rossi and Keiron Le Grice. Abingdon, UK: Routledge, 2017.

———. *Memories, Dreams, Reflections*. Revised Edition. Recorded and edited by Aniela Jaffé. Translated by Richard Wilson and Clara Wilson. Reprint. New York: Vintage Books, 1965.

———. *Mysterium Coniunctionis*. Second Edition. 1955–1956. Volume 14 of *The Collected Works of C. G. Jung*. Translated by R.F.C. Hull. Princeton, NJ: Princeton University Press, 1989.

———. *Psychology and Alchemy*. Second edition. Volume 12 of *The Collected Works of C. G. Jung*. Translated by R. F. C. Hull. Princeton, NJ: Princeton University Press, 1968.

———. *The Red Book: Liber Novus*. Edited and Introduced by Sonu Shamdasani. Translated by Mark Kyburz, John Peck, and Sonu Shamdasani. New York: W. W. Norton & Co., 2009.

———. "The Spiritual Problem of Modern Man." 1928/1931. In *Civilization in Transition*. Second Edition. Volume 10 of *The Collected Works of C. G. Jung*. Translated by R. F. C. Hull. Princeton: Princeton University Press, 1989.

———. *Symbols of Transformation*. Second Edition. 1967. Vol. 5 of *The Collected Works of C. G. Jung*. Translated by. R. F. C. Hull. Reprint, Princeton: Princeton University Press, 1976.

———. *Two Essays on Analytical Psychology*. Second edition. 1966. Volume 7 of *The Collected Works of C. G. Jung*. Trans. R.F.C. Hull. Reprint. London: Routledge, 1990.

———. *The Undiscovered Self, with Symbols and the Interpretation of Dreams*. Translated and revised by R. F. C. Hull. Princeton, NJ: Princeton University Press, 1990.

Kampf, Zachary. "The Rebirth of Tragedy." PhD diss., Pacifica Graduate Institute, California, 2022.

Kapadia, Asif. *Diego Maradona*. Featuring Daniel Arcucci. On the Corner/Film 4, 2019.

Keane. "Bad Dream." On *Under the Iron Sea*. Island Records, 2006.

———. "Crystal Ball." On *Under the Iron Sea*. Island Records, 2006.

———. "Is It Any Wonder?," On *Under the Iron Sea*. Island Records, 2006.

Keats, John. "I Cry Your Mercy-Pity-Love! – Aye, Love." Poetry Foundation. Accessed December 29, 2021. https://www.poetryfoundation.org/poems/50326/i-cry-your-mercy-pity-love-aye-love.

Keller, Helen. "Helen Keller Speaks Out." Accessed December 6, 2019. https://www.youtube.com/watch?v=8ch_H8pt9M8.

Kennedy, Dana. "Blue Skies." Accessed October 26, 2021. http://sportsillustrated.cnn.com/features/1997/womenmag/blueskies.html.

Kennedy, Jr., Robert F. *The Real Anthony Fauci: Bill Gates, Big Pharma, and the Global War on Democracy and Public Health*. New York: Skyhorse Publishing, 2021.

King, Ursula. *Spirit of Fire: The Life and Vision of Teilhard de Chardin*. Maryknoll, NY: Orbis Books, 1996.

BIBLIOGRAPHY

The Kinks. "Dedicated Follower of Fashion." On *The Kink Kontroversy.* Pye/Reprise, 1965.

———. "A Well Respected Man." On *Kinda Kinks.* Pye/Reprise, 1965.

Larsen, Stephen, and Robin Larsen. *A Fire in the Mind: The Life of Joseph Campbell.* Reprint, New York: Anchor Books, 1993.

Le Grice, Keiron. *Archetypal Cosmology and Depth Psychology: Selected Essays.* Ojai, CA: ITAS Publications, 2021.

———. *The Archetypal Cosmos: Rediscovering the Gods in Myth, Science and Astrology.* Edinburgh: Floris Books, 2010.

———. "The Dark Spirit in Nature: C. G. Jung and the Spiritual Transformation of Our Time." In Keiron Le Grice. *Archetypal Cosmology and Depth Psychology: Selected Essays.* Ojai, CA: ITAS Publications, 2021.

———. "Land of Hope and Dreams: An Archetypal Analysis of Bruce Springsteen's Song Lyrics, Part Two." *Cultural Crisis and Transformation: Archai: The Journal of Archetypal Cosmology.* Issue 2. 2010. San Francisco, CA: Archai Press, 2010.

———. "A Last Chance Power-Drive: An Archetypal Analysis of Bruce Springsteen's Song Lyrics, Part 1." *The Birth of a New Discipline. Archai: The Journal of Archetypal Cosmology.* Issue 1. 2009. Reprint. San Francisco: Archai Press, 2011. 145–174.

Lee, Bruce. *Bruce Lee: Artist of Life.* Compiled and edited by John Little. Boston, MA: Tuttle Publishing, 2001.

McGilligan, Patrick. *Clint: The Life and Legend.* Updated and revised edition. New York: OR Books, 2015.

Manilow, Barry. "Copacabana." On *Even Now.* New York: Arista, 1978.

Michaels, Wendy. "Why Jim Carrey Wrote Himself a $10 Million Check Before He Was Famous, Even Though He Was Broke." Accessed November 29, 2021. https://www.cheatsheet.com/entertainment/why-jim-carrey-wrote-himself-a-10-million-check-before-he-was-famous.html.

Mitchell, Joni. "Carey." On *Blue.* New York: Reprise Records, 1971.

———. "River." On *Blue.* New York: Reprise Records, 1971.

———. "Tin Angel." On *Clouds.* New York: Reprise Records, 1969.

———. "Willy." On *Ladies of the Canyon.* New York: Reprise Records, 1970.

Nadal, Rafael, and John Carlin. *Rafa.* New York: Hyperion, 2011.

Nietzsche, Friedrich. *Basic Writings of Nietzsche.* Translated by Walter Kaufmann. New York: Modern Library, 2000.

———. *Thus Spoke Zarathustra.* 1885. Translated by R. J. Hollingdale. Reprint, London: Penguin, 1968.

Oermann, Nils Ole. *Albert Schweitzer: A Biography.* Oxford: Oxford University Press, 2017.

Pagels, Elaine. *The Gnostic Gospels.* New York: Vintage Books, 1989.

Proust, Marcel. *Swann's Way. In Search of Lost Time, Volume I.* Translated by C. K. Scott Moncrieff and Terence Kilmartin. Revised by D. J. Enright. New York: The Modern Library, 1992.

Queen. "Don't Stop Me Now." On *Jazz*. EMI / Elektra, 1978.
Reich, Wilhelm. *Character Analysis*. Third edition. New York: Farrar, Straus & Giroux Inc, 1980.
Roach, Jay, director. *Meet the Parents*. Universal Pictures, 2000.
Ruperti, Alexander. *Cycles of Becoming: The Planetary Pattern of Growth*. Vancouver, WA: CRCS, 1978.
Russell, Dick. *The Real RFK Jr: Trials of a Truth Warrior*. New York: Skyhorse Publishing, 2023.
Saito, Morihiro. *Traditional Aikido*. Tokyo: Japan Publications, 1974.
Sartre, Jean-Paul. *The Words*. Translated by Bernard Frechtman. New York: George Brazilier, 1964.
Schopenhauer, Arthur. "On the Sufferings of the World." In *The Essays of Arthur Schopenhauer: Studies in Pessimism*. Translated by T. Bailey Saunders. Project Guttenberg. Accessed July 31, 2021. https://www.gutenberg.org/files/10732/10732-h/10732-h.htm.
Schweitzer, Albert. *Out of My Life and Thought. With Postscript 1932–1949 by Everett Skillings*. Translated by C. T. Campion. New York: Henry Holt and Company. 1933–1949.
Shadyac, Tom, director. *Bruce Almighty*. Universal Pictures, 2003.
Shyamalan, M. Night, director. *The Sixth Sense*. Buena Vista Pictures, 1999.
Springsteen, Bruce, and the E-Street Band. "Born to Run." On *Born to Run*. New York: Columbia Records, 1975.
———. "For You." On *Greetings from Asbury Park, N.J.* New York: Columbia Records, 1973.
———. "Frankie." *Tracks*. New York: Columbia Records, 1998.
———. "Incident on 57th Street." On *The Wild, the Innocent, and the E-Street Shuffle*. New York: Columbia Records, 1973.
———. "Land of Hope and Dreams." On *Live from New York City*. New York: Columbia Records, 2001.
———. "Mary Queen on Arkansas." On *Greetings from Asbury Park, N.J.* New York: Columbia Records, 1973.
———. "The Promised Land." On *Darkness on the Edge of Town*. New York: Columbia Records, 1978.
———. "Rosalita." On *The Wild, the Innocent, and the E-Street Shuffle*. New York: Columbia Records, 1973.
———. "Wild Billy's Circus Story." On *The Wild, the Innocent, and the E-Street Shuffle*. New York: Columbia Records, 1973.
Tarnas, Richard. *Cosmos and Psyche: Intimations of a New World View*. New York: Viking, 2006.
———. "The Ideal and the Real: Saturn-Neptune." In *The Birth of a New Discipline. Archai: The Journal of Archetypal Cosmology*. Issue 1, 2009. Reprint, San Francisco: Archai Press, 2011, 175–199.

———. "The Ideal and the Real (Part Two): Related Saturn-Neptune Patterns in History and Culture." In *Cultural Crisis and Transformation. Archai: The Journal of Archetypal Cosmology*. Issue 2. 2010. San Francisco, CA: Archai Press, 2010.

Teilhard de Chardin, Pierre. *The Heart of Matter*. Translated by René Hague. San Diego: Harcourt Brace, 1978.

Teilhard de Chardin, Pierre, and Blanche Gallagher. *Meditations with Teilhard de Chardin*. Santa Fe, NM: Bear & Company, 1988.

Teresa (Saint). *The Interior Castle*. http://www.catholictreasury.info/books/interior_castle/ic2.php.

Thomas, Bruce. *Fighting Spirit*. London: Pan Books, 1994.

Tolstoy, Leo. *The Death of Ivan Ilyich and Other Stories*. Introduction and notes by Dr. T. C. B. Cook. Ware, UK: Wordsworth Classics, 2004.

Ueshiba, Kisshomaru. *Aikido*. Tokyo: Hozansha Publications, 1985.

———. *A Life in Aikido: The Biography Of Founder Morihei Ueshiba*. Translated by Kei Izawa and Mary Fuller. Tokyo: Kodansha International, 2008.

Vickery, Tim."Diego Maradona: How Tormenting England Made Him an Argentine Deity." Accessed November 26, 2019. BBC Sport. https://www.bbc.com/sport/football/55074235.

Wagner, Winfried. *Aikido: The Trinity of Conflict Transformation*. Innsbruck, Austria: Springer, 2015.

Wordsworth, William. "Ode: Intimations of Immortality from Recollections of Early Childhood." Poetry Foundation. Accessed November 3, 2021. https://www.poetryfoundation.org/poems/45536/ode-intimations-of-immortality-from-recollections-of-early-childhood.

Note on Birth Data

Where available, birth data for the charts included in this volume were taken from Astro-Databank, an excellent repository of birth charts and short biographies of thousands of notable people, with each entry classified for reliability (see https://www.astro.com/astro-databank/Main_Page) according to the Rodden Rating. The vast database hosted by Astrotheme was also consulted in certain instances (https://www.astrotheme.com/astrology_database.php). In most cases, the charts referenced in this volume are available from both sources. In the absence of reliable astrological data, I obtained birth information at Britannica online and Wikipedia. Where no precise, reliable birth time was available, I used noon charts—cast for 12 pm on the date of birth—to reduce the margin of error.

INDEX

12-Step program
 226
8 ½ (motion picture)
 81f, 202

Abba
 83
Abdul-Jabbar, Karim
 90f
ablutio
 180, 183
abstinence
 172
Ace Ventura (motion picture)
 17
actualization (of form, potential)
 30, 41, 46, 74, 95, 98f, 105, 114, 122, 194, 207
Adams, Richard
 220
addiction
 124, 126f, 130, 185, 222–227, 231, 240f
adulthood
 32, 40, 46, 95, 98, 100, 217
aesthetic dimension/experience
 61, 63f, 84, 143, 158, 165, 168f, 201f, 204
Africa
 106, 109f, 115
agape
 171
Agassi, Andre
 25–27, 29
aggression
 18, 68–72, 74, 177f, 180, 182
aging
 8, 11, 114, 204

agnosticism
 225
aikido
 178, 180, 187f
alchemy
 30, 132, 148, 180, 183f, 198, 202, 238
Alcoholics Anonymous
 226
alcoholism
 104, 126, 130, 136, 139, 223, 227
alienation
 33, 45, 46, 53, 64, 114, 207, 209, 211, 216, 231, 234
alignments/aspects
 (*see specific planets and aspects*)
Along Came Polly (motion picture)
 22
altruism
 115f, 119f, 122
"Always" (Bon Jovi song)
 169
"American Pie" (Don McClean song)
 220f
amplification
 11, 13, 84f, 88, 195, 199, 201
Analyze This (motion picture)
 19
Anderson, Pamela
 165
Anderson, Wes
 22
Andersson, Harriet
 206
anger
 18, 68–70, 73, 85, 178
anima
 19, 21, 40f, 54, 84, 93, 135, 141, 147,

anima (cont.)
157, 165f, 168, 171, 202–204
Annie Hall (motion picture)
11f
Anniston, Jennifer
22
archetypal astrology
204, 242
archetypal combinations
7, 17, 35f, 48, 57, 63, 68–70, 84f, 87f, 92, 94, 115, 120, 124f, 130, 135–137, 148, 151, 164, 166, 170, 176, 178, 200, 210, 219
archetypal complexes
1, 10, 14, 18f, 21, 30, 35, 42f, 57, 60, 62–64, 68, 72–74, 77, 82f, 87, 121f, 135f 141, 157f, 161f, 165, 175, 178, 183, 194, 205
archetypal factors/functions
143, 150, 160, 222, 230f
archetypal figures/images/roles
82, 85, 112, 120, 128, 132, 139, 153, 210
archetypal influences
13, 189, 192, 203, 209, 227, 240, 242
archetypal patterns/dynamics
35, 41, 45f, 222, 243
archetypal principles/powers
1, 10, 48, 84, 114, 135, 150, 166, 238
archetypal psychology
144, 197
archetypal themes/motifs/qualities
1, 5, 11, 14, 19, 55, 57, 60, 76, 89f, 94 144, 153, 210, 212
archetypal worlds/realities
3, 114, 219, 239
archetypes
(see *Jungian and astrological archetypes*)
As Good As It Gets (motion picture)
45
Ashes to Ashes (BBC television series)
129f
assassinations
104, 221f, 224, 229
astrology/astrologers
5, 7, 27, 69, 78, 80, 111f, 132, 151, 153, 194, 200, 204, 227, 237, 240
atheism
154, 207

Augustine of Hippo
223, 230
Aurobindo, Sri
137
authenticity
8, 19, 21, 51, 57, 64, 67f, 74f, 84, 110, 119, 121, 158, 232
autism
229
awakening
21, 29, 46, 49, 57, 67, 132, 150, 223

Bach, Johann Sebastian
107, 133
Bad Dream (Keane song)
212f
Badlands (Bruce Springsteen song)
197
Balague, Guillem
126f, 184
Bancroft, Anne
60
Band Aid (charity band)
115
Bardot, Brigitte
165
Barrie, J. M.
144
basic perinatal matrices (BPMs)
16, 46, 139, 227, 229
beauty
35, 38, 53, 61–63, 78, 81, 84f, 164f, 168, 170, 172, 200, 202f, 208, 213
Becker, Ernest
11
Beckham, Victoria
84
Beckinsale, Kate
165
Bee Gees
82
behaviorism
137
Bergman, Ingmar
204f, 207–209, 216f, 240
Berry, Halle
84
Beyoncé (Knowles)
84

INDEX

Beyond Freedom and Dignity (B. F. Skinner)
137
Bible/biblical
41, 43, 84, 114, 170, 176, 216, 223
Biden administration (US government)
229
Big Bopper
220
Big Pharma/Big Tech
231
biography
6, 96, 106, 111, 179, 222
biology
95, 199
birth data
251
birth process/pattern
46, 155, 168
birth time
93, 144, 185f, 201, 251
Black Books, The
130
Blaze of Glory (Bon Jovi album)
85
bliss
114, 141, 143, 166, 191, 199f
Blondie
84
body
100, 179–182, 188, 199
Bollingen
156f, 235–237
Bon Jovi
85, 93, 169, 186
Boomtown Rats, The
115
Bonnard, Pierre
170
Borg, Bjorn
73
"Born to Run" (Bruce Springsteen song)
195
boundaries
40, 48, 57, 67, 72, 127f, 138, 147, 154, 157, 164, 168, 176f, 184, 227
Bowie, David
82, 128–130, 185, 214
boxing
91

"Boys Don't Cry" (The Cure song)
38
Brand, Russell
185
Brando, Marlon
152f
"Bread and Wine" (Hölderlin poem)
146
break (psychological)
23, 26, 42, 61, 108, 202, 223
breakthroughs
23, 102
breast (in Grofian psychology)
155
"Bright Eyes" (Art Garfunkel song)
220
British culture
63, 86f, 119
Bronson, Charles
70
Brontë, Emily
63, 174
Bruce Almighty (motion picture)
17, 191f
Buddhism/Buddha
7, 115
Buddy Holly
220
budō
179
bullies/bullying
70, 72
burial rites
237
Bush, Kate
173–175, 187
Byrnes, Jack (in *Meet the Parents*)
18–22, 133

Cable Guy, The (motion picture)
192
California
97, 105, 232
Camelot
222, 233f
Campbell, Joseph
85, 94, 96–106, 110, 112, 136f, 144, 160f, 185f, 191, 197–201, 203, 233, 237

cancer (illness)
  228
Capell, Richard
  38, 78
capitalism
  185
"Carey" (Joni Mitchell song)
  165
Carlin, John
  28
Carrey, Jim
  14, 17f, 189–192, 239
Catafalque (Peter Kingsley)
  132
categorical imperative
  48
categories (Kantian)
  48
Catholicism
  222
Cayce, Edgar
  153
censorship
  69, 72, 74, 229f
Cezanne, Paul
  170
channeling,
  127, 153, 233
Chaplin, Tom
  213
charismatic figure/charisma
  121, 132f, 176
chemicals
  227f, 232
chess
  49
child archetype
  11, 37, 47, 55, 72, 142
childhood
  11, 25, 40–43, 45f, 57, 73, 140–146, 148f, 154f, 185, 192, 195, 217, 229
childishness
  41, 149
Christ
  115, 134, 136, 172
Christianity
  43, 106, 109, 119, 122, 132, 135f, 160, 187, 203
Christmas, Lloyd (*Dumb and Dumber*)
  189–191
Christmas Carol, A
  14
Chronicles (Old Testament)
  44
Chronicles of Narnia
  144
Chronos
  58, 75, 216
Churchill, Winston
  86, 230
civilization
  145f, 162f
Civilization and Its Discontents
  155
classics
  63f
Cleese, John
  76
Clinton, Hillary
  71
Clinton, Bill
  168
Clouds (Joni Mitchell album)
  219
coagulatio
  238
Cobain, Kurt
  127, 184
cocaine
  124, 127
cogito ergo sum
  47
coherence (archetypal)
  68, 106
Columbia University
  99, 101
comedy
  11, 13f, 18, 70, 76, 89, 133, 189
compensation
  23, 88
complexes
  (*see archetypal complexes and specific planetary combinations*)
compulsion
  76, 98, 122, 239
configurations
  (*see entries for specific planets*)

INDEX

conjunction (aspect/alignment)
5f, 10, 14, 17, 21, 25, 27, 33, 36, 45–48, 55, 60–64, 68, 70, 72, 76, 79, 85, 89f, 93, 96, 98, 104, 115f–117, 123, 130, 133, 137, 141, 143–145, 148, 150f, 153, 155, 160f, 165, 168–172, 178, 186, 190, 192, 200, 203, 210, 217, 222, 224, 229f, 240f, 243
conscience
8, 30, 95, 98, 223
conscious awareness
5, 20, 148
conscious ego
95, 148, 176
conscious identity
138
conscious personality
18, 120, 132, 136, 153
conscious selfhood
140
conservatism
22, 53, 59–61, 63, 70, 81
conspiracy theories
229f
conventional standards/values
19, 21, 23, 57, 64, 99, 122
conversion experience
223
Corleone, family in *The Godfather*
153
"Copacabana" (Barry Manilow song)
82
corruption
55, 185, 231f, 234
cosmological constant
47
cosmological order
144
cosmology
243
cosmos
199
Covici, Pascal
104–106
Covid-19 pandemic
182, 229f
creative artists
97

creative block
202
creative centers
199
creative genius
79
creative inspiration/energy
76, 135, 180
creative mythology
105, 112, 144
creativity
24
Crocodile Dundee (motion picture)
70
crucifixion
124
Cruyff, Johann
170
Cruz, Penelope
84
Crystal, Billy
19
"Crystal Ball" (Keane song)
161
"Crystal Ship" (The Doors song)
213
crystallization (of the personality)
96, 100f, 105
cults
122, 132, 184
Cure, The
38
cycles
1, 16, 35, 94, 96, 102, 104–107

daimon
122
Dali, Salvador
186
damnation
16
Damon, Matt
167
Daniels, Jeff
190
dark night of the soul
237
Darkness on the Edge of Town (Springsteen)
194

Darth Vader
    29
Davies, Ray
    63
De Niro, Robert
    18f, 152f
deafness
    49f
death
    5, 8f, 11, 14, 23, 34–38, 41, 52, 67f, 95, 104f, 111, 114, 133, 170, 178, 204, 206f, 209, 213, 216, 220, 231, 237
Death of Ivan Ilyich, The
    64–68
deception
    159, 192f, 206, 209f, 229, 234
Decline of the West, The
    102
defensiveness
    14, 16, 32f, 41, 50–52, 56, 68–70, 72f, 75, 150
deities/deification
    121, 123, 161, 204
deluge
    138
delusions
    13, 114, 117, 121, 135, 158, 164, 166, 183, 207, 209, 226f, 229
democracy
    232
Democratic Party (US)
    221, 230
demonic/demons
    122, 149, 239
demoralization
    138, 183, 211
Denial of Death, The
    148
depression
    5, 41f, 138, 210, 238
Depression, The Great
    100
depth psychology
    243
desires
    35, 98, 165f, 168, 171
destiny
    30, 43, 95, 99, 101, 153, 233

development
    18, 25, 40f, 55, 74, 95, 132, 141, 164
devil
    124, 239
dialectic
    49, 207, 209
Diamond, Neil
    31
Diana, Princess of Wales
    119, 221
Diane Keaton
    11, 76, 167
Dickens, Charles
    14, 72, 76
dictators
    69, 72
differentiation
    30, 32, 132, 145, 153, 155, 159, 166, 235
Dionysian
    204, 234, 238
Dirty Harry (film series, character)
    177
discernment
    132, 147, 153, 158, 175
disciples
    121
disciplinarians
    19, 69
discipline
    22, 25–27, 40f, 60, 69, 84, 92, 205, 227
disco/disco queen
    82
disenchantment
    234, 238
disillusionment
    130, 138, 200, 204, 210, 233, 235, 237f, 243
disintegration
    123, 125, 127f, 130, 138, 140, 183, 204, 222, 238
Disney, Walt
    144
dissolution
    32, 114, 122, 126f, 133, 136, 138, 146–148, 154, 157, 161, 168, 171, 180, 182–185, 191f, 204, 216, 222, 227, 235, 238

INDEX

divine, the
  114, 120, 132, 137, 141–143, 162, 169–171, 183, 202f, 209, 226, 232, 237f
divine bliss
  114
divine guidance
  226
divine homesickness
  143
divine mission
  120
divine source/mystery/radiance
  137, 203, 209
divine revelation
  142
divine inspiration
  137
divine will
  183
divinization
  126f
Djokovic, Novak
  29, 182, 188
"Do They Know It's Christmas?" (song)
  115
Dolce Vita, La (motion picture)
  81, 93, 200, 202, 204
"Don't Stop Me Now" (Queen song)
  82
Doors, The
  161
doubt
  11, 18, 23, 47f, 50, 59, 77, 81, 207, 209f, 213–215, 218, 224, 238
Down Came the Rain (Brooke Shields)
  41
dreams
  57, 130, 150, 157, 159, 169, 175, 185f, 189, 191–195, 197, 199, 202, 205, 209, 212f, 215–220, 222–235, 237, 239f, 243f
dream-world
  132, 142
drowning
  138
drugs
  119, 124–130, 139, 185, 215, 222f, 225, 227, 231, 233

dukkha
  7
Dumb and Dumber (motion picture)
  17, 190, 191, 239
Durant, Ariel
  162f
Durant, Will
  162f
duty/duties
  22–24, 34, 41, 53, 66f, 69, 73f, 95, 101, 121, 133, 137, 226
Dylan, Bob
  161

earth (ground)
  141, 146f, 187f
Earth (planet)
  78, 103, 143, 172
Eastern philosophy
  164
Eastwood, Clint
  70, 176–178, 187
ecstasy
  208, 227
Eden
  216
Edinger, Edward
  132
egocentrism
  14
ego-consciousness
  14, 29, 46, 116, 120, 122, 138, 183, 216
ego-structure
  128
Egypt
  44, 160
Einstein, Albert
  47, 118, 184
Ekberg, Anita
  202
Ekland, Britt
  165
elders
  18, 30, 105, 110
elections
  222, 232
Erlking
  (*see* Erlkönig)

Eliade, Mircea
  197f
Eliot, T. S.
  136
embarrassment
  18–23, 29f, 50f, 55, 63
empathy
  56, 73, 115f, 118, 141, 146, 148, 161
enchantment
  114, 132f, 139–141, 143, 145, 148, 151, 155, 157f, 165f, 168, 183, 211, 218, 238
England
  126, 214
enlightenment
  179f, 194, 227
environment
  228, 232
ephemeris
  96, 111f
epiphanies
  102, 160, 206, 223
Erdman, Jean
  101
"Erlkönig"
  37f
Eros
  164–166, 171, 200
  (see also anima)
Esalen Institute
  105
escapism/escapist impulses
  23, 61, 124, 128, 133, 136, 140, 157, 175, 182, 194, 207, 222
eschatology
  107, 119
establishment
  185, 228–230
estrangement
  37, 230
eternal images
  203
eternal life
  138, 206
eternal return
  16, 76
eternal silence
  203
eternal youth
  112

eternity
  173f, 206
ethics
  48, 64, 76, 111, 168, 177
evil
  7f, 155, 176
evolution
  1, 172, 187
exile
  46, 114, 216
existential alienation/crisis/confusion
  45, 101, 202, 213
existentialist thinkers
  45

fairytales
  144, 168, 199, 208, 211, 213, 217–219
Falklands War
  126
Fältskog, Agnetha
  83
fame
  84, 126
family life/relationships
  19, 21–23, 35, 40, 42, 44, 87, 95, 100, 105, 110, 112, 141, 152f, 157
"Fancy" (Keats poem)
  169
fantasy
  23, 61, 114, 121, 128, 130, 132, 141, 157f, 164, 166, 173, 192, 194, 205, 219, 235f, 243
Farrelly brothers
  190
fate
  7f, 34, 43, 105
father archetype/principle
  37, 46, 99
father complex
  22
father figure
  18, 29, 31
Fauci, Anthony
  229f
fear
  21, 29f, 38f, 42, 52f, 55, 59, 69f, 72, 74f, 81, 87, 89, 182, 209f, 227, 241

INDEX

Federer, Roger
  28, 73, 170, 187
Fellini, Federico
  81f, 93, 200–204
female roles
  19
feminine principle/experience
  141, 150f, 169, 172, 187, 203
fetus
  155, 227
fighting
  68f, 74, 86f, 93, 177, 179, 213
film
  (*see entries under film titles*)
Finnegan's Wake
  136
Fiorina, Carly
  61
Fistful of Dollars (motion picture)
  176
Fischer-Dieskau, Dietrich
  37
flamboyance
  17, 82
Fleming, Alexander
  119
flood motif
  138, 148
Focker, Greg (*Meet the Parents*)
  18–22, 44, 134f
Fonda, Jane
  165
fool's journey
  189–191
football (soccer)
  73, 123–126, 184
fortune
  87, 89
Four Quartets
  136
Francis of Assisi
  223, 230
"Frankie" (Bruce Springsteen song)
  195f
Frankl, Viktor
  137
Franklin, Aretha
  84

Freeman, Morgan
  191
Frobenius, Leo
  102, 185
funerals
  104f, 216, 237

G. I. Jane (motion picture)
  70
Gaia
  146
gain-of-function research
  230
Game of Death, The (motion picture)
  90
Gandhi, Mahatma
  118f, 184
Garfunkel, Art
  220, 241
gaudiness
  82, 165
Gautier, Jean-Paul
  79
Geldof, Bob
  115
generosity
  87, 106, 118, 133
genius
  79, 123, 126, 145
geometric relationships/alignments
  10, 32, 53, 63, 115f, 210
  (*see also* aspects)
Gere, Richard
  167f
Germany
  35, 73, 86, 99, 110f, 145f
ghosts
  104, 176, 195, 206
Gibb brothers (Bee Gees)
  82
Gifford lectures
  110
glamor
  81f, 127, 135, 140
gnosis
  160
Gnosticism
  132, 160

God
  47, 87, 89f, 111, 126, 130, 140f, 143, 161f, 169, 171f, 175, 179f, 183, 191f, 207–209, 223, 225–227, 232, 237f
Godfather, The (motion picture series)
  153
godlike power/quality
  126f, 133, 192
gods and goddesses
  89, 130, 144–149, 151, 155, 203, 243
Goerring, Herman
  72
Goethe, Johann Wolfgang von
  37, 78
Gospel of Thomas
  30
gospels
  106f
grace
  133, 170
Graduate, The (motion picture)
  60
Grail legend
  99, 105
grand cross (aspect pattern)
  38, 106, 173
grand slam (tennis)
  78, 182
grand trine (aspect pattern)
  75, 144f, 149, 151, 160, 186
Grim Reaper
  38
Groundhog Day (motion picture)
  14–17

habits
  41, 45f, 150f, 223
Hamill, Mark
  29
Hanks, Tom
  75, 167
hard aspects
  11, 22, 24f, 27, 31, 33, 38, 46, 63, 73, 84, 94, 96, 111, 119, 132f, 138f, 147, 161, 170, 173, 190, 196, 198, 207, 210, 220f, 240
Harry, Debbie
  84

haunting
  14, 178, 205–209, 215f, 233, 237, 240
Hawn, Goldie
  70
heaven
  90, 139, 142f, 145f, 148, 195, 208, 216
hedonism
  81, 200, 202–204
Hegel, Georg Friedrich Wilhelm
  145, 161–163, 170, 186
Heidegger, Martin
  8, 76, 145
Hemingway, Ernest
  63
Hepburn, Audrey
  151, 165
hero archetype/pattern
  25, 29, 54, 58, 70, 102, 104, 115, 122f, 126, 135f, 176, 185f, 195, 199f, 220, 226, 229, 239
heroin
  222, 233
heroism
  29, 54, 74, 115, 120, 122, 130, 132, 136f, 222, 231, 233–235, 238
Hero with a Thousand Faces, The
  136, 199
High Plains Drifter (motion picture)
  176
Hill, Scott
  208f, 240
Hillman, James
  74, 194, 198, 235, 242f
Hinduism
  139
Hingis, Martina
  25, 77
history
  1, 31, 80, 107, 123, 126, 161–163, 165, 186, 197–199, 212, 242
Hitler, Adolf
  72, 111, 170
Hoeller, Stephan
  132
Hoffman, Dustin
  22, 60
Hogan, Paul
  70

INDEX

Hölderlin, Friedrich
    145–149
holism
    88, 92, 159, 197, 199
Holly, Buddy
    220
Hollywood
    70, 165
home
    19f, 22, 36f, 42, 44f, 66f, 112, 140f, 143, 156f, 193
homesickness
    143
Hudson River Foundation/Riverkeepers
    228f
Hopes and Fears (Keane album)
    210
humanity
    14, 31, 43, 52, 115, 141, 153, 171f
humility
    28, 43, 77f, 133, 140
humor
    11, 13, 16–18, 22, 85, 89, 190
Hunt, Helen
    45
"Hyperion's Song of Fate" ((Hölderlin)
    186
hypnotic quality
    122, 132, 139, 166

"I Am . . . I Said" (Neil Diamond song)
    31
"I Cry Your Mercy-Pity-Love" (Keats)
    169f
icon
    124
idealism
    106, 114f 118, 127, 137f, 140, 152, 189, 195–197, 206, 220–222, 229, 231f, 234f
idealistic heroism
    115, 137, 231
identity
    13, 22, 24, 27, 33, 95, 115, 118–122, 124, 127–129, 132f, 137–140, 214
identity confusion
    127, 131, 133
ideologies
    72, 121, 132, 164, 171, 178, 207

idolization/idols/idolatry
    121, 123, 126f, 235
illness
    5, 11, 52, 73, 104, 119, 139, 185, 231
illusions
    101, 114, 132, 135, 158, 166, 192, 195, 206f, 209, 211, 216, 238
imaginal realm/figures
    130, 157, 182, 206, 243
imagination
    67, 73, 135, 141, 144, 149, 151, 160, 164–166, 168, 170, 173, 176, 182, 191, 195, 198, 204, 207, 217f, 234f, 242f
imitatio Christi
    122, 134, 226
imitation
    122, 127, 159
impersonation
    159, 188
inauthenticity
    55, 64, 67
incarnation
    34, 99, 114
inconjunct (aspect/alignment)
    33
    (*see also* quincunx)
individualism
    29, 116, 180
individuation
    1, 30, 32, 34, 41, 46, 50–52, 61, 64, 69, 72, 74f, 84, 94, 98, 120–122, 138–140, 145, 148, 153, 158, 164, 166, 171, 175, 189, 191, 210, 234, 235, 238
ineffable
    159
infancy
    43f, 114, 142, 146
infantalism
    121, 148, 207
inferiority
    11, 19–21, 28, 30, 32, 40, 42, 50f, 53, 59f, 69, 72, 88, 100
inhumanity
    116, 171
inner critic
    30, 40
innocence
    40f, 53, 55, 58f, 72, 79, 142, 144ff, 151, 190, 204, 229, 239

"Innocent Man, An" (Billy Joel song)
  53–57
insanity
  131, 148, 208f, 214
integral history
  163
integral philosophy
  163
integration
  32, 72, 89, 101, 133, 176, 207, 217, 235
intellect
  50, 164
intelligible character
  106
intentionality
  122
Interior Castle, The (St. Teresa)
  89
Intimations of Immortality (Wordsworth)
  141f
intoxication
  227
intrauterine experience
  227
intuition
  48f, 102, 143, 153, 178, 183, 195, 199
Ireland
  136
"Is It Any Wonder?" (Keane song)
  211–214
Isaiah (Old Testament)
  227
Italy
  123–125, 176
It's a Wonderful Life (motion picture)
  168
Ivan the Terrible
  72

Jainism
  106, 119
jeet kune do
  92
Joplin, Janis
  184
journey motif
  30, 35f, 41, 85, 104, 138, 178, 180, 185f, 189–191, 194, 200, 234, 239

Joyce, James
  136
judgment/being judged
  18f, 21, 27, 29–32, 40, 43–45, 50, 54f, 61–64, 70, 72, 98, 100, 110, 125, 151, 168, 175, 204, 209f, 217, 226, 233, 235, 243
jujitsu
  91
Jung, Carl Gustav
  1, 31, 41, 76, 106, 121, 130–133, 135–139, 145, 155–157, 184–186, 197, 210, 223, 225, 235–237, 241
Jungian archetypes
  15, 29, 165
Jungian psychology
  19, 46, 54, 84, 100, 159, 175, 240
Jupiter
  1, 10–13, 35f, 44, 74, 76, 81–92, 106, 115, 117f, 143–145, 155, 159f, 189–194, 196–201, 204, 242f
Jupiterian themes/experiences
  9, 84f, 88f, 92, 106, 115, 191f, 195, 197, 199f, 204
Jupiter-Mars
  77
Jupiter-Mercury
  17
Jupiter-Neptune
  17, 189–203, 239, 243f
Jupiter-Pluto
  44, 77
Jupiter-Saturn
  11, 81, 88–92
Jupiter-Uranus
  35, 115

Kama
  164
Kampf, Zachary
  184
Kant, Immanuel
  48
Kardashian, Kim
  84
karma
  34, 89
Keane
  210–214, 216, 240

INDEX

Keaton, Diane
11, 76
Keats, John
169f
Keller, Helen
49f
Kennedy, John F.
104, 220–222, 233, 237
Kennedy, Robert F.
221f, 233
Kennedy, Robert F., Jr
222–234, 241f
Kenobi, Ben (*Star Wars*)
29
Kidman, Nicole
84, 165
king (in myth)
54
Kings (Old Testament)
44
Kingsley, Peter
132
Kinks, The
63, 79
Kinnear, Greg
45
Kirk, Captain James T. (*Star Trek*)
48f
Klee, Paul
170
Klose, Miroslav
73
kokyū-nage (breath throws)
180
Kruger, Diane
167
kung fu
91

labor
5, 8, 10, 29, 33, 43, 72, 88, 92, 109, 114
Lachman, Gary
132
Ladies of the Canyon (Joni Mitchell album)
173, 217
Lady Gaga
185
Lagarde, Christine
71

lament
151, 210, 216, 220, 237f
lapis
30
Larsen, Stephen and Robin
96, 101, 105
laughter
11
Laurie, Hugh
240
Law, Jude
167
lawbreaker motif
177
Lawrence, Jennifer
84
Led Zeppelin
90
legacy
105, 108, 118, 180
Leone. Sergio
176
L'Équipe (newspaper)
126
lessons
15–17, 29, 53, 55
Lewis, C. S.
144
Liar, Liar (motion picture)
17, 77, 192
Liberace
82
liberal politics/establishment
178, 228
liberation (function of Uranus)
21, 57, 139
libido
148
Lieder (Schubert)
35, 37, 39, 78
life-field
27
lifetime
94, 118, 232
limitations
5, 9, 16f, 23f, 33, 45f, 49f, 57f, 60f, 66f, 69, 74, 81, 87f, 93, 96, 102, 114, 128, 133, 135, 139f, 197, 207, 213

Lincoln, Abraham
    230
literalizing/literal minded
    40, 57, 159, 243
"Livin' on a Prayer" (Bon Jovi song)
    169
logia
    30, 78
logic
    47–49
logos
    159
loneliness
    31, 35–37, 46, 58, 175, 211
"Longest Time" (Billy Joel song)
    58f
longevity
    73
longitude
    111
Loren, Sophia
    165
love
    60, 171f
    (*see also* romance)
Lucifer
    124
lunar
    19, 42, 45, 146–149, 153, 156, 186
    (*see also* Moon)
lying/lies
    13, 17, 158, 192

MacDowell, Andie
    16
madness
    114, 208
Madonna
    165, 202
mafia
    19, 124, 152
magic and myth
    102, 199f
magical quality
    114, 195
magical world of childhood
    141, 144f
magnification
    13, 35, 88, 92, 159, 192

Magnum Force (motion picture)
    177
Major Tom (Bowie)
    129f
malaise
    211, 231, 234
malefic
    7
"Man with the Child in His Eyes" (Kate Bush song)
    173
mana
    133
Manhattan
    11
Manilow, Barry
    82, 93
mansions (St. Teresa)
    89f
Maradona, Diego
    123–127, 184
Mars-Jupiter
    85
Mars-Neptune
    68, 70, 172–188
Mars-Pluto
    57
Mars-Saturn
    17f, 68–76, 90, 230
Mars-Venus
    35
martial arts
    90, 92, 178–180
    (*see also specific martial arts*)
martial qualities
    74, 85, 177
martyr
    57, 120
Marx, Karl
    207
"Mary Queen of Arkansas" (Springsteen)
    195
masculine principle
    70, 152, 172f
masculinity
    70
Mask, The (motion picture)
    17

INDEX

Masks of God, The (Joseph Campbell)
105, 197
Mastrioanni, Marcello
81, 202–204
materialism
154, 185, 207
maternal care
41f, 93, 146
maternal ground/unconscious
136, 148, 157
maternal unity
155
mathematics
47
Matisse, Henri
63
matrix (of being)
41
(*see also* basic perinatal matrices)
maya
114, 132, 135, 165f, 183
McCarthy, Andrew
167
McCartney, Linda
116f
McCartney, Paul
117
McLean, Don
220f
meaning
31f, 50, 121, 140, 159, 161, 166, 197, 235, 237f, 243
meaninglessness
13, 31, 207
media
129, 182, 229f
medication/medicines
42, 119, 194, 214f, 227, 231, 241
meditation
182, 226, 243
mediumship
132, 153
melancholy
42, 219, 235
Mengele, Josef
72
mentors/mentoring
18, 25, 28f, 31, 60, 62, 75, 96

Mercury planet/archetype
10–12, 14, 27, 38, 47–52, 71, 76f, 90, 92f, 106, 150, 157–63, 193
Mercury, Freddie
82
Mercury-Jupiter
85, 192
Mercury-Mars
77
Mercury-Neptune
157–161, 164, 170, 192
Mercury-Saturn
10, 47–50, 52
Mercury-Uranus
231
"Mercy-Pity-Love" (Keats poem)
169, 187
"Mermaid" (Keats poem)
169
Messi, Lionel
126
messiah
107, 120, 126
Messiah (Händel)
43f
metaphor
138, 160, 226, 243
metaphysics
207, 216, 225, 227
Mexico Football World Cup 1986
123
midlife transition
131
Midnight in Paris (motion picture)
135
midpoint aspect
77
military
70, 72, 104, 126, 171
Milne, A. A.
144
Milne, Christopher Robin
186
miraculous/miracles
57, 79, 202, 223f
mirage
195
misogi
180

Mitchell, Joni
  165, 173, 175, 186, 187, 204, 217–219, 241
Mitty, Walter
  23
Monroe, Marilyn
  41, 151, 165
Moon-Jupiter
  10, 36, 46, 87,143f
Moon-Mars
  38, 90, 93, 173, 176, 240
Moon-Mercury
  90
Moon-Neptune
  55–57, 140–155, 157, 167f, 186, 195
Moon-Neptune personal transit
  155–157
Moon-Pluto
  125, 186
Moon's orbit
  186
Moon-Saturn
  11, 19, 22f, 29, 35–38, 40–46, 133, 152, 154, 219, 240
Moon-Sun
  79
Moon-Uranus
  144, 168
Moon-Venus
  46, 90, 115, 144
Moore, Demi
  70f
moral boundaries
  176
moral exhaustion/fatigue
  210f, 237
moral improvement
  15, 122
moral judgments/decisions
  16, 69, 72, 95, 110, 155, 225f
moral ambiguity
  122, 135, 168, 176f
moral pressure/imperatives
  64, 74f, 88, 92, 109, 121
moral qualities/virtues
  29, 58
morality
  23f, 48, 50, 54, 98, 168, 210

Moreau, Gustave
  170
Morrison, Jim
  127, 161, 184
mortality
  5, 8, 14, 34, 104
Moss, Kate
  84
mother/motherhood
  29, 41f, 44–46, 56, 141, 148, 150f, 155, 157
mother archetype
  46, 55, 146, 157
mother complex
  19, 22
Mother Nature
  87, 99, 143
motivations
  54f, 59, 69, 74, 76, , 114, 118, 135, 195, 210, 229
Moulin Rouge! (motion picture)
  84
mourning
  104, 219f, 234
Müller, Gerd
  73
Müller, Wilhelm
  36
multidimensionality (of archetypes)
  200
multivalence (of archetypes)
  10, 63, 68, 74, 87, 243
Murray, Bill
  14, 16, 77
muscular armoring
  69
music
  31f, 35–39, 43f, 53–59, 82–85, 127, 161, 194–197, 210–213, 217–221
musicians
  116, 127
Mussolini, Bennito
  72
My Name Is Earl (television show)
  89
mysterium coniunctionis
  184
Mystic River (motion picture)
  178

INDEX

mysticism/mystical experience
   114, 119, 127, 133, 136f, 140, 172, 184f, 187, 197, 203, 227, 237
mystics
   89, 132, 137, 171
mystique
   133, 135, 158f, 164, 176, 183, 190, 194, 233
mythical method (T. S. Eliot)
   136
mythic cycles
   102
mythic deities
   148f, 151, 164
   (*see also* gods and goddesses)
mythic and the sensual/material
   145, 203f, 242
mythic and spiritual/religious life
   34, 132, 135, 155, 197, 199, 202f, 234
mythic themes
   54, 170, 202f, 242
mythmakers
   132, 161
mythologization
   124, 127, 136, 146, 148, 151, 157, 161, 173, 200, 222f
mythology
   85, 133, 136, 160f, 197, 199–201
mythos (Joseph Campbell)
   102, 237

Nadal, Rafael
   25, 28f, 77f
Nadal, Toni
   28
Naples
   123f, 126
Napoli (football club)
   123f
narcotics
   227
natal aspects/alignments
   11, 35, 41, 44, 53, 57, 70, 82, 89, 98, 106, 123, 137, 152, 166, 170, 173, 178, 182, 207, 209, 222
natal charts
   33f, 40, 160, 194
   (*see also* entries by individual name)

Navratilova, Martina
   25
Nazism/Nazis
   72, 86, 110, 132
Neptune planetary archetype
   1, 36, 49, 55f, 63, 71f, 74, 79, 82, 90, 104, 106, 114–238
Neptune-Pluto
   123, 172
Neptune-Sun
   138, 140
Neptunian themes
   114–238
neuroses
   11, 88
New Mexico
   137
Newton, Isaac
   47
Nicholson, Jack
   45
Nietzsche, Friedrich
   13, 27, 30f, 76f, 120, 137
nightmares
   214–216, 241
night-sea journey
   138, 185
nihilism
   31, 204
Nimoy, Leonard
   48
nirvana
   139
No Boundary (Ken Wilber)
   164
Nobel, Alfred
   106, 118f, 178
Nobel Peace Prize
   106, 118f
no-exit scenario
   16
Noll, Richard
   132
non-differentiation
   139, 154, 204
non-existence
   132
non-ordinary states of consciousness
   46, 153, 182, 208

noon charts
185f, 201, 251
Norris, Chuck
70
nostalgia
135, 140, 145, 148f, 157, 214, 216, 234
numbness
211, 241
numinosity/the numinous
128, 158, 197, 227

obligations
88, 92, 232f
oblivion
206f
obstacles
18, 41, 49f, 54, 73, 89, 189f, 238
oceans
138, 154, 197
oceanic feeling/experience
138, 154f, 204, 227
Odysseus
166
Oermann, Nils
111
O'Keeffe, Georgia
137
Once and Future King, The (by T. H. White)
234
oneness
143, 155, 179
one-sidedness
64
operatic quality
82, 87
opportunism
90f
opposites (relationship between)
21, 155, 190
opposition aspects/alignments
20f, 25, 33, 36, 62–64, 70f, 76, 79, 89f, 94, 108, 115, 118, 137, 144f, 148, 159, 162, 168, 173, 185f, 190, 192, 212f, 220–222, 230, 235f, 240f
optimism
81, 87, 89, 189f, 195, 197
orbits (of planets)
32f, 78, 94, 116, 186

orphan archetype
41
Osment, Haley Joel
240
otherworldly quality
130
outdoors
85
outer planets
34, 78, 186, 210, 239
outer space
130
outsider
230
overdose
231, 233

pacifism
69
Pacino, Al
152, 153
Pagels, Elaine
160
pagoda (in *The Game of Death*)
90
pain
7, 9, 13, 16, 23, 32, 36, 41 50–52, 54f, 57, 65, 68, 110, 124, 135, 139, 148, 150f, 155, 158, 217, 220, 234
pain relief
241
painters
170f, 186, 206
painting
62, 137, 170, 186
Pale Rider (motion picture)
176
paparazzi
81
paradigms
52
paradise
55, 114, 139, 155, 195, 216, 234
paralysis
183
paranoia
216, 227
paranormal
132

INDEX

Paris
　84, 107, 109, 135, 167
Paris salon
　63
parody
　63
participation mystique
　159, 190
Passgard, Lars
　206
passions
　98, 170, 199, 239
passivity
　57, 69, 159, 164
Pasteur, Louis
　119
pathology
　72, 140, 235, 243
pathos
　235, 238, 243
Pele
　170
Pender, Gil (in *Midnight in Paris*)
　135
Penn, Sean
　23
perennial mythology
　160, 197
perinatal matrices/psychology
　46, 139, 155, 227
Peron, Eva
　119
personas
　19, 32, 53, 67, 70, 74f, 82, 88f, 95,
　121, 127f, 138–140, 185, 217
personal identity
　128, 133
personal myth
　135
personal transits
　33, 73, 94, 97, 103, 108, 112, 156, 208,
　214, 226, 234–237
pessimism
　5, 13, 89
PETA
　116
Peter Pan
　144

Philemon
　130
philosophy
　1, 5, 13, 30f, 48, 88, 92, 106, 108, 119,
　162–164, 172, 180, 182, 199
Philosophy of History, The
　162
physical energy
　18, 69, 85
physical sensitivity
　181
physical training
　68f, 90
physics
　47
"Piano Man" (Billy Joel song)
　58
Picasso, Pablo
　63
Pisces
　6, 12, 96, 102
planetary alignments/configurations
　1, 64, 68f, 94
planetary archetypes
　6, 27, 49, 53, 68, 90, 94, 98, 114, 117,
　128, 133, 182, 222, 227, 234
planetary positions
　33, 96, 118
planetary transits
　112
planets
　63, 78, 94, 96, 103, 115, 127, 138, 146,
　229, 235
Platonic Form
　106
platonic relationships
　171
Play It Again, Sam (motion picture)
　88
pleasure
　8, 53, 58, 65, 67, 81, 84f, 155, 165, 169,
　202–204
pluralism
　128, 130
Pluto planetary archetype
　21, 31, 44, 49, 60, 67, 71, 76, 90, 92, 98,
　106, 137, 145, 148, 162, 172, 176, 186,
　230

Plutonic themes/energies
  93, 98, 139, 187, 239
poets
  136, 145, 158, 170, 206
poetic sense
  145, 148, 158, 161, 164, 169–171
poetry
  31, 36f, 136, 141, 144, 146, 148f, 161, 169f
poignant quality
  141, 149, 178, 214–217, 219f, 238
poisoning
  227f, 231f, 234
Police, The
  223
political establishment
  185
political idealism
  231
politics
  70–72, 168, 178, 119, 221f, 233f
pollution
  227f, 231f
Polo, Teri
  18, 21
polytheism
  198
popular culture
  48
popular music
  38, 82
pragmatism
  91
prayers
  191f, 222
preaching
  161
preconscious/prepersonal
  46, 139, 155
pregnancy
  25, 42, 44, 77
prenatal
  227
prescientific
  120
presidency
  222, 231, 233
presidential candidate
  61, 221f, 242

Presley, Elvis
  127
pretending
  127, 140, 225f
pride
  120, 138
prima materia
  30
primal world
  114, 155
Prince Harry (British Royal)
  119
Prince William (British Royal)
  119
Princess Diana of Wales (British Royal)
  119, 221
principium individuationis
  30, 46, 99, 116
Private Benjamin (motion picture)
  70
problems
  22, 39, 47, 67, 73, 88f, 92, 214, 242
problematic side of life
  9–11, 13, 47, 88
problem-solver motif
  73
prophecy/prophetic ability
  120, 126, 153, 164
prophet
  119–121, 130, 132, 153
Proust, Marcel
  85, 149–151, 186
psyche
  1, 27, 72, 115, 131, 155, 182, 199, 238
psychedelics
  182, 208, 240, 243
psychiatric drugs
  231
psychiatric hospital
  126
psychic experience
  132, 153, 182
psychodynamic therapy
  5, 69, 227
psychological function
  176
psychological life
  141, 157, 206, 225, 243

INDEX

psychological maturation
17, 23
psychological resistances
74
psychological transformation/shift
32, 45, 61, 98, 135
psychologists
1, 130
psychonauts
182
psychopathology
207, 214
psychotic episode
227
puella aeturnus
112
puer aeturnus
100, 112, 144, 242
purifying
234
purity
55, 57, 138, 142, 170f, 229

quantum physics
47
Queen (rock band)
82
quincunx aspect/alignment
33, 80, 128, 222
quintile aspect
127

racism
132
rapture
114, 160
rational ego/rationality
48–50, 52, 139, 158–160, 162, 199
realism
8, 24, 60, 92, 189, 207, 210, 217, 219
rebel/rebellion
27, 49, 57, 126
rebirth
139, 184, 238
Red Book, The
41, 130
Redford, Robert
166

re-enchantment
234, 238
Reeve, Christopher
167
regression
114, 121, 139f, 155, 185, 204, 227
rehab
226, 228
Reich, Wilhelm
80
religion
106, 132, 136, 154, 157, 160f, 177, 192, 194, 197–199, 203, 205, 207, 232
religious belief/conditioning
100, 118, 120 153, 169, 207, 211
religious experience/epiphanies
160, 189, 197, 206, 223
religious ideas/teachings
122, 160f, 194, 198
religious orthodoxy
160, 203
religious path
120, 156, 198
religious practice/life
116, 120, 122, 133, 137, 222, 238
religious projections
124f
religious rites
180
religious sects
160
renewal
146, 197, 231, 234
repression
23, 37, 40f, 69, 72, 240
Republican Party (US)
61, 230
resistances
19, 42, 52, 73f, 106
retrograde motion
33, 78, 103
revelation
7, 31, 120, 142–144, 150, 157, 160, 200, 203, 210
reverie
141, 149f
Rice, Condoleezza
71

Rice-Oxley, Tim
  213, 240
rites of passage
  46, 104, 180, 198, 237
The River (Bruce Springsteen album)
  175, 197
Riverkeeper's Alliance
  228
Roach, Jay
  18, 185
Robin, Christopher (from *Winnie the Pooh*)
  144
rock music
  63, 85, 127, 220
Roddick, Andy
  78
Roman gods
  138, 203
romance/romantic experience
  16, 21f, 35, 53–61, 64, 75, 81–84, 88, 98f, 148, 151, 158, 164–168, 170–172, 190, 195, 202–204, 206, 217– 219
romanticism/romanticized view
  120, 127, 135, 151, 164, 174, 210
Rome
  81, 201f
Rosalita (Bruce Springsteen song)
  197
Rosen, David
  132
rose-tinted view
  197
Rousseau and Revolution
  163
Royal Tenenbaums, The (motion picture)
  22f
rule-follower motif
  22, 67, 135
rules
  21–23, 30, 33, 47, 59, 61, 63f, 66, 69f, 74f
ruling ideas/dominants
  48
"Running Up That Hill" (Kate Bush song)
  175
Ruperti, Alexander
  77

sacrifice
  84, 115, 118–120, 122, 136f, 140, 175, 206, 208, 226, 234
Sagittarius
  12
salvation
  122
samsara
  7, 46
sanctuary
  56, 141, 155, 157
San Francisco
  178
Sarah Lawrence College
  101
Sartre, Jean-Paul
  45f
Saturn planetary archetype
  1–113, 114–116, 118, 133, 137, 144f, 147f, 151f, 154, 160, 176, 186, 189f, 194, 204–239, 240–243
Saturn-Moon
  20, 37
Saturn-Neptune
  42, 104, 154, 160, 178, 204–238, 240–244
Saturn-Neptune-Pluto
  178
Saturn-Pluto
  68, 76, 241f
Saturn-Uranus
  38, 68, 160, 177f
Saving Private Ryan (motion picture)
  75
savior
  119f, 123f, 126, 229
Schellenberg, Walter
  72
schizophrenia
  136, 207
Scholem, Gershom
  137
Schopenhauer, Arthur
  5–11, 13, 31, 47, 75f, 88, 105f
Schubert, Franz
  35f, 38f, 78
Schweitzer, Albert
  94, 106–113, 119, 137

Schweitzer, Helene
  111
science
  52, 118, 172, 199, 229f, 236
Scorpio
  123
Scrooged (motion picture)
  14, 17
séances
  132
Secret Life of Walter Mitty (motion picture)
  23
sects (religious)
  160
secularism
  199, 202, 207
sedatives
  231
seductress
  60
self-consciousness
  21, 155
self-control
  148
self-discipline
  29
self-esteem/ self-confidence
  120, 138, 159
self-expression
  24, 30, 115, 122
selfhood
  46, 121, 128, 130, 133, 139f, 239
self-image
  74, 122, 127
self-improvement
  92
self-judgment
  33, 151
self-knowledge
  52, 69
selflessness
  68, 119, 121, 133, 155
self-loss
  120–122, 213, 216
self-mastery
  93
self-overcoming
  234

self-preservation
  32
self-protection
  32, 53f, 59, 87, 219
senex
  5, 14, 24, 40f, 54, 68, 70, 73f, 100, 206f, 242
sense of identity/self
  13, 119, 127f, 132, 139, 213
sergeant-major motif
  77
Seventies (1970s)
  73
sextile (aspect/alignment)
  42, 57, 60, 70, 73, 76, 98, 133
sexual experiences/attraction
  60, 81, 168, 202f
shaman/shamanism
  132, 198
Shatner, William
  48
sheep (Bible)
  43
shepherd (Bible)
  43
showgirl/showman
  82
Shyamalan, M. Night
  240
Simm, John
  214
singer-songwriters
  31, 53, 173
sirens motif
  164, 166, 202f
Sixth Sense (motion picture)
  240
Sixties (1960s)
  63, 176, 221f, 231
Sjöström, Victor
  216
skepticism
  207, 209, 230, 234
Skinner, B. F.
  137
Skywalker, Luke
  29
Smith, Robert
  38f

sobriety/sobering up
 207, 209, 211, 223, 225–227
socialism
 207
societal standards
 19, 30, 74f
sociological function (of religion)
 207
solar archetype
 10, 27, 29, 31, 54, 117, 120, 122, 131f, 137
 (*see also* Sun)
soldier
 68, 237
solitaries
 30–32, 78
Solitary Man (Neil Diamond song)
 32
solitude
 29–31, 37
Solomon, King (biblical)
 44
solutio
 148, 184, 238
soul
 35–37, 41, 43, 67, 89f, 120, 141, 143, 148, 153, 155, 166, 169, 194, 203f, 234, 237f, 242f
soulful quality
 140f, 145, 243
soul-making
 94, 235, 242
space and time
 30
Space Oddity (David Bowie song)
 129
Spaghetti Westerns
 176
speed of planetary motion
 33, 78, 103, 186
spells
 164, 166, 168, 203, 217f
Spengler, Oswald
 102
spiderman
 39
spiders
 39, 185

Spielberg, Steven
 75
spirit and matter
 227
spirit in the world
 116, 207, 229
spirit of Christmas (in *Scrooged*)
 17
spirits
 130, 146, 153, 237
spiritual experience/spirituality
 30, 41, 92, 114, 118–122, 131–133, 137–141, 143, 145f, 149, 153–164, 166, 169–172, 178–183, 185, 194, 197, 199f, 203–210, 222–231, 233–235, 237f, 243
spiritual activism
 185
spiritual alienation/death/wasteland
 41, 234
spiritual ascent
 243
spiritual community
 153
spiritual dimension of life
 160, 178, 180, 182, 203, 233, 235
spiritual discipline
 227
spiritualism
 132
spiritualization
 171, 178f, 203
spiritual-mythic vision
 146
spiritual truth
 120, 158, 160, 200, 210
spiritual warrior
 178, 182
Spock (*Star Trek*)
 48f
sport
 25–28, 73, 78, 184, 187f
Springsteen, Bruce
 35, 161, 194f, 197, 239
square aspect/alignment
 11f, 25, 30f, 33, 35–37, 41, 44, 46–48, 53, 57, 60, 70, 72, 74, 76, 90, 94f, 98, 103f, 115, 117–119, 127f, 130, 136f, 143f, 150, 152, 154–157, 160f, 165, 167, 170, 176–178, 185, 190, 208, 210,

INDEX

square (cont.)
213, 217, 220, 222, 230, 240, 242
Stairway to Heaven (Led Zeppelin song)
90
Stamp, Terrence
167
Star Trek (television series)
48f
Star Wars (motion picture series)
29
Starman (David Bowie song)
129
Starsky & Hutch (motion picture)
22
status
63f, 124, 127, 162, 185, 199f
Stein, Gertude
62f, 79, 135
Steinbeck, Carol
97, 105, 110
Steinbeck, John
97, 105, 110
stellium (aspect pattern)
25, 27
Stewart, James
168
Stick to Your Guns (Bon Jovi song)
85
Stiller, Ben
14, 18–23, 44, 133, 135
stimulus-response conditioning
137
Stone, Sharon
165
Story of Civilization, The
162f
storyteller
161
sublimatio
202–204, 243
sublimation
171f, 178, 182f, 200, 204
submission
136
sub-personalities
131
Sullivan, Anne
49

superiority
77
supernatural
92
surrealism
186
surrender
87, 128, 139f, 161, 183, 192, 223, 225f, 238
Swabia
146
Swann's Way
149–151
Switzerland
110, 187
(*see also* Zurich, Bollingen)
symbolism/symbols
54, 68, 78, 102, 104, 123, 132, 135–138, 159, 161, 170, 174, 186, 197–199, 216, 232, 235, 237f, 243
sympathy
115–117, 119, 139, 229
synchronicity
107, 223
synthesis
161–164, 183f, 235

Tacey, David
132
Takemusu (god)
180
Tai Chi Chuan
178
Tao/Taoism
132, 164, 200, 226
Tarnas, Richard
47, 49, 60, 68, 73, 75f, 93, 104, 106, 112, 116, 137, 150, 200, 204, 206, 210f, 220, 227
taskmaster
8, 16, 72
Taurus
27, 156, 187
technology
231
Teilhard de Chardin, Pierre
137, 171f, 187
Teilhard-Chambon, Marguerite
171

"Tell Her About It" (Billy Joel song)
  59f
tennis
  25–29, 73, 77 f, 170, 182, 187f
Teresa of Ávila
  89, 93
tests
  33f, 92, 225f
"Thank You for the Music" (Abba song)
  83
theology
  107, 110f, 136
Theron, Charlize
  165
Thomas, Bruce
  92f
Thomas, Dylan
  136
threshold
  29, 34, 52, 74, 151
threshold guardian
  74
Through a Glass Darkly (motion picture)
  205–208, 240
Tillich, Paul
  137
timelessness
  141, 144
"Tin Angel" (Joni Mitchell song)
  219
"To the Sun God" (Hölderlin poem)
  147
Tolstoy, Leo
  64–68, 80
toxicity/toxic womb
  227, 231f, 234
transcendence
  121, 124, 126, 128, 133, 137–139, 157f, 161, 164, 170f, 181, 183, 202, 205–209, 216, 227, 235, 243
transcendent
  114, 116, 130, 142, 143, 170, 208, 226
transformation
  1, 29, 32, 61, 68, 75, 100, 111f, 135f, 139, 183, 186, 188, 191, 223, 235, 239, 241
transits
  32–34, 37, 40f, 44, 46, 52, 73, 76, 78, 88, 90, 94–106, 108–112, 116, 118,

transits (cont.)
  130, 138–140, 155–157, 166, 168, 182f, 204, 207–211, 214, 220, 222, 234–238, 241f
transpersonal
  45, 114, 133, 139, 145, 173, 179, 192
trine (aspect/alignment)
  27, 33, 37, 42, 47, 60, 67, 70, 73, 75f, 81, 98, 116, 118–120, 127f, 133, 137, 143–145, 149, 151f, 160, 163, 165, 169, 176, 178, 184, 186, 200, 203
Troy (motion picture)
  167
Truman Show, The (motion picture)
  17, 192
Trump, Donald
  61f, 64, 85, 159, 230
T-square (aspect pattern)
  11, 35f, 38, 48, 71, 74, 77, 90, 92, 106, 115, 144, 152, 176, 213, 222, 242
tyrant
  24, 29, 72

Übermensch
  31
Ueshiba, Kisshomaru
  179, 187
Ueshiba, Morihei
  178–180, 187f
Ulysses (James Joyce)
  136
unconscious
  1, 7, 23, 27, 46, 51f, 64, 67, 69, 76, 88, 98f, 120f, 127f, 131f, 136, 148, 153–155, 157, 171, 175, 197, 203, 236, 240
unconsciousness
  7, 21, 31f, 46, 52, 55, 74, 135, 139, 148–150, 153, 190, 192, 194
"Under Milk Wood"
  136
Under the Iron Sea (Keane album)
  210–213, 240
underworld
  67, 148, 239
undifferentiated condition
  114, 153, 184
Unforgiven, The (motion picture)
  178

INDEX

union (mystical)
  89, 184, 204
unitary
  140, 162, 171, 199, 204
unity (experience of)
  115f, 119, 127, 146, 157, 159, 164, 183f, 227, 235
unity with the environment/nature
  127, 157
unity with the mother
  46, 148, 155
universalism/universality
  194, 199
universalization (experience of Neptune)
  116, 130, 146, 171–173, 179
universe
  47, 162, 172, 178–180, 187, 200
"Uptown Girl" (Billy Joel song)
  57f, 79
Uranus planetary archetype
  1, 20f, 27, 35f, 48f, 56f, 62–65, 67f, 106, 108, 115f, 128, 130, 136, 139, 145, 150, 160, 167f, 173, 176, 185f, 190, 224
Uranus-Neptune
  79, 128, 160, 223
Uranus-Pluto
  93, 149
Ure, Midge
  115
utopian vision
  137

Valens, Ritchie
  220
valentines theme
  168, 219
van Damme, Jean-Claude
  70
Vanity Fair magazine
  228
vegetarianism
  116f
Venus planetary archetype
  14, 21, 25, 27, 36, 53–56, 58–67, 71, 79, 81–84, 90, 98, 115, 137, 144, 151f, 164–171, 187, 200–203, 218, 230
Venusian quality
  54, 58, 67, 170, 204

Venus-Jupiter
  46, 81–85, 202f
Venus-Neptune
  164–168, 170–172, 203, 217–219
Venus-Pluto
  67, 125
Venus-Saturn
  21, 53, 56, 57, 59–65, 67, 75, 151, 219
Venus-Saturn-Neptune
  219
Vickery, Tim
  126
Virgin Mary
  124, 203
Virgo
  15
virtues
  28, 29, 58, 61, 121
visionary experience
  120, 153, 161, 164
visions
  38, 114, 205f, 237
vocation
  95, 100, 111, 153, 158, 160
Vuillard, Edouard
  170

Wagner, Richard
  31, 188
"Wanted Dead or Alive" (Bon Jovi song)
  85
Wales
  136
warrior
  69, 70, 72, 85, 176, 178, 180–182
washing/cleansing motif
  138, 180, 183
wasteland
  234
water
  138, 156, 174f, 197, 203, 223, 228, 232
Waterkeeper Alliance
  228
Watership Down (book, motion picture)
  220
Watts, Alan
  160, 186

"Well-respected Man" (The Kinks song)
63
Welsh culture
136
Western civilization/culture
52, 145, 199
Westerns
176
"When I Was a Boy" (Hölderlin poem)
145
wholeness
120, 155, 159, 234
Wilber, Ken
163f
"Wild Billy's Circus Story" (Springsteen)
239
Wild Strawberries (motion picture)
216f, 241
Williams, Richard
25
Williams, Serena
25
Williams, Venus
25
willpower
223
"Willy" (Joni Mitchell song)
173, 217
Wilson, A. N.
80
Wilson, Owen
20, 133, 135
wine motif
81, 84, 186
Winehouse, Amy
127, 184
Wing Chun (kung fu)
91
Winnie-the-Pooh
144
"*Winterreise*" (Schubert)
37
wise old man archetype
16, 25, 29, 31, 33, 41, 43, 59f, 75, 226
wishes/wishing
10, 165, 192, 210
wish fulfillment
191, 200

Woodman, Marion
137
world transits
90, 210, 212, 220
worldview
11, 13, 47, 52, 80, 88, 185, 192, 194, 243
world-weariness
234
Wuhan
230
Wuthering Heights
63, 174, 187
wu-wei
183

Yoda
29
yoga
160, 178, 198
You Will Meet a Tall Dark Stranger (motion picture)
13
Young Guns II (motion picture)
85

Zarathustra (Nietzsche's)
31, 77
zeitgeist
210f, 231
Zeta-Jones, Catherine
165
Zeus
89
Ziggy Stardust
128, 185
Zimmer, Heinrich
137
zodiac
1, 6, 78, 94, 96, 102, 111
Zürich
155f, 235

ABOUT THE AUTHOR

Keiron Le Grice is a professor of depth psychology and co-chair in the Jungian and Archetypal Studies specialization at Pacifica Graduate Institute, California, where he also designed and co-founded the online doctoral program in Psychology, Religion, and Consciousness. He serves as an honorary lecturer in the Department of Psychosocial and Psychoanalytic Studies at the University of Essex, and was the 2023 Zürich Lecture Series speaker at the International School of Analytical Psychology.

Originally from Nottinghamshire, England, he was educated at the University of Leeds and the California Institute of Integral Studies in San Francisco where he earned his doctorate in Philosophy and Religion. He is the author of several books including *The Archetypal Cosmos*, *The Rebirth of the Hero*, and *The Lion Will Become Man*. He is also co-editor of *Jung on Astrology*, a compilation of Jung's writings on this topic, and co-founder and former editor of *Archai: The Journal of Archetypal Cosmology*, now serving as editorial advisor.

The author's video lecture series on archetypal astrology and depth psychology, covering much of the material included in the volumes of this book, alongside other examples of astrological correlations, are available for purchase via the links below:

Lecture Series 1: Jupiter and Saturn
https://vimeo.com/ondemand/itasjupitersaturn

Lecture Series 2: Uranus, Neptune, and Pluto
https://vimeo.com/ondemand/itasuranusneptunepluto

www.itas-psychology.com

Made in the USA
Las Vegas, NV
30 December 2024

15620490R10162